EDITORIAL ILLUSTRATION

EDITORIAL ILLUSTRATION

CONTEXT, CONTENT AND CREATION

ANDREW SELBY

BLOOMSBURY VISUAL ARTS
LONDON • NEW YORK • OXFORD • NEW DELHI • SYDNEY

BLOOMSBURY VISUAL ARTS
Bloomsbury Publishing Plc
50 Bedford Square, London, WC1B 3DP, UK
1385 Broadway, New York, NY 10018, USA
29 Earlsfort Terrace, Dublin 2, Ireland

BLOOMSBURY, BLOOMSBURY VISUAL ARTS and the Diana logo are
trademarks of Bloomsbury Publishing Plc

First published in Great Britain 2023

Cover design: Lou Dugdale
Cover image © Rebecca Hendin

A catalogue record for this book is available from the British Library.

A catalog record for this book is available from the Library of Congress.

ISBN: PB: 978-1-3500-9686-8
          ePDF: 978-1-3500-9688-2
          eBook: 978-1-3500-9687-5

Typeset by Integra Software Services Pvt. Ltd.
Printed and bound in India

To find out more about our authors and books visit www.bloomsbury.com
and sign up for our newsletters.

Contents

Figure 0.1
Cuban-born illustrator Edel Rodriguez's work has had a significant international impact beyond the usual boundaries of editorial illustration. His work has garnered international interest across broadcast media and in the public arena, through the adoption of his images for protest banners and placards by marchers protesting against political and social issues.

Introduction

Editorial illustration is a form of visual journalism that provides critical commentary and context on contemporary subjects. Its role is to enlighten, inform and educate readerships across a range of subjects that are of public interest. A powerful tool of expression, evaluation and exposé, editorial illustration can be widely seen in newspapers, magazines and journals occupying both print and digital form. Created and presented in tandem with textual journalism, an editorial illustration serves to provide readers with an accurate and balanced account of events through an obligation to discover and reveal the truth about subjects. Authors Bill Kovach and Tom Rosenstiel state in their book *The Elements of Journalism*, that 'All truths – even the laws of science – are subject to revision, but we operate by them in the meantime because they are necessary and they work … [journalism seeks] a practical and functional form of truth' (2007). They argue that in 'a world of expanding voices', the upholding of journalistic standards such as truth and accuracy becomes the foundation on which analysis, comment, context, criticism, debate and interpretation allow larger truths to emergence. To parallel that journalistic expectation, editorial illustrators aim to be objective about their subject, through the portrayal of news, investigative journalism, reviews, regular columns and features with the same degree of fairness and accountability and without 'fear or favour'.

The most successful proponents of editorial illustration achieve global recognition and respect for the work they create well beyond the boundaries of their subject. Their images capture the zeitgeist of a moment and cut through the barrage of information we receive on a daily basis. Their output questions perceptions, provokes outrage and oscillates continually with readers who receive their messages and engage with the wider content in the publication. Far from the old adage of being 'today's news, tomorrow's fish and chip paper' when reproduced in traditional print form, editorial illustrations have a habit of staying around as visual reminders of time in digital editions. Editorial illustrations often have a second life, re-emerging as backdrops to political stories being reported on television news channels, or as comedic, cutting excerpts in social media posts, and as inspiration for placards in protest marches and political rallies. They mobilize the reading and viewing public to monitor the behaviour and standards of authority figures and offer a voice to those not in positions of power or influence. Acting as a succinct visual statement, an editorial illustration can encapsulate the views of the many as a call to arms, a omnipresent reminder and an instrument of change. These examples chronicle not only the responsibility editorial illustrators have to the public that they serve but also how society is reliant on the information that they carry, present and communicate.

Timeliness is a critical factor in the production and dissemination of editorial illustration set against the clamour for newsworthy content that appears incessant and that seemingly accelerates on a daily basis. The editorial illustrator must be prepared to respond to developing situations, by creating work that answers to a range of factors, including the impact of how a story affects readerships and their proximity to events, and whether that content is in the public interest. From the satirical lampooning of political figures using caricature, through to wittily exposing the mistakes and misdemeanours of celebrity, no subject escapes the judicious eye of the editorial illustrator. By extension, illustration is used in editorial settings to uncover and investigate subjects, either in direct action or piecing together images from reliable firsthand witness accounts and verified sources. This form of investigation can create incisive artwork and compelling accounts of situations that require in-depth reporting in often dangerous and difficult circumstances through extended visual essays and reportage, often allowing marginalized or under-represented subjects to have valuable media exposure. Editorial illustration is also used in reflective commentary to review subjects from a distanced vantage point, contextualizing them from a considered and objective position and providing an authoritative, rationalized and reasoned opinion. Whilst reviewing political or economic decisions might be radically different to critically analysing books, films or exhibitions, the need to step back and re-examine content after the passing of time remains a valued and respected tradition of journalistic independence and reliability. Regular columns and features require dexterous visual handling to ensure that the editorial illustration maintains a consistency of voice and message with the columnist. Many readers owe their newspaper brand loyalty to this form of journalism and trust the commentary that prevails in these columns through shared values and espoused beliefs.

Editorial illustration is never neutral in commentary, tone or intention. By definition, no person is ever able to be neutral in all things, shaped knowingly or unconsciously by background and experience. Positions on issues such as race, gender, identity, religion, philosophical and political persuasion are derived from a mixture of lived and informed experiences. These may sit at odds with the demographic of other readers, so aspiring to be accountable and remain credible must rely on concentrating on the facts and using their skills to inform, educate and entertain. Instead, historical credibility has been built on using impartial methods to retrieve information that can be constructed both as content and critique. In that regard, the motivations of journalists and editorial illustrators are not dissimilar. There is a responsibility to provide information in a form that allows the reader to extract knowledge and interpret content in ways that allow them to form their own views and beliefs, but there must be sufficient conceptual breathing *between* the text and the image where contemplation and cognition can occur.

This book therefore positions the study of editorial illustration as a vital contributor to the mass consumption of media communication from the advent of the first newspaper in 1785. Whilst the wider subject of illustration has an impressive and illuminating history of storytelling over many centuries, from the Neolithic rock and cave markings, through the Egyptians and through to historically vital reporting documents such as the Bayeux tapestry, the invention and adoption of printing as a reliable vehicle to reach a wider readership and demographic is central to the story of the birth and rapid development of editorial illustration in particular. Those early attempts to communicate through imagery as essential pictorial forms, scratched into rock,

carved into tree bark or imprinted onto objects made of material soft enough to leave an impression, are evidence of the earliest attempts of our ancestors to forge a communicative language that could be deciphered, learnt and repeated. Civilizations not connected to one another by anything other than a shared celestial existence – ironically made up of coded patterns of stellar constellations by tribes and factions – were devising shapes and patterns of information that in parallel spoke to their peoples. The understanding of how the coding and decoding of text and image is explored in the context part of the book, surveying the historical development of editorial illustration as a form in the context of news media growth around the globe. Crucially, this part also explains how editorial illustration is constructed as an intellectual property and how it is received by readerships through a combination on interconnected and relevant theoretical models, societal developments, arts movements and philosophical discourses.

The content section of the book examines what types of information content are carried by editorial illustrations and in what format those illustrations are permitted to exist in newspapers, magazines and journals. Discussed from the perspective of discovering and developing an illustrative voice in both conceptual tone and graphic language, this section surveys illustrative output recognized as versions of editorial illustration. From conceptual output through to sequential GIFs, animations and emerging realities afforded by augmentation and virtual existence beyond the screen, the text considers the conditions in which those types of editorial illustrations are employed by publications in the presentation and dissemination of subjective content. In the same way that successful, impactful journalism relies on talented insight and crafted writing, editorial illustrators are renowned for the often surprising and ingenious ways that they force readerships to react to visual material, creating responses that are alarming, unexpected or obtuse. The section then examines the intelligence that underpins the conceptual unlocking of an assignment, drawing out the nuances of journalistic expression and repurposing the essence of the message into visual form. This requires a thorough and well-exercised understanding of tools such as visual puns, wit, satire, sarcasm and pastiche and their application in the construction of successful editorial illustrations that capture, dazzle and remain memorable for the reader.

An exploration of what constitutes a visual language is developed through some analysis of preconceptions of the term. The text unearths how visual language is observed and categorized as a multimodal interface through contributions from a cognitive scientific perspective, and how that compares with what we might recognize in expressive forms of writing and music. By drawing parallels with other communicative forms, the conditions that permit images to contain and share meaning are presented as actions that can be applied in the moment, but that also form a substantial and critical role in our stored memory experiences, allowing us to make recall connections and develop sophisticated visual lexicons that are unique and valuable to us as individuals. Such retention and recall mechanisms are particularly pertinent as we move from singular performing editorial illustrations to multi-panel images, or sequences and plural experiences that use imagery on printed surfaces or screens as markers for augmented or virtual reality multimodal experiences.

Finally, the creation section of the book explores contemporary editorial illustration approaches to carving out and developing a professional career. The emphasis is placed on articulating how successfully established and emerging editorial illustrators are professionally presenting their work in a fast-paced, rapidly changing physical and virtual promotional space. The text considers the advantages and cautions of representation by agency, self-promotional websites and social media platforms alongside traditional publishing options such as illustration annuals and targeted self-publishing forays.

From advertising and marketing work, the section then concentrates on the process of winning commissions and negotiating assignments with clients, often against fierce and sustained global competition. The section expands upon the collection of visual research as a continuum for the collation and expansion of a successful professional practice. Examining the close working relationship between the commissioners and creators of illustration, this section champions the process of ideation and visual exploration as being of significant value to the

health and well-being of a professional career in the discipline stretching over a lifetime of opportunity and achievement. Using examples drawn from some of a diversity of makers representing the different backgrounds outlined in earlier sections, the creation section aims to inform and inspire those new to the discipline to create innovative work that will be the next chapter in this journey.

This book has been written in extraordinary times. Unusually in the modern age, the world has experienced a global health pandemic and citizens have been affected by very similar issues and conditions. Unlike the Spanish influenza outbreak a century ago, the immediate impacts of such a phenomenon have been communicated to us relentlessly around the clock, on every conceivable platform and device and in every language. The mass communication of information – and disinformation – has left many exhausted, confused, disenfranchised and isolated by events and experiences, both lived and shared. Reporting of the Covid-19 pandemic raises important questions for us, both as global citizens and local residents in our own communities, about the presentation, consumption and reception of information. Many facts and figures will pass us by and the politicians and health officials who presented that information will be forgotten over time. What will remain are some of the enduring, heartfelt stories and testimonies that were derived from core human interest in each other. Many will have been published as texts, articles and opinion pieces. They will have been produced as hard-hitting illustrated covers that made hairs on the back of necks rise, political sketches that eviscerated and chastised decisions, and heart-rendering depictions of suffering, death and decay. Editorial illustration has a privileged and responsible position in a civilized society to improve the quality of information and opportunity for debate through intellectual curiosity, candour and honesty. This book seeks to espouse and uphold those traditions, serving as a reminder of the great history of the form, the scope for originality in creatively pursuing the upholding of those beliefs and looking to a bright and prosperous future for the discipline of editorial illustration across the myriad of its forms.

Figure 0.2
Creating imaginary worlds where figures fly above skylines is
a hallmark of illustrators such as Lasse Skarbøvik, who creates
images where an inner logic is created to allow readers to believe
content, however far-fetched or illusory it might appear.

Figure 0.4
Illustration by Brian Stauffer for *Nautilus Magazine*,
commissioned by art director Len Small, for a feature piece
about water and our dependence on it as a species and a
world. The article examines how the search for water shapes the
course of our exploration of the universe.

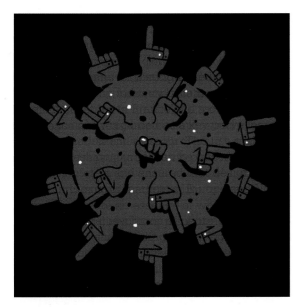

Figure 0.3
American illustrator Adam McCauley's conceptual 'Covid
Shaming Backlash' illustration for *The New York Times* replaces
spike proteins with multiple pointing human hands to suggest the
culture of blame in the early part of the Covid-19 pandemic.

Part One

Context

This section examines the historical origins and growth of editorial illustration as a vital communication medium that brought knowledge and understanding to the masses. The great explorers from Britain, France, Spain and Portugal discovered new countries and cultures in the seventeenth and eighteenth centuries. Their return caused great celebration, but also created increased curiosity and desire for knowledge from wider sections of society who were becoming more literate. Countries quickly realized that more power and control over their place in a new world order could be exerted through colonization of land and sea, establishing trading partners and routes across the globe. Newspapers became a crucial instrument in relaying information and political propaganda that were used to justify and support such aims. At the same time, the ruling classes realized the control of information was critical to controlling society and that newspaper content and opinion was a vital mechanism to exerting control over their subjects.

The Industrial Revolution propelled this surge of interest, with new innovations in printing technology and the distribution of news in the form of emerging transportation links. A wider demographic of the general population were able to be reached and they believed they could seek a better life and attain an improved standard of living through education. The timeline highlights key historical moments in editorial illustration by making the contextual link between world events that have shaped our resulting understanding of political, economic and social histories. Using these documented events, the chapter then examines the dominant art movements that have emerged out of these contextual concerns, what drove them and how they continue to be influential for contemporary practitioners today.

History

The history and development of editorial illustration
and the technical inventions of printing to supply
the publishing industry are inextricably linked. That
contextualized publishing history is mirrored in some
of the cultural developments of the late nineteenth
and twentieth centuries, driven by massive changes
in societal expectations and a rejection in many quarters of elitism. These included the hierarchy of roles of
men and women, their working conditions, the birth
of new and alternative political ideologies, questions
around the role and relevance of religion and spiritual-
ity, and the rejection of traditions which threatened
to stifle progress away from the traditional ruling
classes. By default, these wider questions massively
impacted cultural production, purpose and appreciation, as societies took a greater interest in the world
around them and the way it was presented. With
a more confident and knowledgeable voice – and a
wider demographic of interested parties – important
political, social and moral questions arose around how
art was produced and received, and the shift that
occurred from the elitist 'art for art's sake' preoccupation into an offering that was altogether more about
servicing needs, promoting voice and functioning as
an important tool of communication.

Central to much of this upheaval was the age-old issue about depictions of the 'real' representing truth, which fundamentally questioned the representational roots of creative and cultural production. Idealism, beauty and an appreciation of naturalistic forms and situations were increasingly questioned. Traditionalists fought to maintain and preserve these values as still being relevant in a period where communities had seen such massive industrial change, with promises of brighter and progressive futures both in developing countries, but also in nations whose power had been built on centuries of exploration, victory and enlightenment; or conversely, conflict, oppression and exploitation, depending on political stance. Alternative expressions of the 'real' emerged, from the European-centred Impressionists who literally embraced the real world and attempted to capture its immediate and changing beauty, and the Post-Impressionists who looked to wider cultures' and civilizations' depictions of beauty, where absenting naturalism in favour of depicting the world through staged and deliberate reconstructions of the picture plane using colour and shape was preferred. This break from conventional scale, perspective and placement of elements in compositions was nothing short of a revelation and the term avant-garde was coined to describe a leading edge movement of thinkers and makers intent on change.

Illustration generally was important in this period as many artists and designers realized that publishing vehicles such as illustrated books, posters and manifestos could help spread messages of change and influence readerships. The purposefulness of illustration as a powerful and influential communication medium was recognized and exploited as part of a wider movement looking to

Figure 1.1
Norwegian illustrator Lasse Skarbøvik's is renowned for a graphic language which is widely applied to many genres of editorial illustration, from economics and social commentary through to health and homewares for a global client base. This illustration for the cover of *The Economist* about global finance is a case in point about the global reach and significance of the form. It also serves to capture neatly the relevance of global finance on all our lives as global citizens.

Figure 1.2
Simoul Alva's work is extremely versatile, working across illustration, typography and animation. Using illustration allows editorial designers to control readers by making them pause, reflect and grow accustomed to textual content. It is one of the key benefits of using illustration over photography. This illustration is titled, 'How to Worry Better' *for The New York Times*.

launch ideas, make persuasive cases for change and create new collective identities. Liberating illustration from popular misconception as simply a literal depiction of writing, or 'mere' decoration, was important for the subject. But traditionalists believed that the pursuit of writing had elevated and lauded status as a superior form of expression and were extremely defensive of preserving that position, claiming that illustrators and artists risked cheapening the authors work by making work too accessible. These powerful individuals and collectives, made up of writers, critics, fine artists and collectors of individual artefacts or extremely limited editions, worked cooperatively together to ensure that a hierarchy of culture was embedded in the public psyche.

High-brow bourgeois works, such as the *livre d'artiste* vehicle of highly

finished and beautifully presented artist books that could be purchased by a wealthy minority sat firmly apart from the low-brow crafted and mass-produced publications designed for more of the general populous. Ironically, the range of transferable skills that the illustrator possessed in relation to the fine art

Figure 1.4
Originally from Hong Kong but now residing in Santa Monica, California, Victo Ngai uses her cultural heritage and highly developed conceptual and observational skills in her exquisitely detailed and sensitive illustrations. Her work entices the reader through her sophisticated use of compositional placement of subject matter, creating mesmerizing imagery that is resonant and truly illuminates the page.

Figure 1.3
Simoul Alva's 3D graphic language is versatile enough to encompass the demands of transitioning work from static print-ready images to working as sequences on digital platforms, as demonstrated here for *Medium* about hackers targeting Kindle to disable user tracking and adverts. The online version shows the characters erasing the massages on screen to make the most of the sequential opportunity. Her work is indicative of the digital and global monoculture, with polymath creators working across disciplines as digital natives.

Figure 1.5
Japanese-born illustrator Yuko Shimizu's graphic language draws heavily on her cultural background both conceptually and stylistically. Influences such as traditional Japanese woodblock prints, as well as the storytelling properties of manga and anime combine to give her work a distinctive feel. This illustration utilizes all of those features for the article 'Facebook Under Fire: How Privacy Crisis Could Change Big Data Forever' by Todd Spangler for *Variety* magazine, art directed by Robert Festino.

counterpart was vast, from translating and illuminating written texts, hand drawing typographic fonts as headlines and organizing bodies of visual and textual information to page layouts and mastering a broad range of further competencies around the creation of printing plates ready for printing and distribution. In this regard, the origins of the illustrator can be seen as a multi- and cross-disciplinary visual communication expert. This ability to observe cultural change, and to contribute to and be influenced by cultural output connected to societal change has assumed different levels of concentration in the intervening years, but has resulted in illustrative output always being produced and now being culturally recognized as an important contributor in its own right to the development of communication media.

Today contemporary editorial illustration is at the forefront of progressing the transformation of how information is communicated to readerships. The influence of digitization means platforms and delivery of content have revolutionized the production and dissemination of material from print to screen. Output is more fluid than at any time in the history of editorial illustration and we have grown used to seeing visual content move and become interactive. Much influence has been adopted from the cross-pollination of ideas across and through disciplinary boundaries, from animation, gaming, comics and alternative reality production, including augmented, virtual and mixed-reality experiences for users. Besides introducing new conceptual and technical influences in the way content is presented and consumed, a new pool of talent has been welcomed into the fold, with new skills that are in demand and winning commissions. Creators such as Simoul Alva are producing three-dimensional illustrative output for a range of high-profile clients in static and animated format that services print and digital platforms, across typography, illustration and animation. Yuku Shimuzu and Victo Ngai are bringing new forms of narrative sensibilities to the editorial sphere with work that recognizes and celebrates the influence of Japanese manga and anime culture. The growing influence of global cultural artefacts, products and services are influencing both creators and readerships, a clear sign that there is an appetite and hunger for content and comment that shows no sign of abating.

Timeline

Recognizing that editorial illustration necessarily has its roots in advances in printing and dissemination of information, political and economic development and social history, this timeline charts the birth and development of the form from the period leading up to the first Industrial Revolution that began in Britain in the 1800s, through to the present day.

1785 – *The Daily Universal Register* is published by John Walter in London as a 2 1/2 penny broadsheet. It is rebranded as *The Times* in January 1788.

1818 – *The American Journal of Science* is first published.

1821 – *The Guardian* newspaper, a champion of editorial illustration comment, is launched in the UK.

1832 – *Le Charivari*, the French satirical daily newspaper and forerunner to *Punch* (1841), published.

1832 – *The Penny Magazine*, widely regarded as the first English periodical with wood engraving illustrations is issued.

1838 – *The Times of India*, originally called *The Bombay Times and Journal of Commerce*, is launched in India to sustain and promote the interests of British Empire rule on the sub-continent.

1839 – The birth of photography with experimental methods of fixing light projections permanently is pioneered by Louis Daguerre and Henry Fox Talbot.

1842 – New coverage is transformed in London with the publication of wood engravings by the Brothers Dalziel and others to accompany articles in the *Illustrated London News*.

1843 – *L'Illustration* is published in France, using illustration to visually report on current affairs and cultural events.

1848 – Karl Marx and Friedrich Engels produce *The Communist Manifesto* that highlights inequalities created by economic structures.

1851 – *The New York Times*, one of the world's most revered newspapers for editorial excellence, is published for the first time.

1855 – Frank Leslie's *Illustrated Newspaper* is published in America, capitalizing on the public's desire to see illustrated content.

1855 – *The Daily Telegraph and Courier*, later to become *The Daily Telegraph*, is published in London.

1861 – The American Civil War rages until 1865, with the battles to end slavery widely reported in illustrated newspapers of the age.

1866 – Semiotics research is conducted by Charles Sanders Peirce.

1869 – Photographic reproduction is made possible by the invention of the halftone process, which sees an image broken down into small dots.

1877 – American broadsheet newspaper *The Washington Post* is first published.

1881 – New liberal press laws in France promote popular types of newspaper, including *Le Petit Journal*, that satisfy increasing appetites for entertainment news and gossip, leading to

the publication of the first colour supplement, *Supplément Illustré*, in 1884.

1883 – The pioneering magazine *Life* is published, showcasing photojournalism from 1936.

1883 – The oldest women's interest title, *Ladies' Home Journal*, hits newsstands for the first time.

1886 – The automated typesetting machine Linotype is invented by Ottmar Mergenthaler.

1888 – *National Geographic Magazine* is launched.

1888 – *The Financial Times* is first published in London, and quickly gains a reputation for reporting financial information and opinions that will influence fiscal policies of the British government.

1889 – *The Wall Street Journal,* a bastion of financial and business reporting, launches in New York City and becomes the respected cornerstone of all financial and stock trading reporting.

1892 – *Vogue* is launched, showcasing fashion journalism, illustration and photography.

1892 – Three-colour process printing is invented by American Frederic Eugene, which allows full-colour illustrations to be printed using half-tone screens.

1896 – The *Daily Mail* is founded by Alfred Harmsworth in the UK, who is later ennobled as 1st Viscount Northcliffe.

1897 – *The Saturday Evening Post* is published and makes a household name of the illustrator Norman Rockwell, who creates over three hundred covers – the title ceased publication in 1969.

1899 – The Boer War rages between South Africa and Britain, with the latter victorious by 1902.

1903 – Colour photography is invented by Lumiére brothers, Auguste and Louis.

1912 – The sinking of the *Titanic* is imaginatively and fully reported in *The New York Times*.

1914 – The outbreak of the First World War or Great War sees unimaginable suffering and hardship to millions in Europe, culminating in a truce in 1918.

1916 - Ferdinand de Saussure's semiotic theories are published in France.

1920 – The first issue of *The Reader's Digest* is published.

1922 – The term 'Graphic Design' is introduced by W. A. Dwiggins, becoming part of mainstream psyche by the 1950s.

1923 – *Time*, founded by Henry Luce, and developed by influential editor Britton Hadden, is published for the first time. The title *Fortune* emerges from its business pages to become an influential publication in its own right (1930) after the Wall Street Crash.

1923 – The world's first broadcast listings magazine, *The Radio Times*, is founded by John Reith, general manager of the British Broadcasting Company (BBC), which became a Corporation in 1927.

1925 – The first issue of *The New Yorker* publishes political and social reflections of current events in weekly format, heavily fore-grounding illustrators and cartoonists.

1929 – The Wall Street Crash sees the most devastating stock market crash in history, and its reporting in US newspapers triggers the Great Depression, which dominates Western industrial countries for over a decade.

1933 – *Esquire* magazine launches and publishes groundbreaking journalism, illustration and photography under the stewardship of art director Henry Woolfe.

1939 – The outbreak of the Second World War in Europe, ending in 1945.

1944 – The French newspaper *Le Monde* is founded.

1945 – *Elle* magazine, Helene Gordon Lazareff's brainchild, is launched and becomes influential for repositioning perceptions of how women think, act and perceive themselves.

1946 – The Cold War characterizes the uneasy aftermath of the Second World War, with Russia and the United States wary of each other's developing nuclear capabilities.

1947 – Partition of the Indian sub-continent sees the end of the British Raj and the creation of Pakistan as a recognized political and geographic state.

1949 – The North Atlantic Treaty Organization (NATO) is established.

1950 – A three-year war between the United States and Korea sees the creation of two states – North and South Korea with an uneasy truce reached.

1959 – Xerox markets the photocopier for the first time.

1962 – The United States declares war in Vietnam and wages conflict until 1973, when forces are pulled out after high death tolls lead to increasing public unease and hostility.

1966 – The Chinese Communist Party, under its leader Mao Zedong, declares a Cultural Revolution which promotes communist ideologies.

1970 – *The New York Times* launches its Op-Ed page which will display some of the most intelligent and thought-provoking conceptual editorial illustration.

1971 – Federal Express allows illustrators courier service to deliver artwork to clients.

1971 – Quad/Graphics is founded by Harry and Elizabeth Quadracci, and goes on to become one of the largest magazine printers in the world.

1971 – The birth of email between computers linked to a network that will later see the technology rolled out to small businesses and home consumers.

1972 – *The Washington Post* reporters Bob Woodward and Carl Bernstein expose presidential complicity of Richard Nixon in the Watergate political scandal.

1973 – Newspaper circulation reaches peak consumption in the United States at over 60 million, a figure that began to decline in the late 1980s.

1973 – Wireless mobile network technology that will later support mobile phones is introduced.

1973 – A global oil crises emanating in the Gulf sees supplies severely restricted and huge price increases that affects much of the developed world.

1974 – US President Richard Nixon resigns over the Watergate scandal before he is impeached and convicted by the House of Representatives and the Senate.

1975 – Bill Gates launches Microsoft.

1976 – The fax machine enables illustrators to send visual media facsimiles using traditional phoneline technology.

1976 – Apple Computer is founded by Steve Jobs and Steve Wozniak.

1978 – Industrial disputes over the implementation of new typesetting and printing equipment halt publication of *The Times* in London.

1980 – *The Face*, the influential British style magazine, is launched by Nick Logan in London.

1980 – *RAW* magazine is founded by Françoise Mouly and Art Spiegelman.

1981 – Australian media tycoon Rupert Murdoch acquires *The Times* newspaper as part of his internationally influential News Corporation empire.

1982 – *USA Today*, a daily general interest newspaper, launches in the United States.

1984 – The IRA attempt to assassinate UK Prime Minister Margaret Thatcher and her cabinet at a party political conference in Brighton.

1984 – Apple Macintosh II launces globally, through the infamous '1984' commercial directed by Sir Ridley Scott, which was televised only once during a CBS commercial break of SuperBowl XVIII.

1986 – Adobe Illustrator revolutionizes the way illustrators and other creators can create digital images, spawning other rival software packages.

1986 – A new national newspaper, *The Independent*, launches in the UK as an antidote to what many see as increased political bias in mainstream news media.

1986 – London's Docklands becomes the new home of New International, with national newspapers *The Times*, *The Sunday Times*, *The Sun* and the *News of the World* evicted from their ancestral home in Fleet Street, despite 5,500 staff protesting in the 'Wapping dispute'.

1987 – Former MI5 Assistant Director and operative Peter Wright writes the novel *Spycatcher* which is then the subject of a banning order by the British government. The English press are initially gagged to prevent it's serialization, but this order is later overturned.

1987 – GIFs (Graphic Interface Format) are first witnessed through images and then simplified animations.

1989 – The invention of the World Wide Web by Sir Tim Berners Lee, enabling HyperText Markup Language (HTML).

1989 – The fall of the Berlin Wall between East and West Berlin, symbolizing the break-up of East Germany and the fall of the 'Iron Curtain' as a doomed political project of the Cold War.

1990 – First Gulf War waged on Iraq by United States and coalition forces after Saddam Hussein invades Kuwait.

1991 – The Press Complaints Commission (PCC) is established in Britain through the Calcutt Inquiry to create a self-regulatory industry code of practice on standards and ethics in press reporting.

1997 – Diana, Princess of Wales, is killed in a car crash whilst being chased by paparazzi photographers in Paris.

1998 – Adobe Photoshop is launched, changing the way digital images can be composed, manipulated and presented.

1998 – Peace on the island of Ireland is established with the signing of the Good Friday Agreement.

1998 – Sony creates e-readers, the alternative new technology to rival the printed book.

1999 – US publisher Simon & Schuster releases ebook under the imprint iBooks.

2000 – Sales of USB flash drives commence, allowing digital memory storage of files in a convenient stick-like device.

2001 – World Trade Center attacks kill over three thousand citizens in the worst terrorist attack to take place on American soil.

2003 – The Iraq War launched by coalition forces on inconsistent evidence that Saddam Hussain has weapons of mass destruction.

2004 – Mark Zuckerberg's Facebook platform transcends student campus communications and lays the foundations to becoming a globally recognized social media platform.

2005 – The IRA formally announces an end to its armed struggle on the island of Ireland.

2006 – Twitter is launched, originally with 140 characters per post and no image or video capability; this later changes to reflect the powerful dissemination tool the application has become globally, and character count increases to 280.

2006 – Wikileaks, an organization founded by Julian Assange, begins to publish online data from classified documents that expose national security and intelligence issues at the highest levels of national governments and non-government organizations.

2007 – Apple launch the first iPhone.

2008 – A global 'credit crunch', precipitated by unsecured property foreclosures in the United States, triggers economic uncertainty that sees governments scramble to prop up financial institutions amid catastrophic financial failures of historic banks, such as Lehman Brothers Holdings Inc.

2009 – The social networking platform Sina Weibo launches in China.

2009 – The birth of Augmented Reality is celebrated in *Esquire* magazine.

2009 – WeTransfer and Dropbox Inc., the digital file upload services launch, revolutionizing the way illustrators can send editorial sketches and final artwork to clients.

2010 – Start-up company Instagram launches a mobile image-sharing application that later encompasses video for social networking an promotion.

2010 – Apple launches iPad, with an inbuilt keyboard that offers new reading and viewing experience in the convenience of tablet form technology.

2011 – Snapchat application launches for quick turnaround story content that self-deletes after a matter of seconds.

2011 – *The New York Times* establishes a paywall for digital content on its online platform, limiting access to free content.

2012 – In excess of 2 billion global users have access to the internet.

2012 – Publication of the report by Lord Justice Leveson into "the culture, practices and ethics of the press" in the UK in the wake of the Milly Dowler *News of the World* phone-hacking scandal, exposed by *The Guardian* newspaper in 2009.

2013 – Natalie Nougayrède becomes the first female editor of *Le Monde.*

2014 – Virtual Reality is a source of investment for major technology giants Sony, Facebook and Google.

2014 – Support for the anti-EU UK Independence Party, which will later campaign for Brexit, grows in local and European elections.

2015 – The French satirical publication *Charlie Hebdo,* is the scene of a violent shooting in Paris as Al-Qaeda terrorists kill twelve staff of the alternative French publication for publishing images of the Islamic prophet Muhammad they considered offensive.

2016 – Donald Trump is elected the 45th President of the United States of America after one of the most divisive and bitterly fought campaigns in history, including accusations of voter interference that appear to originate from Russia.

2016 – British voters narrowly vote to leave the European Union in a bitterly fought referendum that sees claims and counter-claims of fake news being presented through broadsheet, tabloid, broadcast and social media.

2018 – Swedish teenage environmentalist Greta Thunberg begins her 'School Strike for Climate' campaign that sees her become a global super-star in the environmental fight to protect the planet.

2019 – A strain of coronavirus, Covid-19, is detected in Wuhan, China and quickly spreads to become a global pandemic, causing major social and economic disruption to many countries.

2020 – Shocking social media footage is released of the arrest and death of George Floyd in Minneapolis which ultimately leads to an upris-ing of racial tension and global awareness of the Black Lives Matter movement.

2021 – Oxford University and pharmaceuti-cal company Astra Zeneca, along with Pfizer Biontech, develop an vaccine to fight the spread of Covid-19.

2021 – Senator Kamala Harris makes history by becoming the first black Vice President of the United States of America.

2021 – Joe Biden becomes the oldest President of the United States of America at 78 years of age, amassing over 80 million votes in the highest voter turnout in US history.

2021 – The United Kingdom leaves the European Union after Brexit terms are finally agreed between the two sides.

2022 – Russian President Vladimir Putin orders his armed forces to invade Ukraine.

Growing influence and awareness

This timeline illustrates the inextricable link between global events and significant cultural or technological achievements, and the resulting production of content in newspapers, magazines and journals. What the timeline also shows is the growing influence that these forms of commu-nication media had on readerships since the first publication of *The Daily Universal Register* in 1785. Whilst we take information availabil-ity, dissemination and discourse for granted in a contemporary mass communication age, where a sizeable proportion of the estimated 7 billion population of planet earth are more connected than ever before, it is truly astonish-ing to think that this communication revolution has happened inside three hundred years. Our

connectedness fuelling our hunger and desire for information is seemingly insatiable.

The timeline reveals that early newsworthy communication was characterized chiefly by scientific discovery, literary criticism and politi-cal observation. This chimes directly with levels of literacy in the developing world at that time and is further underpinned by the founding and growth of learned societies, professional bodies in traditional disciplines such as law, science and medicine. Access to an education meant power, esteem, social standing and mobility. It was also hugely resented by those without such opportunities. Gradually, as literacy increased, a developing second wave of interest stemmed from those outside the traditional learned circles, to encompass other parts of society and forms of knowledge exchange. Women fought for greater rights, recognition and representation in devel-oped societies and class divides started to create tensions and erode as more and more people recognized the power of knowledge encapsu-lated by words and pictures. There was a desire to find out about other subjects that affected people's lives, so society musings, short stories and political satire entered the frame that sought to provide commentary that delivered more than a mere reporting of facts. A greater proportion of this content was fictional, observant and opinionated, mirrored by other output through the arts, literature, music and the new technol-ogy, photography. The demand for information heralded the arrival of illustrated content, provid-ing a toe hold for those with developing literacy and a contextual reference for those with fluency over what they were reading, exemplified by *L'Illustration* in France and Leslie's *Illustrated Newspaper* in America. Inevitably, the race to publish photographs in newspapers intensified, driven by insatiable consumer demand and improvements in printing technology.

The rise and dominance of photography in newspapers and magazines could have been a killer blow to the drawn, printed or constructed image. It is certainly true that non-photographic images have waxed and waned in popularity as denoted through the timeline. Some explanation of that history can be attributed to photo-graphs being adopted as the 'new' technology, through documenting singular, pivotal events or key moments in history. In other instances, the camera opened up new possibilities for photojournalism concentrating on reporting important diplomatic or conflict-related assignments domestically or overseas. Or for enabling the gossiping, chattering classes access to subjects in ways never before documented, including access to subjects such as celebrity and royalty in ways beyond traditional portraiture. Sometimes the camera and resulting photographic image, or images, were seen as a way of extending visual practices that had been forged by illustration. The American Civil War and the discovery of the American Wild West were reported by artists in the field, often risking their lives to capture moments that later defined civilizations and identities. Photography was often seen as a way of bringing an immediacy and truth to those situations, and as the world seemingly became smaller as technological innovation opened transportation and discovery to the masses, familiarity with locations, situations and events installed photographs as being reliable forms of witness and testimony.

In many ways, editorial illustrators actually thrived from the advent and application of photography. Contrary to popular opinion, editorial illustration was still commissioned by newspapers, magazines and journals. Sometimes it was an antidote to the over-reliance on photography, creating a welcome pause and refresh on sections of editorial content that gave the reader a much-needed visual break. On other occasions, illustration was used to deliberately create more contemplative space for the reader. Publications like *The New Yorker* and *Time* magazine used illustration imaginatively and intelligently to embolden their written content, but were also happy to commission illustration or cartoons as standalone commentary, reflecting the qualities they saw in their readership: intellectually engaged, curious and deep thinkers. The versatility of editorial illustration was in its very construction to function as an effective and powerful form of visual journalism. As a result, editors became aware of the power of using editorial illustration as a way of poking fun at the establishment through satirical observation or witty repost. Illustrators could frequently get away with risky social, political, economic or cultural commentary without catching the attention of a subject's legal representation. The immediacy and seemingly undeniable fact encapsulated in a photograph rendered them too inflammatory to publish. Illustration, as a constructed medium, could be controlled to embody and elicit differing emotive responses, from creating a soothing background environment through to biting, cut-to-the-bone comment.

Ironically, photography and illustration have somewhat merged in recent decades with the advent of the computer and its adoption by creators, publishers and consumers. The properties of illustration and photography have been explored by creators collaging and montaging pictorial elements together, through experimenting with Xerox photocopiers and photographic silkscreens. The blur between construction of illustrations and photographs has become hazy. The rise of affordable hardware, software and connectivity has made the 'digital' images pioneered by creators such as Barbara Nessim now become mainstream, allowing illustrators to originate, develop and execute static and sequential artwork in collaboration with designers, art directors and publishers. In some instances, this has also led to co-productions and to the formation of new, exciting and groundbreaking publication and dissemination of content for a generation that resist or distrust mainstream providers of news content. However, the manipulation of imagery has caused an interesting shift in our perception of how images are now received, giving rise to concerns over the legitimacy of doctored images and the content that they purportedly contain. Fakes and forgeries run the risk of undermining accountability and reassurance in the eyes and minds of readers.

Editorial illustration now has to service and function across print and digital platforms in contemporary communication publications. By definition it has to occupy static and sequential spaces in the editorial page or screen grid. Often it has to function across print and digital platforms simultaneously. Increasingly, it will also have to work in response to the reader's actions and impulses. As technology develops, data-driven content will need to be handled in real time. Platforms such as augmented, virtual and mixed reality (AR, VR and MR) will need to be further explored by creators and publishers. The only constant, as illustrated succinctly by the timeline, is that these developments will be in direct response to what we demand as a society, driven to find out more and hungry for information that we can act upon, convey and share at our virtual fingertips. That will only succeed if we as consumers fight to maintain the standards of responsible journalism, quality dissemination and public accountability for the content we digest.

The following sections introduce art movements in a rolling chronological order that align with the birth and development of publishing text and image in what we recognize as publications that have been edited, controlled and disseminated by a publisher. Art movements often grew and evolved out of the connections that creative participants experienced through their involvement and belonging with each other, often as a result of circumstances such as conflict and war, social change and political upheaval, or out of pure desperation for something better. In many instances, counter movements came into being and developed directly in opposition to existing movements, whether through political or philosophical differences, conflicts or new directions forged from compromised resolutions and learnt experiences.

As a result, exact definitions are continually fluid and evolving as we are able to piece together information about the past and consider it with the benefit of hindsight and evidential fact today. In that context, editorial illustrators often identify with several movements in both the educational development of their work and how they sell themselves in a commercial sense. In that spirit, art movements that inspire illustrators should be seen as overlapping or interlocking bridges that connect creators to an evolving universal sphere of influences that govern previous, current and future works in a developing and changing media consumption market subject to explicit editorial demands.

Expressionism

The Expressionist movement was born out of frustrations that writers and artists had with German societal values at the start of the twentieth century. Their combined rejection of centuries of statehood, characterized by rampant class division, was significant in forming an indelible bond between words and images. This was used as a battering ram to fundamentally unsettle the core foundations of the establishment built on the unshakeable faith in royalty, the nobility and entitlement.

The Expressionists sought inspiration for both the philosophical grounding and physical manifestation of their work from the under-represented working classes. Honesty,

integrity and direct communication characterized the output, with writing paired back to allow wider interpretation, and prints and illustrations often crudely and roughly carved from wooden blocks, preserving the sense of originating from the raw material, thereby concentrating the immediacy of message. Artists like Oskar Kokoschka, Egon Schiele and Edvard Munch sought to depict subjects beyond obvious physical manifestation, including states of turmoil and anguish from an inner psychological perspective, rendering them as public and quantifiable, and shocking as a result.

Futurism

In parallel with Germany, Italian society wanted upheaval and release from a feudal existence. The land-owning minority were being attacked on all sides by a new band of ideologues branded the Futurists, who saw revolution in the form of a new aggressive cultural output that stretched from architecture through to poetry. A fascination with the promise of industrial might, leading to the freedom of the working masses from their historical enslavers heralded a rush of ideas and new, dynamic and visionary approaches to communicating that energy and promise to an eager public. Rather than masque the frameworks of construction under a veneer of manufactured finish, the Futurists sought to lay bare their visual designs, characterized by strong, aggressive lines, sharp angles and directional text that exulted the virtues of the age. Art works by Gino Severini and Natalia Goncharova particularly embody these characteristics.

The synergy between cultural forms can be often observed in illustrative output of the period, where typography is used as a tool to illustrate and embed repetitive rhythm, symbolizing the repetitive nature of the precision-made machine of which the Futurist obsession was clear. In contemporary work, illustrators are drawn towards Retro-Futurism, which, as the term implies, embodies the angular constructions and inventive representation of its parent, whilst accentuating a neon colour palette and crisper, more complex mechanical renditions of forms that often defy gravity and logic.

Creating work digitally has created a natural bridge between image and typography and Retro-Futurism seamlessly blends these into integrated offerings that are both capable of being read in static form, and in the truest sense of Futurism, as moving components on digital publishing outlets.

Dada

Inevitably, this political and social unrest caused agitation in Europe, and coupled with industrial advances and nationalistic jockeying for positions of strength in a world quickly opening up resulted in tensions leading up to the declaration of the First World War. Rage and bitterness ensued, fuelled by disputes about geographical territory, misplaced trust in dubious political leadership, economic poverty and anxiety about the future from the masses. Instability in Europe heaped pressure on already historic fear and suspicion between nations, culminating in the assassi-nation of Archduke Franz Ferdinand of Austria in Sarajevo, Bosnia. The horrific result was the Great War (1914–18) which delivered frightening, apocalyptic scenes in the battlefields and the catastrophic loss of life on a scale never before witnessed.

The impending gloom and misery of the conflict gave birth and rise to the Dadaist movement, constituted primarily of communist sympathizers and anarchic creators. The Dadaists sought to produce output that weaved connections between the spoken and written word and visual output, amplifying the point-lessness of conflict and instead imploring that technological advances be applied to liberating the masses. Visual depiction was pared back, with limited colours being teamed with linear forms that often referenced industrial and urban objects and symbols, and produced using frugal printing methods available through circum-stance. As many creatives fled to avoid war zones and hotbeds of conflict, works in this period display a transience and fluidity that gives them energy and vibrancy.

Much of the historical and contemporary conceptual illustration output in an editorial setting has its philosophical and visual founda-tions in Dadaism. The gap between content and visual depiction creating a space for contempla-tion, reflection and analysis is a parallel concern for Dada creators and their conceptual modern-day contemporaries, who might be termed Neo-Dadaists. Crucially, this period created tensions between traditionalist and historical trappings of representation couched in recogni-tion of narrative realism and new, experimental

Figure 1.6
American illustrator David Plunkert's work draws upon Dadaism in his use of mechanical, print-based ephemera to make his images. This illustration is for *Sojourners* magazine for an article about abuse charges against Jean Vanier, a trusted spiritual advisor revealed as a predator. The compositional placement of the wolf inside the silhouette of the figure suggests evil lurking below the seemingly innocent surface.

approaches to the dynamic possibilities of setting imagery against typography as a playful union. The subversive exploits of John Heartfield (orig-inally Hertzfeld), Man Ray and Kurt Schwitters's use of photomontage have ignited interest in this most compelling and immediate of image-making processes. Contemporary editorial illustrators have been much influenced by Dadaism, includ-ing David Plunkert and Lola Dupre.

Suprematism and constructivism

The Russian Supremacists, like their Dadaist counterparts, saw opportunity in the Russian Revolution of 1917 to completely overhaul the public perception of governance and societal norms through artwork and cultural output which was revulsed by naturalistic glorifications of former empire and sovereignty. Suprematism embraced the abstracted form in all its glory, and experimental works played with notions of movement and discovery through composi-tion and colour, which were reduced to simple graphic shapes and bold primary palettes of one colour and black to reinforce values of equality and solidarity. The new communist ideals were highly attuned to being symbolically represented and output was universally produced to spread the message of the new, and reject vestiges of the old.

Later Constructivism developed these graphic motifs into revolutionary ideological messaging that was produced across traditional output such as painting and sculpture, but had more relevance in an illustrative context through publications, posters and murals of the period. Seduced and obsessed by the promise of adopting and harnessing new technological developments, exponents could see the communicative potential of these groundbreaking messages to reach across the geographic span of the country, and potentially beyond. This was heralded as the start of a new world order as 'Mother Russia' would have aspirations to become a formidable superpower on the global stage. Constructivist creators, spurred on by this vision and encouraged by a new government, produced powerful, directional

imagery that encompassed bold, primary-coloured blocked shapes and crisp, sans serif typography to hammer home messages of change, optimism and progress. The introduction of photomontage was both an important tool to diversify the image-makers tools, but also served to position real people at the heart of this political and cultural messaging as supporters and beneficiaries of new policies and ideas about nationhood in the twentieth century.

In contemporary editorial illustration, the work of American illustrator Shepherd Fairey gained global exposure during the 2008 US presidential campaign, with his Obey propogandist-style 'Hope' posters portraying Barack Obama in a positive and powerful political light. These posters, much like Fairey's output, place a heavy emphasis on strong design that utilizes symmetry, limited colour and repetitive graphic code and symbolism to create stunning, memorable images. The hope and optimism they carry was symbolically reflective of the tenet of the campaign generated by the Obama–Biden team that was successful in 2008.

Figure 1.7a–b
Inspired by the Constructivist movement founded by Vladimir Tatlin and Alexander Rodchenko, AhoyThere's cover for *The Big Issue* explores its readership to actively engage in creative activism. The industrial assemblage of materials and the limited, strong colours create a visually powerful graphic cover and at the same time, underpin the ethos and philosophy of *The Big Issue* as an organization and publication. The artwork is designed to encompass the masthead as an integrated component.

Primitivism

Exploits by artists who had been able to travel in the late nineteenth century served as an unexpected catalyst for the genesis of a new movement known as Primitivism. Cultural artefacts and objects, either brought or gifted from overseas travels to far-flung destinations such as Africa, Asia and Polynesia, or that were referenced through the work of artists who had produced during this period such as Paul Gauguin, Henri Matisse and Vincent Van Gogh, influenced a range of artists now entrapped by either conflict or economic hardship. Influential masks, carved figurines, textiles and jewellery were revered for their simple and faithful renditions, part-abstracted and part-observed depictions of a life seemingly free from difficulty and unabashed by the desperate situations that many found themselves in, in Europe and North America in particular. The developed world looked to its undeveloped cousins for visual and moral inspiration and found solace, charm and empathy in cultural artefacts that seemed to embody an innocence and simplicity so absent from the modern world.

As a source of visual inspiration, Primitivism is massively influential and apparent in contemporary editorial illustration production. Inevitably, the simplicity of form helps create message carriers who are strong, unfussy and direct, whilst the symbolism and iconography attached or attributed to these kind of works can be used to suggest underlying messages or create secondary narratives in support of headlines or running text. The scale and proportion in the depiction of figures, together with the opportunity to pose and gesture them in ways beyond physical conventions of the traditionally rendered human form, create opportunities to exaggerate meaning or create illusory connections with other figures, objects or environments.

Primitivism also permits the suspension of disbelief about subjects, so figures can float or fly, engage with living beings or objects that exhibit personalities through a shared language or belief system, and generally not conform to realist models of believability in physical appearance, or in manifestations of logical content.

Surrealism

Further flights of fancy and rejections of conventionalism spawned the movement known as Surrealism, which was embraced by artists, writers and poets looking for an escapism fuelled by the unconscious. This period saw influential publications by the Austrian neurologist Sigmund Freud, and Swiss psychologist Carl Jung, which introduced theories of psychoanalysis to populations looking for alternative approaches to how humans function and behave, as part of a new liberated freedom away from oppression and regimented existences.

Again, Surrealist compositions appeared to form from a dreamlike trance and elements often floated in the picture plane or on the written page, without apparent reason or relationship to other components of an image or ideas expressed through writing. Surrealist work was largely characterized by intuition and spontaneity, or as André Breton, the French leader of the Surrealists described it, as 'dictation of thought in the absence of all control exercised by reason, outside all aesthetic and moral preoccupation' (Breton 1924). Ideas appeared to form in the process of making work, almost as an automatic response to thoughts and feelings. At extreme ends of the movement, exponents swore by mind-altering drugs or hypnosis to fuel their creativity and output.

Surrealism juxtaposed unconnected, haphazard pictorial elements beyond reality in the image frame and forced the viewer to confront them as a collected whole, creating what Freud described as the 'uncanny', where a supposed familiarity with subjects can also make them alien as an experience. This disturbed or unsettled view of the world characterized the period between the two world wars and reflected many people's

Figure 1.8
Serge Bloch's work evokes the feel and spirit of Primitivism with its use of simplified forms, disproportionate limbs and illusory connections with other objects in the picture plane.

anxieties and fears about their predicament. The connected surreal works of Salvador Dalí, Joan Miro, Dorothea Tanning and Rene Magritte offer rich material for inspiration and guidance for illustrators. Surrealist-inspired work often accompanies articles which are extensions of thought, or deliberately obtuse in their structure or findings, creating the perfect environment for thought-provoking but seemingly incomplete communication. Such open-ended works allow for reflection, contemplation and dialogue between the maker and the reader.

Bauhaus

Given that the Bauhaus only existed for less than two decades (1919–33), its reach and significance is astonishing as a movement that sought to bring harmony to a crushed and despondent world following the end of the First World War. Founded by Walter Gropius, the Bauhaus school – the construction house – sought to bring artists and designers together to existentially serve a social role in using art and design to better society. The founding principle of 'form following function' characterized output across a wide gamut of publishing, product design, painting and architecture. Clean simplicity was preferred over ostentatious ornament to aid functionality and create modest, considered solutions.

In publishing design in particular, the 'less is more' mantra favoured by those leading and studying at the Bauhaus began to manifest itself in orderly and rational layout, with the control that could be wielded through typography and layout marginalizing imagery. The obvious omission was photomontage, which was manipulated from mechanically produced photographs to create even more direct and instructive messaging. Design was gaining traction as a recognized and valued democratic process, and in publishing design, where sorting and displaying information through a standardized framework that permitted hierarchies, the role of graphic design emerged as an occupation of note. The term graphic design originates from this period in history (1922) attributed to the American typographer, William Addison Dwiggins. Requisite skills merged the creative interests of placing information into a grid to aid legibility by adjusting typefaces, font sizes and spacing through new approaches to formatting which recognized and preserved the role of negative space in aiding readability, to the technical production needs that mass printing required.

Whilst undeniably reducing illustrative content in this period, the impact of the Bauhaus movement was substantial on contemporary illustrative practice, both on the philosophy that present-day creators have for prioritizing functionality and through the manufacture of visual solutions that are elegant, clean and sincere.

Art Deco

As a direct contrast to the rigour and elimination of unnecessary decoration of the Bauhaus, the Art Deco movement catered for those with more exotic and frivolous demands. The Art Deco movement gained traction following the Exposition internationale des arts décoratifs et industriels modernes staged in Paris, France in 1925. Decoration and ornamentation were celebrated and revered, characterized by a wide variety of output across publishing where the perceived opulence and mystique of East Asia and the Orient was heralded and reproduced in overtly stylized page layouts, detailed illustrations and decorative typographic forms. Art Deco symbolized the roaring 1920s as a form of escapism, optimism and promise for many, and artists and designers were quick to indulge this interest with output that sought to celebrate and cherish natural forms by actively incorporating

Figure 1.9
Finnish illustrator Janne Iivonen's illustrations are drawn in the *ligne claire* (clear line) tradition that was cultivated through the Art Deco movement, and utilize limited colour for maximum clarity. This illustration is about the pleasures of living in Europe for *Die Zeit*.

their motifs into furniture, lighting, urban design and architecture.

The clear-line work seen in editorial publishing derived from the Art Deco period. It allowed a dignified simplicity both of drawn style and clarity of communication of content, and was popular in publications emanating from the United States of America. Many of the illustrators producing work for publications had served in the armed forces in Europe and brought home dreams of escapism, rendered through these positive and life-affirming works that were characterized by a purity of seeping lines and placement of exotic colours. The marriage of illustration with typography as a considered holistic approach to page layout pays homage to the earlier Arts and Crafts movement that espoused the promotion of the craft of production as a wider political and social ideology of collectiveness and cooperation.

Moderne

An amplification of Art Deco, the Moderne movement is significant in editorial design for introducing form and order to covers and internal spreads of publications. Moderne styling imbued a strong, sensual use of typography and illustration to structured layouts, creating dynamic and eye catching motifs that are still a cornerstone of inspiration for many illustrators and designers working today. Taking inspiration from industrial design products such as automobiles, home appliances and retail and domestic interiors, the emphasis on sweeping, curved lines emphasized both the confidence of work being created in this period and the improved manufacturing prowess to take designs from initial drawings and render them in three-dimensional form. This assuredness ran in parallel in the editorial publishing field, with increased circulation numbers of magazines and periodicals as readerships exercised their increased wealth through subscriptions and lifestyle purchases, as retail confidence improved and the economic promise of capitalism proved a lure for many aspiring middle-class readers to better their lives and futures.

Editorial work was closely aligned with advertising work of the period. The dynamic compositions, full-page and full-bleed images that were saturated with colour epitomized the new optimism of the age, with careful crafting of illustrations that celebrated form through iconography, shape, limited bright colour and repetitive marks particularly to indicate action and speed. Moderne also became synonymous with the rise of 'pin-up girl' images of the period that sought to glamorize and sexualize women as objects of desire. Women were depicted in teasingly suggestive poses and rendered through a stylization that sought to subtly exaggerate their femininity and eliminate any imperfections. Inevitably, many argue that these hyper-stylized reproductions objectify and portray women as sexualized commodities. However, their appeal to women in the period they were published has also been described as liberating and powerful by some commentators.

For example, the pin-up illustrations created by Alberto Vargas assumed iconic status, and the subjects of his collected works, dubbed Varga Girls, became associated with portraying women as beautiful, confident and independent icons of the age. *Esquire* magazine, which was founded in 1933, used Vargas's work to underpin the brand values of the men's fashion magazine as a place that celebrated women for their emergent place in an increasingly liberated society. Vargas managed to both depict and empower women, of whom many were readers and self-confessed fans of his work, and some of whom went on to illustrate as a direct result of his encouragement.

The Moderne movement was the springboard for many artists and designers to establish international reputations as commercial artists who could work between disciplines, which is important in a modern-day context when considering cross-disciplinary practice that makes editorial illustration economically viable. A key exponent was the French illustrator and designer A. M. Cassandre who worked successfully for *Harper's Bazaar* as a cover artist and was often commissioned by advertising clients for his strong, graphic depictions of products and services that have led to many imitations and influences.

Postmodernism

The end of the Second World War saw many of the European and Asian industrialized nations having to regroup and rebuild their shattered economies, broken infrastructure and displaced civilizations. Waging war had been financially expensive and morally debilitating. Life was hard and the utopia of Modernism was challenged by a new breed of intellectuals and groups who set

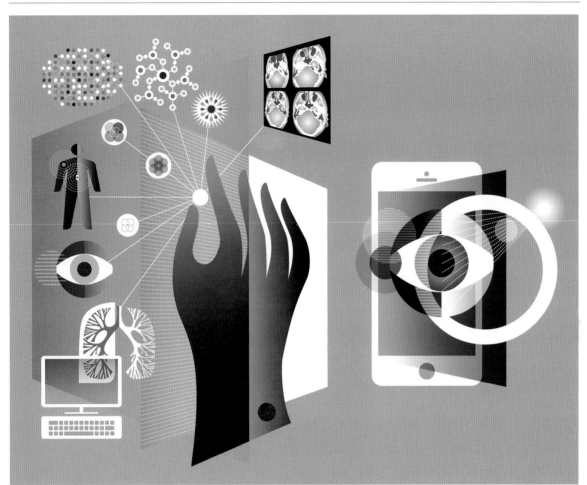

Figure 1.10
British illustrator Paul Wearing is influenced by architecture, interior and textile design of the 1950s and 1960s with its emphasis on colour, geometric shape and texture. His work is instantly recognizable through its attention both to concept and craft, ensuring a wide variety of global clients. More symbolic than literal, Wearing's approach is put to use here to illustrate the article '8 Ways to Look Inside. A sampler of diagnostics from Stanford', art directed by Dennis McLeod. Agency: David Armario Design for *Stanford Medicine* magazine.

out to deconstruct previous theories and instead promote the needs and wishes of causes of their own particular interests. Only the industrialized might of the United States stood relatively unscathed from war economically, but its own internal problems began with suspicions arising from the recent conflict that led to political accusations of communist tendencies, sowing the seeds for rising social tensions around race, gender and national identity. By the mid to late 1960s, the Civil Rights movement, an upsurge in feminism and increasing public hostility to the Vietnam War created a toxic atmosphere of anger, resentment and distrust which exploded both visual depictions of imagery and crucially, amplified content that was opinionated, expressive and contentious.

For illustration, the questioning of Modernist principles offered an opportunity to explore these new vantage points. Diversification of visual approaches became ever more prevalent

as identity in all its forms assumed greater significance. A borrowing and sharing of cultures and counter cultures assumed a new level of energy and expression, as experimental approaches to what constituted living arrangements became hot topics for debate. Sexual freedom and the growth of gay rights, the rejection of mainstream religion in favour of atheism or the exploration and adoption of alternative religious beliefs and customs offered opportunities for self-expression and new modes of societal acceptance. Cults, communes and civil disobedience created massive and deep-felt social tensions in families, communities, neighbourhoods and cities in industrialized societies. Cultural identity became more and more vital to these groups, able for the first time to publicly show their beliefs and protestations and the visual arts played a significant role in both branding and promoting these causes more widely.

Figure 1.11
Paul Slater's
take on
Postmodernism.

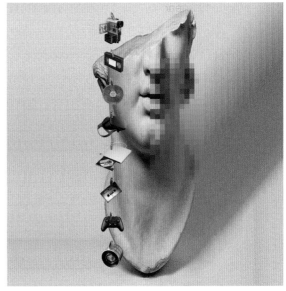

Figure 1.12
Matthew Richardson's illustrations are often thought-provoking
as they deliberately examine and probe connections between
text and image, forcing the reader to attempt to fill in the
gaps. This approach is similar to the Abstract Expressionists who
experimented with found objects, collage and photo-mechanical
processes to make social comment. This illustration is titled 'Diary
of a digital art conservator' for *The World of Interiors*.

Abstract Expressionism

The 1950s effectively marked the beginning of
the revival from the Second World War, and the
Abstract Expressionist movement exhibited the
promise of a better life against a backdrop of division between the prosperous, capitalist United
States and other NATO allies, and the communist Soviet Union and their Eastern bloc allies.
Conflicting ideologies about how the modern
world should function, act and behave were
witnessed through nuclear and space ambitions
that sought to exhibit power and influence by
creating a new world order. Political ideologies
were manifested through words, deeds and
actions and the cultural landscape became an
important marker for the successful winning of
minds. To this end, the Abstract Expressionists
received significant political and financial support
for their endeavours, as the United States sought
to show that non-figurative paintings and sculpture were forthright outputs that spoke of the
promise and progress of capitalism.

Through the war had forced many artists, designers
and cultural thinkers to escape occupied Europe,
and the United States, and New York City in
particular, welcomed these new immigrants to an
already diverse melting pot of cultural practice.
Major cultural players such as Piet Mondrian,
Marc Chagall, Marcel Duchamp and Max Ernst
made their home in the Big Apple, and influenced
the action paintings of Jackson Pollock, Franz
Kline and Willem de Kooning, and the abstracted
colour field paintings of Robert Motherwell and
Mark Rothko. Sculptors such as Alexander Calder,
Henry Moore and Louise Bourgeois rose to international prominence too in this period.

Perhaps more influential for the illustration fraternity was the work being produced
by Eduardo Paolozzi and Richard Hamilton in

Britain, and contemporaries Jasper Johns and
Robert Rauschenberg in America, who pioneered
the way for the Pop Art movement. Their output
referred to how consumerism, driven by free
market capitalism, was enveloping a generation
by use of appropriating found objects, collage
and photo-mechanical processes to make social
comment. Abstraction created tensions that
revealed different political and sociological ideologies between the increasingly separate East
and West, creating the trigger for the birth and
development of the Pop Art and Conceptual Art
movements of the 1960s and 1970s.

Pop Art

Undoubtedly a highly influential movement in
many circles, the Pop Art phenomenon of the
1960s is a highly visible marker of the changing
times affecting society. The work of the period
was highly experimental, both in pushing how
images were conceived and produced, and also
testing their legibility and communicative effect
on an audience. The commodification of consumerism acted as a touchstone for many, including
the now infamous Andy Warhol, whose creative
roots were as a commercial artist and whose

mass-produced agenda shaped much fine art and illustration content of the forthcoming decades.

The recognition and proliferation of Pop Art as a movement was important as it raised the profile and cultural awareness of popular culture to heights not previously seen, breaking the long-held view of 'art for art's sake' and creating an environment where many creative producers and makers felt empowered and compelled to make contributions, whether through painting, writing, sculpture, poetry or music. Illustrative expression was equally driven by content and aesthetics. Crucial to this period was the work produced by artists such as Jasper Johns and Roy Lichtenstein, with the latter expressing and glamorizing comic books as a legitimate and immediate form of communication and storytelling, and thus blurring historical boundaries between high and low art. A generation of image-makers including Sir Peter Blake, Eduardo Paolozzi, Alex Katz and Julian Opie introduced and developed Pop Art as a legitimate

form of editorial communication well suited to the zeitgeist of the times. They have inspired contemporary illustrators such as Malika Favre and Michelle Thompson.

The shackles of publishing, so often a field unattainable and impenetrable for the masses, were suddenly freed and many underground publications began to spring up to cater for the surge in demand. Burgeoning subject areas such as feminism, social history, human rights, political activism and peace studies flourished in this period, and with low production budgets and contributors happy to see their work in print, a relative free-for-all attitude seemed to embody the times. Alternative titles could be produced using relatively cheap paper stock and screen-printing methods, whilst more stable offset printing as also not beyond the reach of many. Dissemination of these alternative publications was kept local and regional, attracting a devoted readership looking for radical, alternative content to that found in the seemingly out-of-touch broadsheet newspapers and periodicals being produced at the time. Crucial to the success of these alternative outlets was the whole counter-culture

Figure 1.13
British illustrator Michelle Thompson's iconic cover of British Prime Minister Boris Johnson for *The Sunday Times Magazine* pays homage to Andy Warhol's Pop Art portraits of the 1960s. Original photograph by PEROU. This illustration generated many political assignments for Thompson after its publication.

Figure 1.14
Using striking colour and bold, geometric pattern reminiscent of the Pop Art movement, Malika Favre's fashion illustrations create a dynamic presence on page and screen.

movement, driven by the non-conformist Beat Generation, where independent record stores, bookshops and wholefood retailers all stocked and actively promoted publications of this nature. The connectedness of communities and the malleability of output served to draw and bind groups together, creating new communities with ideals, aspiration and adventures all of their own.

Psychedelia

As the diversification of publishing continued, the experimental nature of music, art, writing and performance manifested itself through psychedelia in the mid- to late 1960s. As the term implies, much of the output of this period was narcotically induced, with hitherto barriers to social and cultural freedoms being constantly challenged and remapped. The psychedelic movement appealed to an increasingly disenfranchised 'baby boomer' generation of young adults, who questioned the political and social norms of their parents and rebelled to create an alternative, egalitarian society that rejected discrimination. There are clear associations between the music of the period and the visual material that accompanied it in album cover or promotional poster form, and the underlying beliefs and motivations of the hippie cultural movement.

The west coast of the United States, and specifically the city of San Francisco, was the epicentre of this movement. But psychedelia had a cultural reach that extended, albeit briefly, much wider and had profound implications for the towns and cities of middle America who were witnessing threats to their everyday way of lives. Bands such as the Grateful Dead, The Doors, Janis Joplin, Jimi Hendrix and Jefferson Airplane established massive followings for their experimental, hallucinogenic music, which was illustrated by Victor Moscoso, Rick Griffin, Alton Kelley, Stanley Mouse and Robert Wesley Wilson. Images created reveal both the aesthetic and decorative preoccupations of the period with signature over-embellishment of imagery and curvilinear typography into largely indiscernible forms that were deliberately designed to challenge legibility and understanding.

Crucially, the psychedelia movement sought to reinvent the pictorial picture plane by drawing on, appropriating and amalgamating visual sources from previous visual works. Genetically, much psychedelic work has inherent similarities with the Arts and Crafts movement, spliced with Art

Figure 1.15
Milton Glaser's iconic poster of the American singer-songwriter Bob Dylan from 1966 is perhaps the most recognizable visual statement from the counter-culture period. Dylan's curly hair provided the starting point for the swirling, multi-coloured flurry that symbolizes the reach and significance of his music and alludes to the mind-bending drugs associated with psychedelia.

Nouveau and some discernible connections with the Vienna Succession. In contemporary editorial work, the origins of psychedelia still manifest themselves through works which are highly decorative, prioritizing natural forms through the surprising juxtaposition of visual elements, bright and often jarring colour palettes which are synonymous with the Op(tical) Art movement, giving images desired degrees of impenetrability.

Conceptual Art

The inclusion of Conceptual Art, even to recognize it as an art movement, is a step too far for some cultural commentators, but it is important to include it in a book dealing with editorial illustration. Conceptual Arts grandparents were Surrealism and Dada, and the strong links between the intangible and the unexplained serve as a foundation stone for a movement whose primary motive was the outright rejection of materiality and physical representation. Underpinned by the great twentieth-century postmodernist and poststructuralist philosophers such as Gilles Deleuze, Jacques Derrida, Michel Foucault and others, Conceptual Art raised the significance of the overarching idea of the work being vastly more important than its physical manifestation. Artist Sol LeWitt explained that, 'When an artist uses a conceptual form of art, it means that all of the planning and decisions are made beforehand and the execution is a perfunctory affair. The idea becomes a machine that makes the art' (LeWitt 1967). As a result, an apparatus was required to scaffold the work and the use of language became that significant framework, allowing a conceptual position to be proposed and the argument for a critical case to be asserted.

From the origins of Marcel Duchamp, who dismissed aesthetics and production values in pursuit of provocative questions about the merit and value of art as a cultural contribution, conceptual artists have sought to meanings through reassembling the starting point for works. In editorial illustration work, conceptual

Figure 1.16
Javier Jaén is rightly regarded as one of the most iconic conceptual illustrators of his generation, here capturing the zeitgeist of the times for *The New York Times*.

illustration production assimilates some of the ideas around the associative power of language with opportunities to imbue or suggest narrative directions within images to imply other meanings. An example of this type of approach is John Baldessari who subverts film stills by deconstructing and rearranging their forms, integrating text and completely altering their original intention and meaning.

In a contemporary context, the illustrator Javier Jaén uses found objects and assemblages to completely reorder and alter meaning in his playful, witty constructions which provoke surprise, attention and recall from readerships. The works are deliciously ambiguous and detached from their original purpose, yet immediately readable and understood.

Pop Surrealism and Lowbrow

The 1970s saw an inevitable diversification in cultural production of all kinds with all the experimentation and discovery of the previous decades. Art, design, music and writing all went through a progressive period of expression, enveloping new ideas and seeking direction from increasingly eclectic sources. Humankind had travelled into space and conquered the moon, there were promises of political and social change through upheaval manifested by post-colonial rebalancing and greater international cooperation in the twilight of the Cold War. As the decade progressed, visual artists, designers and other cultural producers drew on the dream-like nature of Surrealism and the immediate, imagined reality of Pop Art to create a deliberately low-brow output of work that evoked the mass population's subconscious sensibilities and concerns.

Illustration work produced by exponents such as Mark Ryden and Camille Rose Garcia evokes a tangible sense of tension between highly finished and realized painted painterly forms in judderingly obscure landscapes as unerring environments. Content is often obliquely suggested, creating a dilemma for the unsuspecting reader. The images make for intriguing, and sometimes uncomfortable, viewing, with permission granted to spectate on subjects that are depicted in sometimes compromised or vulnerable situations. Here, the Surrealism philosophy of challenging the unconscious or subconscious mind of the viewer seems to find a renaissance.

In a similar vein, the Lowbrow movement also uses audience discomfort as a way of presenting awkward questions around taste and decency from the margins of culture deemed by many not to be cultural at all. Lowbrow creators take inspiration and draw subject matter from the latent underbelly of society and culture that exists within the margins, often propagated by exponents who have little or no recollection that they are cultural contributors, and whose output would be deemed inexplicable, illogical or dispensable by society at large. Punk music, kitsch artefacts and underground graffiti are examples of source material that Lowbrow artists continually refer to in the making of their work. As a result, output is often designed to be challenging, uncomfortable and conflicted. On the other hand, it often produces work that is surprising, fresh and responsive to mood and atmosphere and can be seen to be therefore reflective of cultural tendencies, tensions and trigger points. The work of illustrators such as Gary Baseman and J. Otto Seibold embodies a Lowbrow approach, where cultural output is varied by publishing vehicle, product or accompanying narrative, but has philosophical clues to the origins and motivations for making the work that resonate with a lived experience and observation of urban street life.

Folk Art

The recognition of Folk Art precedes, by some distance, the latter part of the twentieth century but in the context of how it influenced illustration output, its introduction here is pertinent. Folk Art draws its inspiration from honest depictions and renditions of everyday life in indigenous and peasant communities, celebrating the pursuit of the ordinary through utilitarian or decorative artefacts and objects which are created by self-taught makers who may have had skills passed down to them through previous generations. The genetic origins of Folk Art work are strongly bonded to the peoples that created them and for the peoples that will encounter and receive them. As such, Folk Art is for all people, regardless of class, community, culture, ethnicity, gender, religion and status.

Folk Art displays wonderful cultural variance and a multitude of approaches based on creative and storytelling traditions of its creators, and this synergy between the underlying narrative and the aesthetic output is what has influenced many illustrators who admire the integrity of the work and the deeply held convictions about its production. Furniture, textiles, painting, sculpture and ceramics are produced as objects for everyday sale in small quantities due to their handmade origins and whilst mechanical processes of production are not strictly ruled out, the availability of materials and production tools has historically determined the scale of production that can reasonably be achieved.

In recent years, Folk Art has attracted much interest from collectors as an embodiment of local and regional craft-based traditions which speak to unique ecosystems of communal social history. As a result, work that has historically and traditionally been seen by geographically based admirers has been propelled into global awareness through increased travel and global trade. In some instances, this creates tensions for makers and purchasers who are keen to preserve regional cultural identities, since that is the core essence of the work produced. However, Folk Art makers and purchasers are acutely aware that the production of artefacts is a vital and necessary form of income that is often the difference between being able to manufacture items or not. Many illustrators collect Folk Art not only as inspiration for their own work, but as a 'giving back' to local economies in the spirit to which they themselves are commissioned.

Illustrators such as Jeffrey Fisher, Jonny Hannah and the Clayton Brothers are all influenced by Folk Art and, indeed, many would describe their output as a contribution to this movement. The humility and integrity of the work creates a strong bond between creator and viewer, with simplistic objects, figures and other

Figure 1.18
Jonny Hannah's work is inspired and driven by telling stories of the people. In essence, his illustrative output goes far beyond being inspired by Folk Art. Instead, he is a leading figure in the field, who produces editorial illustration as part of a much larger set of cultural contributions that span books, objects and artefacts. A prolific producer, Hannah's work is rooted in traditions and tales, wonderfully illustrated here in his *Sunday Telegraph* homage to William Shakespeare's collected literary works.

pictorial elements manifested through naïve shapes, repetitious motifs and iconography that is irregular in measurement and finish. Many illustrators utilize a combination of raw materials and handmade processes in the construction of these kind of illustrations and the construction method itself can be a contributing factor to the overall success of the image. The Folk Art colour palette historically took its ingredients from the raw materials of a particular region, including natural dyes drawn from plants and crops that were available. The resulting pigments spoke of the land that they had originated from, giving Folk Art a tangible sense of belonging to specific locations. Illustrators draw much influence from the colour palettes of these offerings, inspired by their unusual juxtapositions and surprising choices that create deep, rich evocations in commercial work.

Outsider Art and Art Brut

A much discussed, and, in some quarters, controversial term, Outsider Art has an interesting output that is influential for illustrators aesthetically, whilst being distant from how

they conduct their practice professionally. Raw Vision, a leading authority on Outsider Art, describes the movement as 'the awareness of forms of creative expression that exist outside of cultural norms' [https://rawvision.com/pages/what-is-outsider-art]. Significantly, producers and creators of works that fall into this realm are experiencing some kind of psychological or emotional trauma that destabilizes or detaches them from conventional society, and who certainly would have little recognition or awareness of what they create as 'art', nor comprehend the idea of a collected public display. Instead, much output is driven by an inner need of individuals to create as a channel of focus of their energy or as some form of therapeutic release.

Works can be characterized by extreme subject matter, which can often depict subjects displaying scenes of violence, raw sexuality, repression or anger, depicted through an intensity of obsessive mark-making, and often repetitive motifs that suggest a distant state of thought and action in the mind of the creator. Equally, some works display a compulsive interest in subjects or motifs which can manifest itself through unswerving attention to detail through rhythmic or hypnotic production, emphasizing a complete immersion with the psychological self that spawns a torrent of visual output.

Art Brut, by extension, translates as 'raw art' and describes works that are unadulterated by other arts production or cultural influence. Closely linked to the Surrealists, the collected art works of psychiatric patients in a Swiss asylum administered by Dr Hans Prinzhorn which were published in 1922, created a fascinating glimpse into the world view through the eyes of those patients. The accompanying book, *Bildnerei der Geisteskranken* (Artistry of the Mentally Ill), profoundly affected the French artist Jean Dubuffet and with André Breton, the influential writer, philosopher and creative pioneer, they amassed a significant collection of works to be investigated and explored as alternative but culturally significant oppositions to centuries of artistic cultural tradition. The visual output of artists such as Bill Traylor, Henry Darger and Madge Gill have influenced illustrators such as Martin Haake and Noah Woods, who openly talk about the effect that Art Brut and Outsider Art have had on their work in both the extension of inner self-expression and physical manufacture of artwork.

Digital and global monoculture: The transition from analogue to digital

From the late 1980s into the new century, the postmodernist agenda of expanding horizons and crossing boundaries between disciplines created a new wave of experimentation fuelled by the accessibility and new capabilities of digital technologies. The introduction of what are now considered studio necessities – a digital camera, computer, scanner and reliable internet connection – liberated not only the production of creative work, but its delivery and dissemination to a whole new audience who were not bound by geographical constraints. Fundamentally, it gave illustrators more power and purpose in the workplace by questioning roles and responsibilities and exploding the myth of illustrator as service provider. Cross-disciplinary practice has collided with theory into a global phenomenon that has legitimized many new, experimental forms of creative practice and given rise to a whole new breed of creatives who see the power and reach of the World Wide Web as a democratizing platform to showcase and be informed, educated and entertained. Multimodal practice involving the interaction between visuals, sounds and movements has forced the consideration of a new dimension – time – into the creative arsenal of production tools.

The game-changing introduction of the Apple MacIntosh computer in 1984, complete with the now infamous Ridley Scott-directed commercial referencing the novel by George Orwell, that promised freedom rather than control. The advertisement propelled Mac into the stratosphere of creative professionals and wannabes who saw creative potential beyond word processing and spreadsheets of rivals. Aided by an intuitive GUI (graphic user interface), which cleverly utilized the icon of a helpful smiley face and a mouse, studios, workshops and spare bedrooms were transformed into creative workspaces. Creative software packages such as MacDraw and MacPaint were bundled together to give creatives the chance to explore and experience the difference between vector and bit-mapped graphics respectively. Other software houses sprang up, offering alternative packages that utilized the stability of the operating system but creating choices for artists and designers to originate, develop and execute their creations, and to organize their offerings through slick desktop publishing programmes. The spirit of the late 1960s counter-culture movements that sought to remove obstacles to progress and leap ahead with experimental, localized innovation was rekindled or revitalized through a growing movement of hungry and enthusiastic digital pioneers.

The American illustrator Barbara Nessim is correctly regarded as a pioneer of the digital editorial illustration. Her work, 'The Gift', for *BYTE* magazine in September 1984, is recognized as the first commissioning of a digital editorial piece of work, combining fluid line and vibrant block colour. These early works excited illustrators and publishers, and spawned a growth in collaborations between creatives and coders to invent software packages which would expand the scope and refine the editorial market for excited makers and their readerships. For example, Adobe's launch of Illustrator in 1986, and Photoshop in 1998, are regarded as seminal moments in contemporary illustration practice and have featured in the development of professional profiles, and of wider cultural output since. The very irony of cross- and multidisciplinary practice, as foreseen by Marshall McLuhan, is that tools like Illustrator and Photoshop have the processing power to render images as identikit realities, making their output almost indistinguishable from a photograph.

The term 'global monoculture' is an interesting spanner to throw into the current art movement landscape. Unquestionably, the adoption of digital tools has profoundly affected cultural output globally, from the digital sampling of music to the repurposing of photographic images into montages detached from their original intention. Many commentators argue that digitization has homogenized creative thinking as well as production, since creatives are generally using the same platforms, software packages and tools to create flat, vector-based material which they characterize as devoid of individual personality and feeling. The immense power of programmes to learn user preferences in terms of tool choices, and gestures of using digital tools like brushes and pens through built-in artificial intelligence, is a situation many creators remain wary of and in some instances, are actively hostile to, as an act of de-libertizing and controlling their creative freedom.

The automation of the wider working society, where the likely changes to labour forces in the

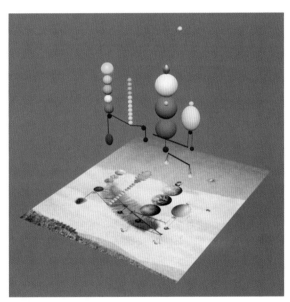

Figure 1.19a–b
A glimpse of an augmented reality future for publishing, in this cover titled 'Prediction Machine' by Matthew Richardson for *Morningstar Magazine*. The cover triggers a VR visualization by Mesmerise Studios which engages users and creates experiences that allow the content to function in a multi-sensory way for readers. Such approaches seek to immerse their audience as a participator in content rather than merely an observer of material.

near future will profoundly affect the origination and production of many goods and services, is seen by some as threatening creative freedom. However, much like the often prophesized death of print, the creative industries embrace of these digital tools offers scope and depth of opportunities for those willing to embrace associated fields such as motion, augmented, virtual and mixed reality (AR, VR and MR) through cooperative enquiry and collaborative practice between maker and recipient. As such, relationships between creation, adoption and reception of content stand to alter complexion in the years to come and editorial illustrators need to be at the vanguard of those developments.

Universal truths: Illustration prejudice

Illustration has been described critically and cruelly as the 'Cinderella of the Arts'. Why does it have this tag? What damage has resulted from its pejorative description, and what have illustrators' done to challenge this unhelpful perception? A straight comparison between 'Illustration' and 'Art' is neither helpful nor required in this context, since they serve particular and specific functions, have different histories of patronage, and various communities of reception. Consequently, they have evolved quite differently. What is clear, however, is that prejudicial views exist both of the subject of illustration, and the content that has been historically attributed to and displayed by illustration, including racial stereotyping, gender bias and political incorrectness of both the message and mode of manufacture carried by images that needs further examination and reconciliation.

To establish some grounding in the context of editorial illustration, where a relationship must exist between image and text, there is very clearly a difference in interpretation of the core values and attributes between Art and Illustration. Whilst the production of Art is multifarious, its origin is not ordinarily defined by a specific purpose. Editorial illustration exists to elucidate, inform and expose content for a reader. That is not to imply that issues do not pertain to, nor exist, in the Art world – they do. But historically, that field has found methods to use these tensions to mobilize modes of production, or at the very least, to open debates around sensitive and controversial issues to critique, contextualize and circumvent views from or with the wider viewing public. Illustration, as part of the wider commercial arts, has often returned instead to its economic value as a justifiable and defensible means of existence, rather than actively fight a corner and be considered as a major cultural contributor in its own right.

In itself, this a peculiarly inward position, since the wider public have a sophisticated awareness of the role and function of illustration as a conveyor of political or commercial messages, and are able to name famous illustrators, or their output, as significant contributors to national output of cultural heritage. For example, Norman Rockwell, perhaps the most famous illustrator of his age, was immediately identified as the cover artist for the *Saturday Evening Post,* and in the context of the American public, a more prolific artist than his contemporaries Jackson Pollock and Jasper Johns. Primarily, this fame was due to amazing circulation figures as periodicals like *Life, Women's Home Companion* and the *Saturday Evening Post* had provided entertainment to many American families prior to the arrival of television in the 1950s.

Some elitist views on illustration accompanying text can be traced to gender-based issues around nineteenth-century constructs of the perceived masculinity of text versus the femininity of image-making as a predominantly decorative form. Illustrated text in the early 1800s was increasingly popular. New publishing technology saw the introduction of images to accompany text, creating a welcome break from text-heavy content for readers. The technology and resulting products created a new kind of demand, and lucrative financial return for publishers and those authors rich enough to be able to employ illustrators. Most authors, poets and playwrights were male and from privileged backgrounds, and enjoyed a healthy status quo of being successful and financially stable. The heights of fame and celebrity that their published works ensured were most certainly worth preserving.

Maintaining a position of authority was not only a necessity in terms of controlling what was published, but a seeming rite of passage for male literary creators in this period to maintain the lifestyle and social standing to which they had become accustomed. Many male authors, poets and playwrights regarded these new illustrated texts as a threat, both to the standing of their craft in higher cultural circles, and to the hierarchy of their output as a superior form of intellectual content. The developing taste for illustrated text would inextricably threaten their livelihoods and their place in the social strata. Illustrated texts were gaining popularity in the public psyche and presented a threat to an established existence enjoyed by the privileged few, and it came as no surprise to see the establishment resort to attacking illustrated texts by undermining confidence in the voracity and quality of their content.

Early attacks by English poet Charles Lamb, roundly criticized writer Samuel Roger's illustrated edition *The Pleasures of Memory* for being 'decadent and ostentatious', according to Brian M. Kane (Doyle, Grove and Sherman 2019: 224), where Lamb is reported to have stated that, 'the "sister arts" or the "feminine arts," should never be intertwined with the "manly art" of writing'. It should be noted that the illustrators in question were J. M. W. Turner and Thomas Stothard, two of the most eminent artists producing work in the early 1800s and both Royal Academicians. The *Quarterly Review* ran the article 'Illustrated Books' where former editor John Murray questioned both the ability of illustrators to illustrate the text and the quality of their efforts. This thinly veiled attempt at disparaging the place of illustration at the expense of writing sought to downgrade the image as a mere aide to understanding the written content, in what Murray referred to as a 'second childhood of learning' (Kane, in Doyle, Grove and Sherman 2019: 224).

Kane proposes that the pejorative 'juvenile' tag that stigmatizes the reception of illustration by many has its roots in this comment. Even the celebrated English poet William Wordsworth, in his sonnet 'Illustrated Books and Newspapers', sought to chastise the illustrative text for being a feminine invasion into a male-dominated space and relegating the imposition of images to a previous time when cavemen daubed images on rockfaces. The idea that a 'manly' text and a 'feminine' image could exist in unison conjured up unspeakably grim societal conventions which were abhorrent to him. Sadly, his popularity and the impact of his views was debilitating for illustration in the wider appreciation of cultural value.

However, an appetite for illustration to accompany text had been established and the seeds of curiosity had been sown. Whilst there would be a gulf in equal representation of the sexes in publishing for some time, the illustrated text garnered significant and growing interest amongst those desperate to further themselves. Illustrated texts helped many to self-educate and improve their literacy, established the legibility of content as a determining factor of laying out information coherently, and expanded knowledge for a generation desperate to improve their lot. In turn, the illustrated text would contribute a powerful voice and advocacy for kindling the movements of social upheaval of the late 1800s,

Figure 1.20
Far from being the 'Cinderella of the Arts', dynamic editorial illustration relies on how the illustrator considers the reader's relationship with an image. Here, Malika Favre uses an unexpected upward viewpoint to engage the reader with the subject for the cover of *The New Yorker*, but, moreover, places women in a position of power and professional authority in historically one of the most male-dominated professions in the world, making a clear stand for equality and a reversal of gender biased representation.

mobilizing people to question and challenge issues such as workers' employment rights, women's place in society and the right to universal education.

What damage has been done?

The popularity of editorial illustration waxes and wanes in line with other forms of visual communication that are subject to fashion. Editorial illustration has certainly enjoyed golden moments that coincide with better economic fortunes, strong editorial direction from publishers and editors and incisive journalism by talented reporters who possessed sharp writing skills. For example, the Golden Era of the 1950s benefited from post-war America's relative wealth after the Second World War and the growth of commercial advertising spend in the media positively benefited the spend on editorial assignments. Conversely, the 1990s saw a proliferation of stock editorial illustration used over and above bespoke commissions, fuelled partly by recessive budgets and easy access to digital archives for a fraction of the cost of hiring a skilled creator.

Most apparent and problematic in these two examples is the undeniable shift to the increasing absence of mentorship from art director to illustrator, which raises education issues on one level, but also exposes lack of knowledge and understanding about creating genuine creative environments beyond financial boundaries. Tighter budgets and pressurized working patterns through more efficient digital interfaces have created additional pressures that can negatively affect the voracity of comment and the quality of manufacture of editorial illustrations. By extension, one can argue this damages the credibility of the wider field of critical, investigative journalism.

Knowledge creation is a recognized and valued pursuit in many disciplines, so why not in the creative industries? The lack of an established theoretical position as a serious, hard-hitting cultural output means that editorial illustration as a form experiences these fashion swings more frequently and violently than forms such as photography. Being on the margins potentially makes serious contribution difficult, stimies collaboration and suffocates the experimentation, innovation and creative development of new and established practitioners. This creates associated problems with the visibility of illustration as a cultural producer of note, affects the professional standing of career illustrators and is reflected in the number of students wanting to study illustration as a major discipline in higher education circles at college.

Certainly, a dearth of academically informed and debated literature has not helped editorial illustration (and the wider subject outside editorial parameters), both within the discipline of graphic design, or in the wider cultural appreciation of visual communication arts as a serious cultural contributor. As the latter wider discipline, the reflection on communication – especially from a practice-informed perspective, is poor – and points to a neglect from critical fraternities like art or design history to engage with illustration, say in the way that has been garnered around architecture or product design. In these two disciplines, there is much serious writing about the technical and aesthetic considerations around the design and construction of domestic and commercial buildings and products, and a celebration of the best exponents of those fields in academic journals, peer-reviewed writing and specialist publications. Moreover, there is a wider appreciation in the role architecture and products play in our everyday lives, including how we view, consume and value their output, and what social, economic and political impacts that have on wider society. By comparison, illustration is a mere bystander.

What have illustrators done?

The situation is thankfully changing. Greater numbers of students want to be educated to higher degree level, perhaps in response to changes in high school curricula which have veered towards STEM-based subjects in recent years as a result of government intervention. Illustration as a subject is easily able to embrace and engage STEM-inspired learners with its heavy emphasis on problem-solving and analytical frameworks to investigate and interrogate subjects. Additionally, there are an increasing number of PhD registered students and doctoral-qualified candidates applying for higher education positions in institutions across the world, whether in education or wider industrial contexts.

Specific illustration-focused academic journals have sprung up, backed by publishers to ensure distribution channels are accessible across the globe. An increasing number of symposia, conferences and live or broadcast events are staged to encourage presentation of new thinking, convergent and divergent approaches to the craft, reception and critique of illustration and a wider appreciation of how the subject of illustration has distinct qualities, innate attributes and particular modes of thinking in its own right. In commercial circles, illustration is being increasingly championed as being a viable and trusted route to explain and inform across publishing platforms as a joined up and strategic process. For example, we have seen inventive approaches to the way that data is presented, from the 2020 US presidential

Figure 1.21
Armando Veve's hauntingly ethereal illustration for *The New Yorker* perfectly captures the spirit of Elizabeth Kolbert's article 'Where Have All the Insects Gone?' which investigates the perilous decline of insects by scientists and heralds worrying signs for all creatures, including humans. Art directed by Alexandra Zsigmond, the illustration shows the chemistry been commissioner and creator, revealing the level of intellectual investment and intrinsic knowledge of audience that this quality of work demands.

election campaign results to instructions to the general populous on preventing the spread of the Covid-19 coronavirus.

Reclaiming ground from other disciplines and having the confidence and courage to own the field of illustration studies as an explicit focus is important, but equally vital is understanding and exploiting this knowledge in the pursuit of recognition in other interfaces, such as user experience, service design and animation, where there are clear roles for illustration to play in the creation and establishment of new knowledge. Further still, the collaborations now taking place between academically trained illustrators and scientists, engineers and policy makers can see illustration gaining exposure, awareness and recognition in many areas that need global attention and development in the forthcoming decades, such as economic mobility, social care reform and health education. It is these explorations that will signal the next step in illustration being recognized as an important and valued contributor to areas such as social anthropology, memory studies and health management to name but a few.

Current Issues and Debates

In an ever-changing communication world, the nature and role of editorial illustration is shifting and continues to re-characterize itself, to keep abreast of global developments and report them to an evolving demographic of readers. The nature of contemporary news communication unfolds at a dramatic pace, requiring constant classification, contextualization and elicitation in ever-decreasing passages of time. In the wake of such constant and quickly evolving content, the role of editorial illustration is to expose and explain news content, by informing, educating and entertaining readerships, and by default, sharing those experiences across engaged cultures, ethnic groups and genders.

Editorial illustration is well placed to highlight global issues, whether providing a visual commentary on cataclysmic pandemics, instructing readers on important health or finance-related matters, or educating them about new technological advances in science or manufacturing. Major global developments inevitably have local impacts to all societies and communities. The editorial illustrator collects complex discoveries and developments, distilling them into simple visual images that enable them to be understood and facilitates their application at local levels. Editorial illustration is truly a barometer of the pressure of our communication times.

However, part of the revered testament of an editorial illustration, and its lasting legacy as a form of journalism in its own right, lies in the need to absorb and reflect on news content and provide a distanced, but nuanced perspective with the critical benefit of hindsight. The need to pause, reflect and reconcile views on content is an important facet of editorial illustration practice. Sadly, the lack of a nuanced position is all too prevalent in other parts of the communication media, readily exposed by the immediacy of social media platforms, where the countless examples of false reporting, misrepresentation or worse, the vacuum of reliable factual foundations, should give real cause for concern.

A considered editorial position should not only react to events, but contextualize them against historical encounters and previous experiences, see them through the lens of resulting actions, and thereby suggest and unlock potential visions. Unlike photographic content, editorial illustration is not only able to factually represent, but can also be constructed to imaginatively depict futures as hypothetical situations and is thus a highly versatile and valued medium.

The power of editorial illustration

The unique role of editorial illustration is to provide a visual commentary on the world around and beyond us. Regardless of whether the subject is political, economic, social or cultural commentary, editorial illustration's purpose and embedded power is to present information visually that can question attitudes, change opinions and alter behaviours. Editorial illustration examines both the major headlines and the fine margins of content, by introducing new findings, exposing points of difference and posing unanswerable questions. It is hugely powerful as a graphic device to immediately shock, excite and inform, yet is also capable of creating potent, deep and lasting impacts.

The lure for editorial illustrators is clearly the potential reach and significance of work being published. Unlike an artist who has gallery representation, editorial illustration's communication channels are global, multi-lingual and pan-cultural. Illustrated messages are traditionally conveyed through newsstands, but harnessing the global distribution power of publishers, also conceivably through every newsstand on the planet. Images are then experienced by a secondary readership by being seen on platforms, subway trains, airport departure halls and doctor's waiting rooms, through the newspapers, magazines and journals of fellow consumers. Messages can be further subverted by readers into placards, banners and posters by enthusiastic fans, enraged readers and motivated followers, giving content yet further extended diasporic life.

Illustrated content is also shared on broadcast platforms through newspaper reviews, editorial discussions between expert correspondents and as backdrops in studio discussions and debates. Work is even witnessed in public forums such as

Figure 2.1
Stanley Chow's masterful graphic language creates immediately recognizable portraits of political figures, celebrities and famous profiles using an economy of visual elements, here depicting the historic inauguration of President Joseph R. Biden and Vice President Kamala Harris which will have a global impact.

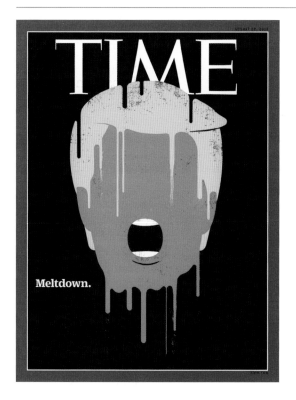
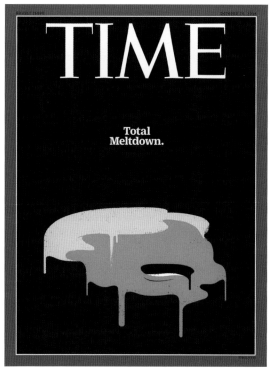

Figure 2.2a–b
The August 2016
Time magazine
'Meltdown' cover
by Edel Rodriguez,
art directed by
D. W. Pine, is a
successful example
of reducing graphic
elements down
to bare essentials
through the process
of condensation in
order to communicate
a complex idea
about the Trump
presidential style,
and becomes
a metaphorical
extension of the
administration
descending into
chaos. The theme is
continued through the
use of characterizing
the passing passage
of time in the 'Total
Meltdown' cover from
October 2016.

concerts, festivals and live events. Online content further seeds new directions for consumption using social media channels that are either networked, or through users who have multiple presence across platforms to share and respond to media-rich posts.

The presence of editorial illustration in the public realm is truly extraordinary and is only likely to grow and diversify, as the public demand more diverse content coverage, greater analysis and closer scrutiny of content in the quest for knowledge, information and truth. Editorial illustration commands respect in the journalistic traditions of upholding freedoms of speech and the right to hold particular views, but is able to navigate subject matter with dexterity and sensitivity precisely because it is a constructed visual form that can exercise certain freedoms and swerve obstacles and restrictions.

Responsibility: Freedoms and restrictions

In the communication media, powerful freedoms come with great responsibility. The journalistic reach and significance of editorial publications affords tremendous power to persuade and influence readerships. There is a balance to be struck between breaking news, reporting behind the

scenes on dangerous events, exposing scandalous actions and publishing provocative opinions about news items that are in the 'public interest', whilst respecting the rights of individuals to free speech and civil liberties. Globally, press freedoms are at markedly different places on the tolerance scale – state-run news operations sit in a very different space to free press associations who operate a self-policed moral and ethical code for journalists, reporters, photographers and editorial illustrators to abide by, to provide accountability for their actions – but this is a fluid and ever-changing affair.

The freedom of the press should be one of the most powerful and fiercely guarded democratic values of any sovereign nation. Countries that permit a free press are effectively championing their democratic traditions and values as nations. They are confident about the transparency of their governing principles, including judicial standpoints incorporating the record of human rights of their citizens, their promotion of agreed social values or their economic accountability and credibility. However, this position is continually open to question and challenge. Countries that have strong media magnates must guard against reporting bias, borne out of political interference, corruption or even worse, state espionage. Strong leaders and groups with politically, economically or socially charged ideologies run great risk of deliberately oppressing, distorting or stifling news reporting, leading to biased communication, and potentially serious repercussions through resulting protest, riots, imprisonment, potentially leading to torture and even death.

For example, the Al-Qaeda terrorist attacks on the publishing offices of French satirical weekly newspaper *Charlie Hebdo* in January 2015 are a startling and very real reminder of the cultural difference in reception of editorial viewpoint surrounding press freedom and responsibility. Emanating from a rise in religious fundamentalism, the swift rise of such terror networks operating on a global scale has become one of the sharpest reminders that not all citizens enjoy the freedom, prosperity and opportunity that many take for granted in democratic countries. The estranged Jihadist extremists, that have ironically emerged from peaceful religions such as Islam, are spurred on by radicalized followers often from underprivileged backgrounds, but financially sponsored by wealthy individuals, conglomerates or states that are accused of being autocratic and ideologically imbalanced.

The *Charlie Hebdo* acts were perpetrated by two brothers purporting to resent the depiction of the Islamic prophet Muhammad in a satirical cartoon carried by the newspaper. Offended by the depiction of the prophet in human form and portrayed in a way that slandered Islam religious and cultural values, the brothers orchestrated a brutal massacre of editorial staff at the newspaper's headquarters in Paris. The three-day murder hunt finally left twelve people dead and a further eleven injured before the gunmen were finally apprehended. Despite a long history of difference around depictions and interpretations of religion, resulting in well-publicized assassination calls (or *fatwās*), the fragility, inequality and uncertainty of French society in this period was brutally exposed.

The attacks caused global outrage and disbelief that terrorism of this nature could be planned and undertaken in a stable Western democracy. The attacks sadly demonstrate the constant flux of tolerance and acceptance on shared moral and ethical standpoints can lead to bigotry and, in exceptional circumstances, fundamentalist extremism. At the boundaries of what societies commonly agree on decency

and respect for shared values, editorial illustration has a crucial role to play in addressing and wrestling back some semblance of control, exploring the potential repercussions of unwarranted and unprecedented actions, and reminding readerships of acceptable ethical, moral standards by promoting alternative or other points of view.

Co-creation and knowledge exchange

Historically, editorial illustration has been at the vanguard of hailing and introducing new knowledge to readers. Whether championing new scientific discoveries, presenting advances in technologies or explaining economic modelling and health applications, illustrations have created wonder, excitement and anticipation for varied readerships. Editorial illustrators have been employed to explain both what has been discovered in ways that are tangible, and to speculate about what further exploration could uncover next. Inevitably, the exchange of new knowledge also has the capacity to unsettle some sections of a readership, by challenging conventions, questioning current modes of practice and disrupting thinking.

As a result, readerships have sometimes expressed concern, fear and outrage in response to articles and accompanying illustrations, with well-founded beliefs unravelled and becoming the subject of doubt. The rise of awareness in, and usage of, social media as a commentary platform to supplement traditional publishing practices has radically changed the communication landscape. This is likely to be accelerated in the next few years as more and more people have access to global connectivity.

The huge power of social media, not only as a carrier but as an influencer, creates an interesting crossroads for how knowledge is both created, exchanged and received as commentary. Historically, editorial illustrators were commissioned to respond to articles, making images in response to the writer's viewpoint which had a tangential relationship to the publisher. The method of recourse to questionable published material was commonly a letter to an editor. In a flourishing social media environment that production workflow is not only extended but fundamentally uprooted and shaken to its foundational core. Now the readership can affect prior editorial decisions by influencing content choices and modes of enquiry. Writers are reachable through personal social media handles and are aware both of readers responses to previous content, but also to their attitudes to that content, created by others through associated remarks that form an extended commentary.

At the other end of the publication production line, the reception of published material in a digital domain now has an immediate frame of response. Comments are posted within seconds of material being published. Those comments are then shared, commented upon and shared again, traversing geographical, political, social and cultural borders or boundaries. The pace and volume of such criticism is astonishing, creating a highly charged and potentially volatile melting pot of commentary that can be easily fragmented and estranged from its originally posted intention. But rather unlike responses in traditional media, social media critique has a history long after the remnants of printed matter have blown from the kerb sides, pavements and sidewalks. The World Wide Web has a nasty habit of retaining information long after the original contributing correspondent has forgotten the affair. This may be a current debate, but it is one that will have a long-lasting legacy.

Placement: Power and prestige

Clearly, editorial illustration cannot exist in a vacuum, both in terms of content or of publishing structure. Visual content must have some form of context, but it is important to state that such contexts can be both tangible and intangible. A tangible context will be a cover, an article or an extended editorial spread across pages of a newspaper, magazine or journal. Illustrations sit in harmony with other edited communication content; a publication masthead if the illustration is used on the cover; under a headline in an article, surrounded by running text and with the addition of graphic devices such as pull quotes or text boxes that break up repetitious content; or interspersed with other articles if employed over pages or spreads. In these situations, harmonious experiences are more difficult to achieve, since content in other articles may not have the same subject matter, nor editorial tone.

In some publications, advertising content can also break up the potential flow of content and needs to be carefully considered, designed and accommodated. However, intangible contexts also exist in the form of stored and experienced

Figure 2.3
A subtle depiction of same-sex relationships in the public domain, examining the history of LGBTQIA(+) rights at William Mary College in this sensitive illustration by Marc Burckhardt. Illustration is deliberately commissioned here as a way of subtly introducing a sensitive and potentially controversial topic, with context and empathy in the way the subject matter is composed and relayed to the readership.

'tacit' knowledge that individuals and readerships have acquired through their own life experience or that of others. This tacit knowledge encourages familiarity and recognition with content that is seemingly 'known', although it can also conjure up inaccuracies and misnomers. Ironically, some of these inaccuracies can be caused by the juxtaposition of one editorial cover against another in close proximity. Placement of images then can directly affect the reception and retention of messages in the eye of the audience.

Covers for magazine and journals, or the front page of a newspaper, are highly powerful and immediate canvases from which to espouse provocative and hard-hitting visual statements. Illustrations are commissioned to exemplify the idea that an image can be used 'to paint a thousand words'. As carriers of important, significant information, these illustrations have several layers of meaning and their creators must distil a mass of content into a striking image with possibly little in the way of textual explanation. The illustration performs multiple functions:

capturing potential readers attention to purchase the publication; creating a sense of anticipation and intrigue in laying foundations for readers to discover new knowledge or supplement what they already know; and creating a memory that anchors that knowledge in the brain which can be retrieved and shared at a later juncture. Such statement covers can have both immediacy and lasting residual impact, demonstrating the power and influence of editorial illustration as an effective and economic communication medium.

Editorial illustrators accept that work commissioned for covers requires particular discipline, concentration of ideas and a thorough and profound level of craft to manufacture work of this kind. The intellectual and aesthetic challenge of producing such work needs well-honed skills and an ability to work in total collaboration with the commissioning editor to achieve desired results. Covers are seldom given to emerging editorial illustrators, who must first learn their craft on the inner pages and build up a trustworthy and reliable reputation before being let near a cover. To regularly achieve the status of being commissioned for repeat work as a cover artist is an honour that is revered amongst editorial illustrators and recognition that you are creating work that signifies the publication and represents the values of the publisher themselves. Seeing your work on a magazine cover for the first time is an exhilarating and humbling experience.

Editorial illustrators who achieve such heights are largely unanimous in their view that complacency is the worst enemy, and that achieving such heights is not a guarantor of future work. Christoph Niemann, the celebrated German-born editorial illustrator, describes the process as 'Structure, patience and editing. Editing, editing, editing. I always want to make something so that in the end it feels like it was the only possible solution. Inevitably' [https://elephant.art/all-work-and-no-play-with-christoph-niemann/]. Building such a reputation means developing a strong partnership between the illustrator, art editors, creative and publishing directors that may span many years and publications as careers unfold.

In a cover context, publications such as *Private Eye* use illustration deliberately to make powerful arguments and statements through the use of satirical cartoons, grabbing the readers' attention and inviting closer inspection. Here, illustration serves several functions as a signifier and carrier of information. Firstly, the illustration demonstrates its appeal by welcoming readers with a familiarity that reassures and comforts; secondly, the image is able to communicate ontological truths and mix these with phenomenological content or some fantastical interpretations to create a smorgasbord of visually convincing content; thirdly, the illustration permits and entices a different reception to a photograph, which is loaded with being a carrier of accuracy and 'truth'.

Such versatility is important, as illustrations can be constructed and produced to successfully navigate away from legal complications or claims of bias that might be inferred through the use of photographic representation. Many editorial illustrations have thus escaped certain reprimand or censorship that photographic content would not.

Medium, message and mediation

The presentation of editorial illustration content, once solely represented through the printed page, now has a digital variant as publishers move magazines and newspapers online. The traditional publication design rule book, which catered for static material, has now had to be reconsidered to accommodate fluid, interchangeable content. From the predictability and finality of print, publishers and readerships are now exploring the fluency and open-endedness of digital platforms. Creating illustrations for both platforms is a challenge, since there is potential for the same image to appear as a 'fixed' unit in print, whilst masquerading in animated or hybrid form digitally. Clearly, illustrators who can adapt work to suit both platforms are going to be in demand.

Many have speculated about the inevitable decline of print, but recent research suggests it is unlikely to become extinct particularly amongst a readership who value publication as a physical product, much in the same way that a certain demographic of music lovers have battled for vinyl. By the same token, digital publishing has many yet-to-be-posed and unanswered questions concerning viability of revenue streams for publishers, its adoption as the preferred reading mode of choice and stability of how published data, and the resulting usage preferences and navigation paths of its readership are ethically handled and stored. It is difficult to exactly predict future trends, but it is likely that a more diverse readership will want a wider range of published forms. What cannot be in doubt is that the demand for original and compelling content to occupy column inches or digital frames will continue to grow. As traditional publishers expand onto new platforms, it is likely that smaller, independent specialist publishers will also see opportunities to seed and nurture new offerings to take advantage of diversifying readerships.

In the traditional world of printed editorial content, layout designers use design hierarchy as a way of informing the reader about the importance of content. Using an underlying design grid to separate headlines, sub-headings and body text allows the reader to navigate through content effortlessly, and gain knowledge and understanding from the content presented. The designer uses a mixture of text, images and iconographic devices to direct the reader across the page, corresponding with the content being communicated. This blended experience results in the reader having a connection with the subject matter. Placement of the editorial illustration here may create shock, awe or wonder if it is used at a dramatic scale or with a forthright, typographically strong headline. Typically this might be used for political, economic or health-related articles. By contrast, thoughtful and considered placement in amongst corresponding textual content can create an empathy with readers through a more relaxed and slower-paced communication experience, suited to leisure pursuits and activities such as gardening, hobbies and crafts. The elements on the page combine through skilful placement to create a calming space to lose oneself, appreciating and reflecting on the content at large.

In a digital realm however, the placement of editorial illustrations becomes a very different proposition. Digital communication platforms seldom operate to conventional publishing standards and are in flux as the technology develops and readerships become more adept at searching, finding and interacting with content in digital forms. These emerging publication platforms enable new reading experiences, such as pop-up windows and animated or motion-based content to be placed in the viewing plane, potentially disturbing and disrupting the reader's control. Such placement of content is deliberate of course, but is not merely confined to creating an innocently enjoyable reader experience. Platforms are far more agile not only presenting content in ways that enhance reader enjoyment and pleasure, but are systematically designed to

capture complex information concerning reader preferences, behaviours and even feelings based on interactions between consumer and content providers, distributors and advertisers.

Using complex algorithms created by coders and developers that use artificial intelligence tracing software to scan consumers reading behaviours, it is possible to log what has been read, avoided and saved for later, to see how much time was spent perusing an article and to see how the reader navigated through the content on display. The ability to then see what advertisements created interest, led to further actions or even resulted in click throughs to advertising products and services expands knowledge or readers behaviours and extrapolates previously private information from them in increasingly sophisticated ways. There are clear moral and ethical implications that are continually surfacing in this regard, with consumer rights and civil liberties organizations taking great interest in developing frameworks to guard against data breaches, fraudulent transactions and personal privacy. New approaches to gathering information about what readers are reading – and what they are responding to – has huge moral and ethical implications that are set to transform the way that content is packaged and consumed in the future.

Perception versus reality

The readership's perception and decoding of editorial illustration creates tensions between depictions of reality and fiction. Believability and truth are certainly terms that are subjective in communication media and reflect the bandwidth that editorial illustration has to operate across in a publishing context. Subject matter that has an ontological foundation differs from that which is phenomenological and, by default, is separated from subject matter that is fantastical.

In the most basic sense, an ontological truth lies in its proven tangibility. For example, the study of particular scientific forms and structures is termed 'morphology' and recognizes that the visual realization of a structure is beyond proof and has been verified. Revered scientific publications like *New Scientist*, *The Lancet* and other scientific journals that publish peer-reviewed, world-leading research, present visual findings to contextualize articles that fulfil the requirement for accuracy and exacting attention to

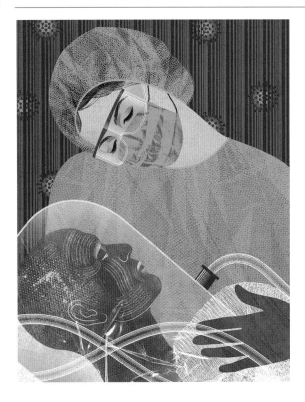
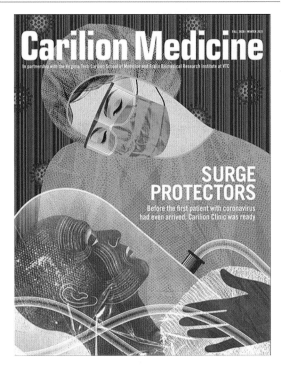

Figure 2.4a–d
Anna and Elena Balbusso work together as the Balbusso Twins producing editorial illustrations for a wide variety of international clients. These examples show how illustrations are composed to accommodate text as part of the integral design. The final artwork for the cover of the *Carilion Medicine* journal allows space for the masthead and main headline in areas that do not interfere with important pieces of visual information such as faces and hands. Similarly, the inside spread illustration is designed to accommodate a text box by allowing the figure on the far left to seemingly peer around the box and directly connect with the reader. The Balbusso Twins' work often strips away stereotypes and repurposes figures, events and situations away from stereotypical depictions.

detail. Their illustration may come in the form of images generated by the study of data sets, such as computer-generated visual modelling of life forms or images captured under a microscope, or by close observation of structural forms by highly specialized illustrators who are employed to capture subjects accurately through scale, colour or tone. Their subject matter's presence is beyond reproach.

Subject matter that has ontological truth can also be applied by editorial illustrators into fictitious settings. A good example would be visualizations of marine creatures or dinosaurs where species are faithfully rendered in terms of scale and appearance based on known factual information but are shown as an infographic design to depict environments when clearly, they would not have all been present together in reality. Such depictions are helpful in qualifying characteristics but imagining behaviours or traits for the reader. In these examples, it is clear that the presence of supporting contextualizing information, whether as running text in the article, or through key fact boxes to accompany the illustration, is crucial to convincing the reader of the validity of information being presented, where there is no margin for error. The editorial illustrator is responsible for portraying these subjects with an eye for detail and an acute awareness of the potential intellect of the readership. In such circumstances, publications develop a trusted reputation for publishing informative content of quality and prestige.

There are many occasions, however, where subject matter cannot be immediately seen, but rather experienced and sensed. Phenomenology – literally the study of 'phenomena' – examines conscious experiences from a subjective or first point of view. Its underlying philosophy is to rationalize our observations of unusual occurrences and events that may have been sensed or experienced that we know to be believable but have not witnessed them firsthand. In an editorial illustration context, a phenomenological approach is commonly employed to educate and explain complex concepts in manageable form. This is often achieved through the presentation mode of illustrations such as diagrams, cross-sections, and maps and charts.

Far from being basic visual elements, editorial illustrators create rich and diverse images to bring abstract and illusory concepts to life for a readership. Their ability to visualize and depict often complex sets of information in innovative and novel ways often brings phenomenological subjects to life and creates resonant, memorable illustrations. For example, the birth and evolution of coral reefs in the natural world, innovative building materials being employed to construct skyscrapers and the rapid development of international trade and commerce during the Industrial Revolution all benefit from a phenomenological approach to displaying visual information.

Editorial illustration can also encompass fantasy where subjective viewpoints are manipulated and distorted to satisfy demand from publishers to represent obscure or intangible situations. Broadly, work produced in a fantastical context either exists because factual reference is inaccurate, obsolete or simply missing, or because there is a deliberate attempt to suppress information and conjure up alternative views by the publisher and creator. In this context, editorial illustrators might play with pictorial elements such as colour or scale to emphasize and exaggerate elements within a composition such as science-fiction-based subjects where new definitions of worlds need to be created, or in the depiction of mythical beasts and creatures. In such circumstances, editorial illustrators are charged with injecting key factors such as drama, suspense and wonder into their work. The fantastical must still be believable and in order to do so, has to operate within a set of codes and conditions that have been established.

This enables the illustrator to define a set of permissions that underwrite the illustration, including whether gravity exists, or whether business figures can fly. Work may be abstracted or highly stylized, but regardless of the visual language deployed, a conscious bond created between creator and reader through the editorial illustration will permit spatial pictorial environments to be understood, actions to happen convincingly and time to pass unchallenged. Work created by illustrators such as Sara Fanelli and Jeffrey Fisher use a fantastical approach to make illustrations that are mesmeric, intriguing and full of wonder.

Creating work that embeds and imparts knowledge needs to be authoritative. The responsibility for such authority rests collectively with the publisher, the commissioner and the editorial illustrator. Images are constructed from knowledge that is new, acquired or informed and the blend of that knowledge produces editorial illustrative output that is both didactic and elegant. From purely factual didactic information sets that are grounded in learnt or experienced knowledge, illustrators use elegant forms of visual stylization to imbue and embody subject matter to appeal and resonate with the readership to communicate the essence, purpose and seriousness of the content. In doing so, the reputation of the editorial illustrator, the writer of the article, the publication and the publisher all receive endorsement and enhancement through bringing a successful and insightful body of knowledge to the audience.

Fake news

In recent years, the term 'fake news' has emerged and quickly become part of our everyday popular culture. Spread on the internet or through other media channels, fake news is embodied by false stories that are deliberately created and conflated to influence political

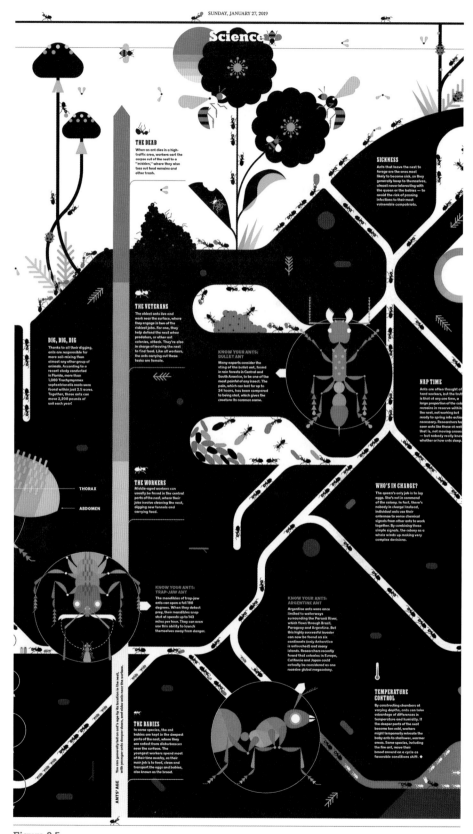

Figure 2.5
Editorial illustration as infographic, painstakingly crafted by Francesco Muzzi to show how ants thrive and prosper as entrepreneurs of the insect world. Art Direction by Leticia Sarmento; Creative Director Deb Bishop for *The New York Times*.

**KNOW YOUR ANTS:
ARMY ANT**

More than 200 ant species are called army ants, but the best example is found in Central America and the Amazon jungle. These ants don't build a permanent nest. Instead, they construct a nest by interlocking their bodies, keeping the queen and larvae safe, while allowing the colony to remain ready to move in search of more food.

SICKNESS

Ants that leave the nest to forage are the ones most likely to become sick, so they generally keep to themselves, almost never interacting with the queen or the babies — to avoid the risk of passing infections to their most vulnerable compatriots.

NEIGHBORS

Ants aren't the only creatures that make a home underground. Sometimes ants nest near burrows excavated by other animals, like rodents, and they're more than happy to incorporate those spaces into their architecture. Nobody knows, however, whether the ants evict the previous tenants or simply take advantage of an abandoned hole.

**KNOW YOUR ANTS:
HONEYPOT ANT**

Like bees, honeypot ants collect nectar — only instead of storing it in their homes, they store the liquids inside their bodies. Special workers gorge on so much flower nectar (and occasionally body fat from prey insects) that their abdomens enlarge. If food becomes scarce, these ants can vomit up the liquids for the colony to feast upon.

NAP TIME

Ants are often thought of as hard workers, but the truth is that at any one time, a large proportion of the colony remains in reserve within the nest, not working but ready to spring into action if necessary. Researchers have seen ants like these at rest — that is, not moving around — but nobody really knows whether or how ants sleep.

FOOD VAULTS

Some harvester ants store seeds in special chambers called granaries. By stockpiling food, they can have enough when circumstances outside the nest, like bad weather or lots of predators, prevent them from foraging.

POOP

Like humans, most ants avoid coming into contact with poop. Some deposit their feces outside the nest, while others have special chambers that function as town dumps. Some fungus-farming ant species use their droppings as manure for their gardens, but only certain "sanitation workers" are allowed to handle them.

**KNOW YOUR ANTS:
ANT**

ts consider the bullet ant, found s in Central and a, to be one of the of any insect. The an last for up to as been compared t, which gives the ommon name.

WHO'S IN CHARGE?

The queen's only job is to lay eggs. She's not in command of the colony. In fact, there's nobody in charge! Instead, individual ants use their antennae to sense chemical signals from other ants to work together. By combining these simple signals, the colony as a whole winds up making very complex decisions.

FARMERS

More than 200 types of ants grow their own food by farming fungus on decaying plant matter. They prefer to do their farming in taller, egg-shaped chambers. That's because the fungi grow in vertical strands, eventually forming curtains that hang from the ceiling.

**KNOW YOUR ANTS:
ARGENTINE ANT**

Argentine ants were once limited to waterways surrounding the Paraná River, which flows through Brazil, Paraguay and Argentina. But this highly successful invader can now be found on six continents (only Antarctica is untouched) and many islands. Researchers recently found that colonies in Europe, California and Japan could actually be considered as one massive global megacolony.

**TEMPERATURE
CONTROL**

By constructing chambers at varying depths, ants can take advantage of differences in temperature and humidity. If the deeper parts of the nest become too cold, workers might temporarily relocate the baby ants to shallower, warmer areas. Some species, including the fire ant, move their brood around on a cycle as favorable conditions shift. ◆

views or social behaviours, often utilizing the use of humour as a way of making messages stick in the memory. The term exists not only as a label for these untrustworthy and unreliable narratives but has also been adopted as a critical term in its own right. We are routinely exposed to politicians and influencers using claims of fake news as a powerfully immediate approach to successfully unsettling and disrupting the status quo.

Fake news is used to alert and spread questionable facts that can lead to telegraphed actions, thereby undermining the scrutiny of serious journalism that embeds trusted sources as a key differentiator to often untrue stories with little or no foundation. This can manifest chain reactions on social media such as Facebook, Twitter and Snapchat that can mobilize supporters to act in serious and unpredictable ways. For example, the storming of the US Capitol Building by President Trump supporters in January 2021 was a deliberate act of sabotaging democracy fuelled by fake news proliferating about the result of the recent presidential election.

In actuality, the term fake news is not a new phenomenon but has instead re-emerged to fill a vacuum or void seemingly left by conventional reporting. The roots of the term can be traced to the manipulation of photography to trick or mystify viewers from the late nineteenth century. The visual roots of fake news clearly have a resonance with editorial illustration, since the reconstruction of images, and their reappropriation for other purposes, is validated by considered editorial decisions. In a digital communication world, traditional purveyors of truth such as public broadcasters are increasingly under threat of destabilization by particularly motivated individuals and groups seeking to cast doubt on the validity of political and economic reporting.

Whilst traditional newspaper publishers and broadcasters point to their very guiding principles of existence, including their moral and ethical obligations to act as a free press in a civilized society complete with editorial leadership and boards of trustees, and their affiliation to a self-regulatory framework of codes and conditions, by contrast social media platforms have little accountability as private companies. The rapid development of these social media platforms, with greater enriched visual content through often reappropriated still illustrative or photographic imagery, memes or GIFs has been unregulated and poorly

self-policed. This permits the ideal conditions to affect the transmission of information, creating a tinderbox effect through user likes, comments and reposts that have the power to radically alter reception and meaning of information.

Reconstituted imagery, or that which is repositioned in a different editorial context from its original intent, is a powerful tool in questioning truth and generating uncertainty because of the power images have to enter our consciousness and the way we store those images as known memories and experiences. Having a lexicon of imagery helps us visualize but not necessarily contextualize where those memories originate from. The fluidity of our cognitive ability is an asset on many levels, but also opens the door to uncertainty and doubt – two key attributes that purveyors of fake news thrive upon. The dilemma of fake news as a form of intentional and unmitigating interference lies in the murky origins of its sources. These sources are not established and identifiable groups, but rather loose confederations of conspiracy theorists who draw together over simultaneous events, such as QAnon believing that the Robert Muller investigation into political interference in the 2016 presidential election was deliberately inconclusive and masked more sinister proof, or the anti-vaccination lobby who oppose Covid-19 relief.

As the Republican candidate for the President of the United States of America, Donald Trump ran a vicious and feisty election campaign in 2016, pouring scorn on political commentators and opponents claims as fake news, instead suggesting narratives through the use of simple visual and textual slogans that would bombard the electorate and undermine the opposition. Using controlled media outlets and his own social media presence, his campaign sought to unsettle voters by actively attacking media outlets and appealing to the uncertainty and fear of the unknown in vulnerable parts of the electorate. Even in presidential office, Mr Trump has furthered this stand-off by seeking to control the media by using platforms such as Twitter to espouse views on all manner of subjects that are seemingly at odds with much of Congress and the House of Representatives, and on occasion, the very constitutional values he purports to uphold. Unsurprisingly, his efforts have attracted considerable global criticism, ridicule and protest and his tenure has provided editorial illustrators with countless opportunities to respond in ways

Figure 2.6
The stark graphic symbolism of hatred and fascism affecting American democracy is powerfully played out through limited colour in this hard-hitting cover titled 'Hate in America' for *Time* magazine, created by Edel Rodriguez and art directed by D. W. Pine.

that are satirical and witty, incredulous and cruel. Many of the illustrators, including Edel Rodriguez, Brian Stauffer and Michelle Thompson have become household names as a result.

The Leveson Inquiry

One of the closely followed public inquiries in the contemporary era was the Leveson Inquiry 'into the culture, practices and ethics of the press' which concluded in 2012. The Inquiry's remit was to, 'examine relations of power between the press and the public, politicians and the police' (Sabbagh 2012).

Since the 1700s, newspapers have been an important part of everyday life in developing countries with democratic intentions to allow and enable free speech of their citizens. The birth, development and adoption of newspapers has closely mirrored the social, political and economic stories of nations at pivotal points in their respective histories, such as the American Civil War, French Revolutions and global events

such as the Great Depression or the Cold War. What we now take for granted as an unregulated – or free press – has a history that is littered with political cultural interference through partisan briefing, propagandist actions or through outright stranglehold, as seen with the Nazi occupation of Paris in the early 1940s and the complete control of the French press. Many would argue that the ideology of a free press is a principle which is cherished but fundamentally flawed as a self-policing concept.

Rising out of the English Civil War period, where the transmission and exchange of news was politically driven and advantageous, British newspapers were licensed during the following Restoration period but the parliamentary act was revoked in 1695, creating what we now know as the free press. While broadcast media in the UK was later subject to regulation due to its perceived power to infiltrate and influence opinion and attitudes, the press has operated a form of self-regulation ever since. In the subsequent years since the publication of *The Times* in London in 1785, national newspapers flourished and grew to cater for an insatiable demand for news and comment until their commercial heyday in the 1950s. At that point, other forms of news coverage began to rise in prominence, first through the national British Broadcasting Corporation (BBC), and later through independent competitors, funded by corporate advertising revenue. Newspapers' influence on the day-to-day lives of citizens were challenged by the emerging broadcast media as sales began to decline. A new format of newspaper, the tabloid, began to compete with the established broadsheets for readers.

In the post-Second World War period, the Press Council was established following the first royal commission overseen by the then new Labour government. Whilst the broadsheet newspapers respected guidance emerging from the Press Council, the more aggressive 'tabloid' publications were an altogether different proposition. Reporting the major shifts in society happening through the politically charged and increasingly revolutionary 1960s, tabloids filled the content vacuum left by the more sobering offerings of the broadsheet newspapers by providing a heady mixture of punchy, attention-grabbing headlines and condensed content. The 'red top' publications – so called because their mastheads were printed in red for easy identification – vied for popularity and sales by seeking out stories emanating from popular culture, celebrity and stardom, from entertainment and sport and increasingly into public life as the democratization of mass media became unstoppable.

The tabloids were instrumental in propelling the Profumo scandal of the 1960s, which rocked the British establishment to its core with allegations of political interference, sexual misdemeanour and potential national security concerns. The government minister John Profumo's affair with British model Christine Keeler opened the flood gates for subsequent titillating features on politicians and people in public positions of authority private lives. On the most simplistic level, these stories had to ignited by some form of information exchange; however, in practice, the lengths and methods used to extract such information became ever more complex in the intervening decades. Then disaster stuck with the murder of British schoolgirl Amanda Jane 'Milly' Dowler in 2002.

The now defunct *News of The World* tabloid newspaper, owned by media tycoon Rupert Murdoch's News Corporation stable of media companies, reported the death of 13-year-old schoolgirl Milly Dowler. In so doing, the news stories revealed specific information that raised serious questions about how underpinning factual evidence had been acquired from a missing person. *The Guardian* newspaper ran an investigative article that claimed to expose serious editorial malpractice at the *News of the World,* including the revelatory accusation that information was hacked from Dowler's mobile phone messages. *The Guardian* further claimed that phone hacking and intercepting messages was an accepted and managerially approved way of extracting vital information that gained information but violated personal privacy. The Press Complaints Commission, another self-policing press body developed from the original Press Council, investigated the claims in 2007 but concluded that they had not been misled. However, suspicions and allegations forced the hand of the British government once again and Prime Minister David Cameron was compelled to ask Lord Leveson to investigate in 2011.

The Milly Dowler revelations sent shockwaves of anger and revulsion through the British public and prompted Lord Justice Leveson's Inquiry into phone hacking. The inquiry heard from 184 witnesses over more than six months and accepted forty-two written submissions as part of its evidence-gathering process. The Inquiry concluded that phone hacking as a method for obtaining information was rife and touched many corners of life, from politicians, celebrities, holders of appointments to public office, institutions and even members of the general public who had come to the attention of the press. Self-regulation effectively continues the role of the press to police itself and ensures that the press continues to operate in a constitutional ecosystem of self-governance. This ensures no statutory intervention by the state and ostracizes any form of censorship on free speech upholding the principles of the 1689 Bill of Rights. By contrast, a clear intent to protect free speech in the press in the United States is enshrined in the first amendment of the American Constitution.

The Leveson Inquiry brought issues of interference to prominence in the minds of the media-consuming public, but there is unease and suspicion of the power of the press and their place within society. These tensions manifest themselves at national, regional and local level in developed and developing countries and are the source of dispute because of the multiplicity of the media. Whilst Leveson offered guidance on printed media, many aspects of digital media were not within the scope of the Inquiry, and are arguably some of the most prominent areas where we have seen abuses of power and the erosion of trust in the subsequent years since its publication in 2012.

Writing in his first volume of memoirs, former US President Barack Obama has observed that 'truth decay' is a seeping wound at the heart of many democratic agencies who pride themselves on fair and balanced reporting of facts. The role of, and regard for, civic literacy as a way of understanding and embracing common societal goals is challenged by the polarization of political sides through the publishing of unsubstantiated factual accounts through platforms that have no journalistic integrity or foundation. A case in point would be the ongoing debate about whether Facebook is a social media platform or a publisher. The debate is likely to intensify with current political and social ramifications of global events such as Covid-19 and movements such as Black Lives Matter showing no signs of immediately abating.

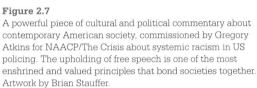

Figure 2.7
A powerful piece of cultural and political commentary about contemporary American society, commissioned by Gregory Atkins for NAACP/The Crisis about systemic racism in US policing. The upholding of free speech is one of the most enshrined and valued principles that bond societies together. Artwork by Brian Stauffer.

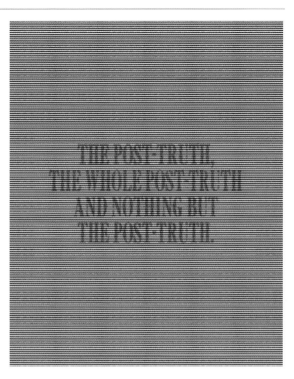

Figure 2.8
Spanish illustrator Javier Jaén's take on the post truth phenomenon, at the heart of how democracies publish, disseminate and digest their news.

Representation

Editorial illustrators have a duty and a desire to represent the natural and constructed practices of society. Despite being more globally connected than we have ever been as human beings, we espouse, adhere to and abide by very different societal values. These values are informed by codified, underpinning beliefs that have arisen out of political, religious, economic and cultural histories from different parts of the world that often collide and conflict with our own lived experiences. Editorial illustration can be said to historically act as a visual barometer of how societies have been viewed and recorded, and whilst there are positive examples of actively promoting under-represented factions of these societies, there are other instances where on first inspection, editorial illustration has effectively upheld and promoted misconceptions and negative stereotypes. In some instances, the wider context of the content surrounding the illustration, or advertising within proximity that has unattached

messaging, has served to promote a position of incongruity at best.

The universalizing concept of the 'everyman' in imagery emerges from an environment where male figures, or where figurative representation was automatically assumed to be male, symbolically represented humans as an encapsulated whole. This embodiment primarily existed because of the masculine-dominated media production industry but was further underpinned by the repression of women by societies as a whole. The rise of prosperity, seeded by the Victorian Industrial Revolution in the Western world in the 1800s, led to a massive industrialization of the workforce and raised expectations of living and working conditions at a localized level, and generated calls for greater social mobility through changes to the way people expected to be governed. Civil society was changing profoundly, with many of the tried and tested political, religious and sociological norms being challenged by a mobilized and determined female voice.

The formation of groups such as the Suffragettes in the early part of the twentieth century and their absolute resolve to create rights for women divided society. For the ruling classes, these groups represented a clear and present threat of change and a loss of power; to the Suffragettes and their supporters, the opportunity for change and for new societal acceptance was not an aspiration, but a reachable and achievable target that would lead to the emancipation of women and true recognition of their worth in society at large.

From these historic reforms, many movements aimed at reclaiming lost ground and forging new paths emerged and staunchly continue to this day. Our news media covers issues and debates around feminism, equal rights, fair pay, religious tolerance and for better awareness, representation and respect for marginalized groups in our society. A live and ongoing debate around the classification and representation of singular, plural and transitional gender identities is an important debate that will see a profound shift in communities over the forthcoming decades. The communication news media has been both a positive tool and a negative weapon in regard to progressing discussion and debate about representations of equality historically. Its survival and growth depends on how key players in the media embrace and cultivate such representations in the future.

On the one hand, broadsheet newspapers have been actively championed and celebrated causes by writers and creators who use column inches to raise awareness, mobilize support and report on the activism that they have driven. Readerships have been enthused by what they have seen and read, empowered to act in their communities and coax, persuade and campaign for change. On the other hand, other broadsheet newspapers have ridiculed and sought to undermine such campaigns at every opportunity, rallying an opposition and effectively trying to drown out or pour scorn on such arguments. Here, readerships have become incensed by views being expressed, and have actively sought to discriminate and block change by undermining and obstructing effective debate and action. These examples illustrate the emotive power of issue-based journalistic content that requires a range of transferable skills to empathize, understand and respond in a manner that promotes tolerance and respect, but also retains integrity for publisher, creator and audience.

Figure 2.9
As the Black Lives Matter protests rose in 2020, the discussion about racism and its victims continued in our homes. Felicia Fortes illustration captures the different emotions experienced when parents and guardians discuss racism with children, by evoking warmth and security through composition of characters, their body postures and the colour palette. The illustration was published in the Swedish newspaper *Göteborgs-Posten*.

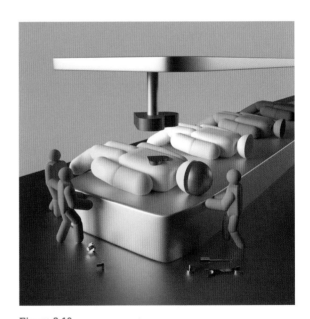

Figure 2.10
Illustrator Simoul Alva tackles the thorny issue of unconscious bias in this image for the print and online versions of *The New York Times*. As part of equality, diversity and inclusion training, some white male participants at an unnamed company appeared for a training session wearing shirts with targets pinned to their fronts – a sartorial statement about their apparent persecution. Alva's solution is to use the symbolism of the production line to embed virtues such as giving a soul and having a heart to the workforce.

Gender and identity

Regrettably, the recognition of gender equality in editorial illustration is still an issue to be widely understood and resolved through diverse practice, with depictions of gender still couched in outmoded, ill-informed and stereotypical interpretations of appearance, behaviour and purpose. As the twentieth century unfolded, the pre-conceived representation of men, women and marginalized genders in mainstream communication media more broadly was the subject of much criticism and angry exchange. Despite gender identity and representation being an historic equality issue, attributed to societies' enforcement of attitudes and tolerances for gender to be considered as identity, the problem has vexed many practitioners, critics and audiences alike.

Decades of indifference, and in some instances, clear bias, led to crude and ill-informed and clumsy representations that were dismissed as being irrelevant, and in some case, offensive. As a result, the issue of gender equality and acceptance has become a highly charged, volatile and explosive arena that demands reshaping delineation, provoking discussion about what might be considered acceptable gender recognitions to wider society. The issue is pertinent in a global context, recognizing that citizens who may wish to exhibit or identify with gender difference face barriers, persecution and worse from oppressive law enforcement that finds acceptance, or even tolerance, threatening.

Gender stereotyping is employed as a term to describe pre-conceived ideas about the purpose and roles that men, women and other genders might have in society. These individuals are effectively assigned to conformist roles through stereotyping, so dustmen would be expected to be male and dinner ladies would be female. These ideas are largely formed in childhood and become an accepted norm, so it is important to connect that image representation in early years can be an educational factor in pressing for acceptable and rational change in societal attitudes in future. These interventions could be through changing depictions of physical appearance and through occupations or activities in illustrations. Much gender stereotyping is prominently visual, but can be a profoundly invisible issue due to unconscious bias on the part of either the illustrator or the reader, or in some instances both parties. Publishers have systems and processes to alert around unconscious bias issues through editorial controls, but editorial illustrators should be educated to be in a position where they are conscious of gender equality and fair representation through their own image ideation, development production processes for this not to be an issue.

Given that an illustration has to be constructed, the building of an image means that allowances can be made in the design of the composition, placement of the visual elements, use of scale, colour, contrast and tonal variation to effectively 'stage' subjects and give them visual prominence. This in-assignment clearly gives editorial illustration an advantage over photography, and although tools like Adobe Photoshop can undoubtedly affect the reception of a photographic image, this manipulates the source image rather than thoroughly rebuilding it from the ground up. With editorial illustration increasingly finding its way onto digital platforms of publishing, greater opportunities exist through the 'animating' of forms to change and morph identities in the same image plane. This flexibility is particularly useful for where non-binary figurative representation is required, or where figures perhaps identify with two or more gender identifiers, in a 'they/them' based context.

Crucially, editorial illustration frequently casts figures beyond their mere representation and by default, they cannot simply be innocent forms within a picture plane. Instead, imbued by the situation of the image in which they appear, regardless of whether they are represented realistically or abstractedly, they serve a function as message carriers for a deeper and more profound range of content-driven ideologies and beliefs. Figures are often totemic, meaning they serve to act as visual protagonists to promote particular perspectives and have a purpose for appearing in an illustration. To extend that theory, editorial illustrators must understand that figurative forms being represented are an extension of their personal beliefs as creators, and that those ideologies are further amplified through the editorial angle taken by the publication and publisher. Having empathy for subject matter, especially in the role, purpose and articulation of figurative forms, is of vital importance and worth investing in the ongoing debate about how society is 'seen' and 'experienced' in editorial illustration.

Figure 2.11
American illustrator and cartoonist Eleanor Davis powerfully exaggerates both the scale and articulation of female characters to redefine and re-state constructions of female identity in contemporary society, in this cover titled, 'A Woman's Place' for *The New York Times Book Review*.

Figure 2.12
An impactful, striking cover that foregrounds women's voices by Mailka Favre for *Resist! Magazine*.

Equal rights, equal values

Whilst historically there are disproportionately few examples of human rights being given equal precedent in news reporting, the influx of a younger, more socially mobile and roundly educated publishing professionals has started to democratize the communication media employment landscape. Recognition that a greater balance of the publishing workforce now originates from diverse cultural and gendered parts of society that more evenly reflects the public that it serves should be a welcome and much-needed development. To be accepted into a non-prejudicial field where difference is both recognized and valued without question, the publishing industry should act as a useful marker in meeting the needs of a diverse readership who are motivated by having freedom to choose from a wider pool of content. Beyond gender stereotyping, the issues of feminism, LGBTQIA(+) rights and gender empowerment, BAME representation, pay and related recognition and promotion are hot topics that can be championed through editorial illustration as an inclusive platform.

Editorial illustrators actively need to think about how content they are portraying rebalances equality for a diverse readership, without illustrations feeling forced or contrived. High-quality research methods, coupled with a positive working relationship that regularly contributes ideas and opinions between publisher and illustrator is the key to creating more representative work. The illustrator actively needs to think about how figurative subjects will be portrayed physically and how they will be employed in an image and proactively promote marginalized groups to roles and responsibilities. For example, transgender chefs might lead a kitchen brigade which immediately forces considerations over role, appearance and purpose. A high-powered executive of a leading multinational company represented as a woman redresses the balance of aspirational, professional career role models and becomes an encouraging and motivating factor for would-be professionals or women considering entering the workforce after a career break. These examples create a progressive and challenging social commentary amongst the readership, whilst ensuring illustrator's work is seen positively by potential commissioners who are looking for talent that can create work that is inclusive, progressive and non-judgemental.

Ethical issues

The question of having an ethical stance in editorial illustration, and in communication media more generally, is a recurring and

Figure 2.13
Editorial illustrators are chosen for commissions because their
approach and their output evokes a mood that creates incredible
empathy with readerships. This thoughtful and sensitive piece
by Swedish illustrator Patrik Svensson is a poignant example,
accompanying an article about grieving at work for the Harvard
Business Review, commissioned by Susannah Haesche.

Figure 2.14
Eva Bee's illustration shines a positive light on representations of
disability by suggesting involvement and acceptance in active
pursuits.

necessary debate. Whilst accepting that illustrators do not routinely make ethical decisions
that affect fundamental life-or-death concerns,
their images nevertheless introduce and instil
far-reaching and potentially influential communication messages. As a result, an ethical stance
is needed to anchor responsibility and accountability, since no illustrator can have an entirely
neutral stance over such a broad spectrum of
subject matter they are likely to encounter in a
working career. To suggest otherwise is naïve in
the extreme.

Deciding which clients to work for, or which
subjects to cover or avoid, is a very personal
choice in the creation of illustrations that will be
consumed by society at large. Being associated
with ethically difficult clients or subjects on the
margins of acceptability can be career damaging,
so understanding the complexities of ethical awareness is vital. For example, being commissioned
by a publication like *Playboy*, the long-standing
adult periodical, when you have ethical and moral
problems with the portrayal of women as objects
of desire will create a dilemma about taking on
such an editorial illustration job. The context of this
example is that historically, *Playboy* has commissioned some very influential illustrators who have
made significant work and enjoyed substantial
financial reward for their services.

An individual's ethical or moral concerns will
dictate responsibilities in the creative process
and it is better to declare objections or concerns
in advance. While some creators believe that
the essence of editorial illustration means that
a separation between the ethical position of a
publisher and their own personal ethos is possible
for commercial gain, there is potentially a great
deal of reputational damage to agreeing to work
that has questionable ethical credentials. Beyond
the main clients themselves, illustrators also have
to consider other contributors and their ethical
positions. For example, some clients will not use
illustrators precisely because they are closely
associated with subject matter such as petro-
chemical manufacturing or drugs or arms dealing
and do not want the reputational risk of being
aligned with those emotive subjects. Navigating
ethically questionable subject matter when new
to the field is difficult, and accusations of 'selling out' remain a concern for many creators.
For the most part, editorial illustrators must be
guided by their own long-term convictions rather
than basing decisions on a job-to-job basis. For
example, if there is acceptance that editorial illustration to a greater or lesser extent uses visual
imagery to manipulate responses from a readership, then all practitioners sit on that spectrum
and make personal choices about what particular
frequency their standpoint is aligned to.

Questions of ethical awareness are also
prevalent in the origination and production of
illustrations. Collecting research data beyond
article content may involve gaining ethical
clearance from suppliers to utilize research data

Figure 2.15
Playboy, the adult entertainment magazine, is historically linked with using editorial illustration in contrast to their usual photographic offering. Here, Brian Stauffer is commissioned to illustrate the pornography industry's potential connection and conversion to virtual technology in the future.

in a scientific context. This is a highly specialized area and reputable publishers will have a process that can be followed to elicit such information. More problematic, and indeed in some circumstances highly contentious, is the issue of appropriating or even outrightly plagiarizing source imagery. Pablo Picasso once remarked that 'Good artists borrow, great artists steal'.

Whilst it is undeniably the case that no idea is truly original, illustrators use creative licence to 'borrow' ideas from a wide variety of different sources knowingly or un-knowingly. For example, lifting the framework for an illustration concept, but imbuing it with different subject matter from the original may be considered an acceptable creative exploit, and is commonly referred to as a pastiche; the image imitates the style of the original creator or the period in which the original was made. The sensibilities employed to originate the idea from a memorable or discovered source and to then adjust the codes and conditions by which the new illustration functions are where the ingenuity and skill lie in manifesting a new version inspired by the old. However, taking the original and reframing it as the creator's own is clearly not acceptable and if

published, becomes an infringement of the original creator's intentions for the work.

Illustrators encounter problems with appropriation in the creation of work that is collaged or photomontaged, where there origin of source material is layered with ownership and rights issues. Illustrators working in these domains need to have watertight proof that their source material has been cleared by the original rights holder to be used if it is a direct copy, or slightly deviates away from the original purpose of the work. The publisher also has a moral and ethical responsibility in regard to the ownership of imagery and appropriation away from original purposes if the image is sampled from a previous source. Many publishers, especially newspapers and political magazines, will have a legal team keeping a close eye on content which is sensitive or potentially libellous. The golden rule is to make serious and well-documented approaches to ascertain ownership and permission to use works. Some publishers will supply illustrators with cleared material but if in doubt, check your legal position before submitting artwork for publication.

Reflections of society

Historically, illustration has been widely used to show ethnic variance that is the very essence of society itself. From the depictions of the ancient Egyptians as hieroglyphic forms, and the engravings of African slaves being captured, rounded up and deported in what was termed, ironically, as the 'Enlightenment era', through to countless images of marginalized groups, illustration has documented and categorized ethnicity as a contributory factor to a mature and established society. However, the area is complex and difficult to navigate, ably demonstrated by issues surrounding stereotyping that not only characterize themselves through physical manifestations of the appearance of a figure's personal clothing or situating figures in stereotypical environments that lead to assumptions and prejudices about the depiction of roles.

Such hieroglyphic forms and historical engravings give us a glimpse into previous worlds, yet we are still discovering new knowledge that allows us to draw conclusions about those segments of society and how their lives impacted on our own. It is often said that the press mirrors society, for good or bad, and usually both. In some senses, the argument for maintaining a free press is enshrined in this position, but history will judge whether what we regard as a 'free press' in the Western world is actually free, or blighted by a few powerful media figures who have a self-interested monopoly on ownership of content, political directions of major industrialized powers and control over their populations beliefs and aspirations.

Recognizing the importance of editorial illustration in representing public discourse about gender, ethnicity, equal rights and under-representation of minorities also shines a beacon of light on the viewpoint of individual illustrators' terms of reference in the cultural production and appropriation of images. As creators, personal standpoints are inevitably reflected in the work that illustrators create. In certain instances, moral, political or religious beliefs may prevent editorial illustrators from undertaking particular jobs for organizations due to their moral or ethical standpoints on particular issues. Tobacco companies, alcohol and adult content are subject examples that have been the source of recent debates around contentious content, but in the last few decades that has extended to religious fundamentalism, extremist politics and celebrity staking of innocent victims. Whilst editorial illustrators are employed by publishers to convey messages, having a standpoint is necessary and increasingly prevalent in editorial work, and an authorial voice is considered a valuable and necessary asset in the current climate of news and news analysis commentary.

Regardless of what editorial illustrations are made, each fundamentally add up to summarizing our societal values and beliefs at that given moment in time. In future years, social historians and commentators will interrogate publications, pore over published articles and examine editorial illustrations to chart our attitudes and behaviours, portray what we considered acceptable or otherwise and determine our

Figure 2.16
Yuko Shimizu powerfully positions the figure of a woman wearing a symbolic red superhero cape in front of a metropolitan business district as a provocateur feature about equal rights, 'Will We Ever Be Equal?' for *Real Woman* magazine.

place as contributors to civilized societies. These collected works will ultimately archive our sociological identities at an interesting point in publishing history where the worlds of print and digital intersected.

History will reveal our political alignments and differences, show our collective economic interpretations and exhibit what we choose to accept and reject as cultural norms. History will uncover political instability amongst states considered superpowers with leaderships who were intent on controlling and manipulating communication. Perhaps more fundamentally still, history will show how we grew as educated and cultured citizens in a world which was grappling with an urgent and profound climate crises, caused as a result of historical industrial and commercial practices, and not heeding the many warnings issued by scientific experts.

Theory

This chapter explores the theory that underpins editorial illustration. The opening section is dedicated to horizon scanning the overall media landscape of the discipline by examining the fundamental relationship between text and image. The chapter considers how we read and understand that relationship in our pursuit of news, information and entertainment, by examining the ways text and image constructions form messages through the study of semiotics to decode messages and meaning. The chapter then develops an exploration of how images and text are linked together in the minds of readers through our understanding of how, when, where and why we receive images. Utilizing this knowledge, the chapter moves on to introducing key figures who have shaped our historical and contemporary thinking through text and image and how these philosophies connect to the social, political, economic and cultural world captured around us.

The big picture: A theoretical overview

Editorial illustration is governed by how and why images are derived and constructed from text. It is shaped by when and where illustrative content is subsequently received by readerships. Different schools of thought inevitably exist about such relationships, depending on a number of contributing or contrasting philosophical theories that have emerged, gained traction and been debated since. These might include, but are certainly not limited to, the time that those theories were formed, or the parallel political, sociological and economic contextual surroundings of a particular age that has transformed, revisited and revised them.

Theories help make sense of developments in a subject, expand upon ideas either applied to illustration, or to the communication arts more generally, and on occasion influence the subject from neighbouring and connected fields including the social sciences, the physical sciences and other humanities. Theoretical applications makes the subject of illustration stronger as an identity in its own right and a valuable contributor to wider discourse about the history, development and future of communication design studies, both in terms of its conceptual communicative function and its physical graphic manifestation. Crucially, they signal the maturity of a subject and allow a position of recognition and respect. Conversely, cultural critics see the field of illustration generally as young and relatively inexperienced in originating and developing its own theoretical discourse. Equally, the subject of illustration is arguably inexperienced at receiving criticism and generating countering theoretical models of its own.

As a result, illustration has many theories applied to it that are misleading and, worse, lack relevance. This places the subject perilously close to not being taken seriously as a cultural contributor and significant ambassador to future communication media development in arguably one of the most profound periods of change since the original Industrial Revolution. Creating a robust and defensible theoretical position of genuine, unique enquiry, where specific vocabulary and critically engaged discourse can be applied or assigned to aspects of illustration, will create a cohesive ecosystem that positions the subject with gravitas and conviction.

The last twenty years have seen a concerted and determined effort to address this issue, with academic peer-reviewed journals dedicated specifically to illustration, academic institutions and professional bodies hosting conferences and symposia and a dedicated library of books released by major publishers that examine all facets of the subject. Illustration has also been examined by linguists, social historians, cultural theorists and creative industry commentators. Illustration is now being widely taught under the ecosystem of integrated practice and theory that is relevant and pertinent to the subject and away from historic models that saw these two pillars of learning divided or misaligned. A greater number of highly educated graduates are available for hire with theories that are applied through the professional practice acquired in a fast-changing creative industry that is much more adept at signalling new trends, prototyping radical approaches and welcoming collaboration across age, ethnicity, gender and beliefs.

This section introduces some of the major theoretical discourse that students and developing professionals are likely to encounter. The following theoretical positions span the time that editorial illustration has existed. The introduction presents concepts related to visual beauty and aesthetic judgements of quality of art, and the rebalancing of craft as an integral part of a valued society that are championed by Immanuel Kant. The over-development and invasiveness of mass media and the resulting destabilizing effects on society is explored through the section on Marxism, whilst Walter Benjamin's output is investigated through the representation and potential politization of subject matter and resulting speculation about the problematized relationship between creator and audience.

Moving forward, issues of representation through to important debates examining the misrepresentation of sexuality and gender in mass media are pursued through the writings of Laura Mulvey and Judith Butler. This section signposts areas where further exploration would be useful in an illustrator's pursuit of knowledge

Figure 3.1
French illustrator Serge Bloch's cover for *Time* magazine cleverly mixes illustration and typography through the photographic use of red thread harmoniously tying in with the magazine's branded border.

Figure 3.2
Matthew Richardson's editorial illustration work, like his other image-based output, is heavily invested in exploring the theories by which images resonate and produce a recall with readerships. His work provokes questions, often using theory derived from literature and film as part of a developing narrative to challenge his readers.

about the academic standing of editorial illustration and its cerebral connections to associated subjects for further study. Having a working knowledge of the underpinning theory is designed to give confidence to the process of explorative development. Serious enquiry is encouraged to equip professionals with the intellectual tools and connected production armoury to achieve a successful career that evolves and cements recognition for work produced.

The relationship between image and text

Understanding the terms and conditions in which editorial illustrations operate is fundamental to working successfully in this field. To do

that, it is necessary to examine the distinct relationship between image and text and establish some principles about how they work in synergy to entertain, educate and inform readerships. It is also important to clarify that successful work in his field exists where dialogical connections can be established between image and text to relay information that is enticing and insightful. To maximize these chances, an investigation into the roles of stakeholders in the intentional communication of content is desirable, and it is important to distinguish the difference between photography and illustration as two important but distinct forms of discourse in editorial publishing.

In her doctoral thesis, Dr Nanette Hoogslag proposes four 'attributes' which must be present in the production and consumption of print-based editorial illustration, namely: manifestation, translation, reflection and engagement. Hoogslag argues that for editorial illustration to communicate successfully to the readership, these attributes must align in a particular 'constellation' (Hoogslag 2014: 23). This statement is vital to understanding the conditions where editorial illustration can successfully occur.

Hoogslag introduces the principle of manifestation as 'the capacity through the materiality of illustration to refer and reveal the technological and material affordances of a specific platform. The editorial illustration points to the newspaper and all it represents in its final reproduced form, but also the manner in which it plays with and contrasts these affordances and uses them for semiosis' (23). Manifestations of illustration are, of course, multifarious with proponents open to create editorial illustrations through various choices of media that are relevant and can be supported through printed or digital platforms. Hoogslag proposes that the principle of translation as 'The ability to translate the essential text into a poetic visual language whilst simultaneously relating to the written story through both a dialectical proximity and a direct textual-visual relationship. To achieve this it uses the readers' own coded language (after Roland Barthes)' (23). This principle is vital in allowing an editorial illustration to operate as a conduit through which textual content in an article is synthesized through the visual code of an illustration to be interpreted by the reader. It is here where the image is received and decoded to make cerebral connections back to the copy text. Crucially, these two principles transition the shift of emphasis from the creators of text and image to the reader, who have lived and learnt experiences to draw from when decoding this information stored in their respective memories.

Hoogslag then proposes that the principle of reflection should encapsulate

'the ability of editorial illustration, as a relational object, to reflect all those who have a stake in the visual image. This includes the producers of the publication, the picture editor, 'the materialisation and dematerialisation' of the illustration described as 'the relay of intent', through the manifestation of the story as the intertextual relationship (Barthes) and the position of illustrator in relation to authorial presence and the receiver' (Hoogslag 2014: 23).

This principle observes the position that all stakeholders have a part to play in the *performance* of an editorial illustration. In receipt of this information, the principle of engagement 'is the ability to use visual impact and rhetorical means to arrest the reader's attention and create an ideological bond (Hall 1973). It is the quality of the Lacanian imagined *ideal* (Žižek 1997–2007) in which the image is used to establish a bridge and then consolidate a bond between the readers' reality and the underlying ideological message of the publication' (Hoogslag 2014: 23). Engagement in this context creates resonance between the publisher, editorial contributors and readerships and creates attachment that might be recognized through brand loyalty or trust in published content. Such attributes are vital in growing and maintaining readerships for circulation, engagement with other key media partners and all-important advertising revenue.

Whilst acknowledging that print media as a platform is fixed, Hoogslag proposes that these attributes themselves are able to fluctuate in the mind of the reader and cement the notion that the reception of information is a semiotic act of communication between the creator, producer and receiver. Editorial illustration, she argues, resides in a constellation composed of these four attributes, where the reader is enticed into a 'space of deliberation' between the editorial illustrations intent and the reader's existing knowledge. Hoogslag's constellation theory is important as it recognizes a clear communication between producer and consumer of

information in a harmonious, symbiotic relationship supported by the environment of published matter. Digital platforms are more fluid in construction and reception, so whilst the principles described above may still apply, the amorphous nature of the digital domain is more open-ended and should be subject to further study. For example, we know the parameters of print-based publishing have a published outcome retrievable by date, volume or edition. Digital publications can be updated by both content makers and by readerships commenting on published content which potentially stretches and distorts the original intention of an article, and to extend the cosmic analogy, other distant parts of the publishing universe are possible to reach and explore.

Semiotics

Illustrations act as carriers of information, but readerships are characterized by their difference, whether by gender, ethnicity, religion, political persuasion or other societal divides. Our learnt and perceived differences would suggest we do not necessarily interpret images in the same way. We have become extremely adept, sophisticated recognizers of information through a variety of communication media and have stored this information as existing knowledge. We use this knowledge to decode and unlock meaning from images and translate them into experiences that aid deeper understanding. But because difference equates to variations in ideology, values and beliefs, we exhibit differences in expectation about how we receive and recognize communication within images. In order to understand this process of creating and receiving images, an understanding of semiotics is required.

The *Oxford English Dictionary* defines semiotics as 'the study of signs and symbols and their use or interpretation'. In the context of editorial illustration, this definition is helpful because it places emphasis both on the creation and reception of signs and symbols, cementing the notion that the creation and reception of images is a negotiated and shared act. The term 'sign' can be read both literally and abstractly: a sign can be a direct, information-imparting road sign on a highway, informing a driver to stop. Equally, a sign can be implied, witnessed by a partially hidden symbol, a gesture or even a place. Illustration is employed as a vitally important

THE NEW YORK TIMES **OP-ED** TUESDAY, MARCH 18, 2014 DY A19

ROGER COHEN

The Unlikely Road to War

A 19-year-old Ukrainian nationalist from a remote farming village, raised on stories of his family's suffering during Stalin's great engineered famine, embittered by Moscow's long imperialist dominion, enraged by the slaying of a fellow student in Kiev during the uprising of 2014, convinced any price is worth paying to stop the Russian annexation of Crimea, takes the long road to Sevastopol.

He is a simple angular man, a dreamer, who as a young boy had engraved his initials on a retaining wall of rocks at the back of his family's plot. When asked why, he replied, "Because one day people will know my name."

On the farm, he works hard by day and reads voraciously by night. He is consumed with the long suffering of the Ukrainian peasant laboring in near feudal conditions. Neighboring countries have gained their independence and dignity after Soviet occupation. Why, he asks, should Ukraine not do the same?

To this teenager, the issue is simple. The imperial ruler in the Kremlin knows nothing of Ukraine. The 21st-century world is changing, but this high officer of the imperium is determined to wind back the clock to the 20th. A good student, the man travels to Kiev, where an older brother works. He falls into the "Young Ukraine" movement, a radical student circle in which feelings run high over the shotgun referendum that saw the people of Crimea vote with Orwellian unanimity for union with Russia. At night, he fingers the hand-engraved Browning pistol that was once his father's.

A plot is hatched. The Russian defense minister is to visit Sevastopol with his wife to celebrate the wise choice of the Crimean people and speak of the Russia's civilizing influence over this beautiful but backward region. Fanfare follows. "Wide Is My Motherland" booms from loudspeakers as the minister's procession of black limousines snakes along the waterfront. The assassin is waiting at a point where the minister and his wife are to greet local dignitaries.

What a teenager teaches us about the fragility of peace.

Two shots ring out. One cuts through the minister's jugular vein. The other penetrates his wife's abdomen. The minister's last words are spoken to her: "Don't die, don't die, live for our children."

Events now move quickly. Russia annexes Crimea. It declares war on Ukraine, takes Donetsk in short order, and annexes the eastern half of the country. The United States warns Russia not to advance on Kiev. It reminds the Kremlin of America's binding alliance with Baltic states that are NATO members. European nations mobilize.

Desperate diplomacy unravels. A Ukrainian counterattack flounders but inflicts heavy casualties, prompting a Russian advance on the capital. Two NATO F-16s are shot down during a reconnaissance flight close to the Lithuanian-Russian border. Russia declares war on Estonia, Latvia and Lithuania. Invoking Article 5 of the North Atlantic Treaty — an attack against one member shall be considered an attack against all — the United States and its European allies come to their defense. China, in what it calls a preemptive strike, invades Taiwan, "a potential Crimea." Japan and India declare war on China. World War III has begun.

It could not happen. Of course, it could not happen. The institutions and alliances of a connected world ensure the worst cannot happen again. The price would be too high, no less than nuclear annihilation. Civilization is strong, humanity wise, safeguards secure.

Anyone who believes that should read Tim Butcher's riveting "The Trigger," a soon-to-be-published account of the long road traveled from a remote Bosnian farm to Sarajevo by Gavrilo Princip, the 19-year-old Bosnian Serb nationalist whose assassination of Archduke Franz Ferdinand in Sarajevo on June 28, 1914, ignited what Churchill called "the hardest, the cruelest and the least-rewarded"

Out of Control

By Gregg Easterbrook

WASHINGTON

WHEN mass murderers took over the cockpits of four American airliners on Sept. 11, 2001, one of the first things they did was turn off the transponders, so the planes would not register properly on civilian radar.

A few months later, the Council on Foreign Relations published a book, "How Did This Happen?" about the mistakes leading to that awful day. I wrote the aviation security chapter, which highlighted vulnerabilities in the way airliner transponders operate.

If the transponders had not gone silent on 9/11, air traffic controllers would have quickly realized that two jetliners en route to Los Angeles had made dramatic course changes and were bound straight for Manhattan. Instead, controllers lost precious time trying to figure out where the aircraft were.

At the time, I would have bet my life's savings that the transponder, which broadcasts an aircraft's location and identity, would be re-engineered to prevent hijackers from turning such units off. But nothing was done. Almost 13 years later, Malaysia Airlines Flight 370 sparked a lengthy worldwide search when, it appears, another transponder was turned off.

The issue today is exactly as it was on 9/11. Pilots like their locations to be known — for ground assistance, and because the transponder warns other nearby planes of their course and altitude. Only a hijacker at the controls of an aircraft would want the transponder silent.

Flight 370 was not unique: Most of the world's jetliners have transponders that can be turned off. On the 777-200, the type of plane used on the flight, there's a simple rotary switch near the first officer's left hand. All someone has to do to turn the transponder off is rotate the dial.

Of course, transponders aren't the only way to detect a plane: There's always radar. In the movies, radar screens show incredible detail about everything. In real life, radar is easily confused, doesn't see small planes, and may have trouble determining altitudes. Transponders solve this by reporting an aircraft's altitude, speed, directional heading and identification code to air traffic controllers and nearby aircraft, using an electronic format that syncs with radar. And the identification codes tell controllers which blip is which flight, something radar has no way to detect.

Some military radars can provide Hollywood-style detail, but military radar is not usually watching civilian flights, and when it is, it needs the transponder code to know what it's looking at. One reason it took nearly a week for American intelligence to conclude that Flight 370 had gone far off course is that analysts had to pore over reams of raw data trying to figure out which tracks were from that particular jet.

Why is there a transponder switch in the first place? Until recently, transponders had to be off when a plane was on the ground, to avoid sending signals that disrupted airport radar. The designs for some private aircraft — but not yet the large commercial planes — deal with this by using automated transponders that turn on when the planes become airborne, then turn off when they slow to taxi speed.

Lately, major airports have installed ground-scanning radars that don't get confused by transponders on taxiways. Large jetliners like the 777 typically operate from such airports, and when they do, they never have a reason to switch the transponder off.

Why do airplane transponders still have a manual shut-off?

The transponder's off switch is a vestige of an earlier era, before reliable chip-based electronics. Older model transponders sometimes sent out spurious altitude readings. "Air traffic control would call and tell you to 'cycle' the transponder," meaning switch it off and then back on in a reset sequence, noted Patrick Smith, a veteran pilot and the author of the 2012 book about air travel, "Cockpit Confidential."

In case cycling does not correct the fault, all jetliners have backup transponders. Flight 370 had a backup transponder — but as with most such units, someone in the cockpit must switch the backup on. No one did that on Flight 370.

The solution is a location-broadcasting system that the flight crew cannot switch off. Over the next few years, much of the world plans to adopt an aviation tracking standard called ADS-B, which should make it harder for a plane to stop reporting its position. Automated transponders should be part of that transition.

Of course, automation of complex systems can have unintended consequences. But most of the flight time of modern jetliners occurs on autopilot — every day, millions of lives worldwide are in the hands of autopilots for extended periods. If automation can be trusted to fly the entire plane, why can't it be trusted to keep the transponders in the correct setting?

Autopilots can be turned off, because a malfunctioning autopilot may cause a crash. A malfunctioning transponder might broadcast flawed data, which is a concern. But a switched-off transponder can spell doom.

Five of the last 10 major air disasters — the four 9/11 flights, and Flight 370 — began with the transponder's being switched off. A few design changes can make that impossible. □

Gregg Easterbrook, a contributing editor at The Atlantic, wrote the chapter on aviation security for the book "How Did This Happen? Terrorism and the New War."

BRIAN STAUFFER

DAVID BROOKS

How Cities Change

Shavar Jeffries was born in Newark in 1975, the son of a 19-year-old mother who was unprepared to take care of him. He spent the first nine years of his life shuttling between different relatives. Then his mother came back into his life and moved him to California.

Shortly after they moved to Los Angeles, there was a problem with the lock to their apartment door. Jeffries' mom called the locksmith and soon began a relationship with him. One evening the locksmith was looking over her phone bill and found a number he didn't like. He smacked her in the head and sent her hurtling across the room. The beatings continued from then on.

Once his mother picked up Jeffries from Little League wearing big sunglasses, her eyes blackened underneath. Another day she tried to bar the locksmith from their apartment, but he kicked through the door. She moved to Burbank and got restraining orders, but on Nov. 25, 1985, the locksmith stalked her workplace and killed her with a sawed-off shotgun.

Jeffries was brought back to Newark and lived for a few months with his father. But one day he came home and his father had vanished, without leaving a note. By this time, he was numb; he just figured this was the way life is. His grandparents took him in and he spent the rest of his childhood with them, living on a street called Harding Terrace in the South Ward of Newark.

William Spear, who grew up on Harding Terrace a few years later, describes the street the way Jane Jacobs describes Greenwich Village in the 1950s: There were eyes everywhere. "You couldn't cut class, because the neighbors would see you and call you on it," Spear recalls. The neighbors couldn't and can't stop the worst violence — Spear's brother was killed in 2012 when a street fight sent bullets flying through a block party — but they could keep some kids in line.

Jeffries' grandparents brought stability to his life. He became active with the Boys and Girls Club. He did well in grade school, won a scholarship to Seton Hall Prep, then won scholarships to Duke and Columbia Law School, got a prestigious clerkship and began a legal career.

And then, having escaped Newark, he moved back to the crime-ridden South Ward. He has worked as a civil rights lawyer. He was the founding board president of a charter school in the Knowledge Is Power Program called Team Academy. He became an associate law professor at Seton Hall and took a leave from that to serve as assistant attorney general. In 2010, he ran for the Newark school board and became its president.

Now Jeffries is running for mayor of Newark against City Councilman Ras Baraka. The race has taken on a familiar shape: regular vs. reformer.

Baraka has the support of most of the major unions and political organizations. Over the years, he has combined a confrontational 1970s style of racial rhetoric with a transactional, machine-like style of politics. Baraka is well known in Newark and it shows. There are Baraka signs everywhere there.

Jeffries is the outsider and the reformer, promising to end the favor trading in government and modernize the institutions. Three months ago, it looked as though he had no shot of winning. And, according to close observers, he has not organized a particularly effective campaign. But he is an eloquent speaker and has strong people skills. His candidacy has become something of a cause célèbre among New York Democrats who fear Baraka would reverse the strides Newark has recently taken. Jeffries is still the underdog, but the election is much closer than it was.

A contest for urban reform.

The election on May 13 will be decided on two issues, one cultural and one structural. Jeffries is being portrayed as a Duke- and Columbia-educat-

Is Ukraine the Next Yugoslavia?

By Jochen Bittner

SIMFEROPOL, Ukraine

HERE is a disturbing thought: What if Vladimir V. Putin no longer has the power to prevent bloodshed in Ukraine, even if he wants to?

The idea first crossed my mind during a chat last week at a checkpoint on the main road from Simferopol to Sevastopol in Crimea.

The checkpoint guard was like a warlord from central casting: an impressively dense beard, long black hair and fur hat. On his sleeve, a badge with a golden death's head.

But it turned out that the guard, Bratislav, had a good sense of humor. He was Serbian and a member of the Chetniks, a nationalist paramilitary, he told us. He and four comrades had been called in a few days earlier from Kosovo by pro-secession "Cossacks from the Don," he said, pointing to the half-dozen grim men behind him wielding batons and Kalashnikovs while checking other incoming cars.

— including the Orthodox bishop of Simferopol, Klyment. He feared that the Balkan wars may be "nothing" compared with what lies ahead in Crimea, with its volatile ethnic mix, and possibly even mainland Ukraine.

Perhaps this is just the anxiety of the moment. But there are worrying parallels.

Just like when Yugoslavia fell apart, the people of Crimea today are being forced to choose national allegiances. Although it was clear from the start that the so-called referendum on Sunday could only lead to a union with Russia, the passion with which pro-Russians and pro-Ukrainians have been arguing for their positions has surprised both sides.

The referendum has been a catalyst for disintegration. Different cultural and ethnic identities that used to coexist peacefully already appear to be mutual threats. In the eyes of many of the 60

Uncontainable ethnic hostilities may be

mea it is the Tatars, a Muslim ethnic group who suffered deportation and mass murder under Stalin. They, too, like Bratislav the Chetnik, claim they want to maintain peace. But can they guarantee it? What about false friends from the realm of jihad, who might view defending their brother's Crimean homeland a worthy cause?

The best man to put this question to is probably Fazil Amzayev, the head of the media office of Hizb ut-Tahrir in Ukraine. Banned in most countries of the world, Hizb ut-Tahrir is a political organization that dreams of a global caliphate, denounces democracy and calls for theocracies in states with a Muslim majority.

A Crimean Tatar who grew up in Uzbekistan, Mr. Amzayev met me in a tearoom in the town of Bakhchysarai, a Tatar stronghold southwest of Simferopol. The 32-year-old wore a leather jacket, had a well-trimmed mustache and spoke fluent English.

No, he said, he couldn't rule out the possibility that jihadists might be attracted to Crimea should Russia start to "systematically" suppress Muslims.

For the time being, Mr. Amzayev maintained. Hizb ut-Tahrir is doing ev-

Figure 3.3
Brian Stauffer's illustration for the Gregg Easterbrook article 'Out of Control', art directed by Matt Dorfman for *The New York Times* Op-Ed page, shows a clever take on missing Malaysian Airlines jet 370 which mysteriously disappeared on a flight from Kuala Lumpur to Beijing in March 2014. Here, the negative space performs the part of the missing plane.

contributor to the communication of signs and symbols, with massive variance of approach and options of receipt of information. The frequency and pitch of how signs and symbols are used by the illustrator can result in wildly differing presentations of output and indeed, received information for the reader.

Semiotics and semiology began to be identified in the seventeenth century by English philosopher John Locke, but it was American Charles Sanders Peirce, a leading philosophical figure in the study of semiotics, who determined a classification system for image-based signs in 1867. Pierce categorized signs into the following typology: *icon, index* and *symbol*. The typology is based on the different ways the sign can refer to its object. Hence:

Icon – A sign that resembles or intimates its object, whether it physically exists or not. A helpful example in an international context is the red cross, which is widely associated with medical help and rely on a shared understanding of the sign.

Index – A sign that recognizes its object through an actual connection involving them. The examples of a Stetson, a handgun and rope could be an index for a cowboy, as signs that are linked by association.

Symbol – A sign that refers to its object through interpretation as a recognizable representation made by a pictorial graphic element. An example might be a road sign depicting a symbol of a circle of three arrows to indicate a forthcoming roundabout.

Signs as icons, indexes and symbols can be utilized independently or in union. To use the earlier example of a highway as part of a unified system of signage, a forthcoming bend is indicated by a directional arrow on a physical road sign (icon), in a location ahead of the actual bend (index) and represented by a black graphic arrow shape on a white background (symbol). This example seeks to highlight that layers of multiple meanings can be directly communicated and implied in the same image, potentially creating a cacophony of information to be decoded by the reader, and in theory raising the possibility of drawing down different meanings.

Like Peirce, the Swiss linguist Ferdinand de Saussure also was a leading figure in the origination of semiotics, and sought to prove language as a sign-system. Saussure identified that a sign has two inseparable components in linguistic settings: the *signifier*, represented by speech marks and the *signified*, exhibited by a concept or idea underlying the sign. Applied to aesthetic, communication imagery, the principle permits a sign to be literally deemed a *signifier* as in image seen in context. It also allows a sign to be *signified* by the concept, idea or meaning the signifier represents, which invites interpretation and imagination on the part of the reader, but also reveals incompleteness. In an editorial illustration context, readerships are given clues in the text and in the images that require interpretation as a flavour or essence of content, so ensuring that any translation is, at best, ambiguous and incomplete. Peirce's and Saussure's work was examined and tested by early twentieth-century French philosophers Jacques Lacan, Michel Foucault, Roland Barthes and Jacques Derrida,

Figure 3.4
An inventive piece of editorial cover design and a semiotics lesson in *The Guardian Saturday Review*, courtesy of Javier Jaén's compositional placement of a banana skin as a trigger for a collection of tumbling, unstructured masthead and headlines about fiction losing its sense of humour.

amongst others, and their thinking pervades much of our understanding about received images today.

Determining editorial control is therefore key to establishing the correct order and spacing for these signs to be received and understood by the reader. In this context it is worth establishing the difference between cognitive and denotative reception of images. As the term implies, cognitive reception connects things we recognize through our perception, learnt knowledge or logical reasoning. The subject in an illustration may be a child, but that subject has a series of connotations such as family, fragility and innocence. The depiction of the subject will affect and potentially impose views on how we receive that image about whether the child is vulnerable, or in grave danger. By contrast, denotative reception identifies objects and subjects by the literal meaning drawn from an illustration. Here, the child is an offspring and a young human. Controlling the cognitive and denotative aspects of image reception is vital to ensuring messages within illustrations are constructed as intended, whilst recognizing that no communication within an image is ever complete.

Linking image and text

Editorial illustration relies on, and operates around, a symbiotic relationship between the linked modes of image and text. This linkage creates multimodality – essentially the application of multiple literacies in one medium – and is absolutely vital in editorial illustration. Establishing a multimodal framework essentially enables representation and communication to be drawn from language where all work resides. John Berger famously stated that 'seeing comes before words' (Berger 1972: 7), referencing the fact that the illustration is seen before the accompanying text is read. This perhaps sits at odds with the assumed hierarchy of an image accompanying text in a traditional editorial design setting. The French philosopher Roland Barthes describes this image–text relationship through the close proximity of image, headline, introduction, body text and captions as 'an amplification from one to the other' (Barthes 1977a: 29). Barthes saw the image as an extension of the story in the text, but since editorial illustration ordinarily does not include captions to explain or contextualize imagery, this premise is arguable. However, his observation that images immediately impose and dictate

meaning (Barthes 1977d) support the notion that the inclusion of illustration in an editorial context both invites the reader to partake in a communication experience, and can fundamentally and profoundly shape that experience.

Authors Gunther Kress and Theo van Leeuwen recognized that images that accompany text can operate in close proximity, but that images do not exhaustively have to translate every word. Instead they argue that '... the visual component of a text is an independently organised and structured message, connected to the verbal text, but in no way dependent on it ...' (2006: 18). Using this principle, it is possible to argue for the multimodality of editorial illustration as a construct between the semiotic underpinning of the space between the editorial intent of the publisher and picture editor, the creator of the image, the writer of the text and the resulting experience of the reader. This space is better understood in printed editorial matter, but raises further questions about liminal space in online publications.

Here, dimensions are not fixed, the chain of multimodality must be expanded to include rolling, updated content and responses to published matter creating an expanded field of image and text relationships. The recognition of multimodality is crucial to understanding the historical success and contemporary offer of editorial illustration, especially since new digital platforms will entice readerships to experience content in ever more encapsulating and immersive ways, through augmented, virtual and mixed realities. In that sense, Barthes argument about the image being a continual presence to accompany text only works in the fixed ecology of the printed page – rolling, sequential or data-driven imagery that acutely challenge that hypothesis.

While there is a recognized space between image and text to offer reflection and grow appreciation of content and understanding of meaning, there is also clearly a need to ensure that a shared understanding of the aims and objectives in communicating that content is agreed. This requires a negotiated position between publisher, contributors and readerships. Kress and Van Leeuwen refer to these stakeholders as 'multiple interactive participants' (2006: 114). Such relationships are vital to the creation and reception of an editorial illustration but they are also challenged. The production chain of stakeholders may not be located geographically close, nor do they necessarily share the same working patterns

Figure 3.5
A clever use of language by Janne Iivonen in this illustration titled 'High Low', with a subtle play on the fortunes of those who have and have not. Iivonen's work is inspired by North American visual culture from comics, TV shows and music videos that he read and watched whilst growing up in his native Norway.

and operational structures, as full-time employees and freelancer illustrators for instance. However, the stakeholders should ideally form a synergy of understanding between the publisher, the author of the text, the illustrator and the readership about the ideological position of content.

In this context, the editorial illustration can operate as a symbolic construction in the mind of the reader (Corner 1983) made up of the content of some of its parts. This stance allows aspects of the constructed illustration to be presented to the reader as part of an overall intention of that synergy of understanding between stakeholders, whilst recognizing that some visual or textual clues may not correspond as they are too deep or obscure. It is, indeed, a negotiated position between the modes of image and text designed to stimulate interest, and to promote a greater understanding of ideological opinions on the presented subject.

Image reception

The relationship between image and text naturally provokes questions about the type of image that accompanies text, and explicitly the choices between photography and illustration as forms of engagement and enlightenment for the reader.

Clearly, each form has merit and both are used in the context of editorial design. But each has a set of functions that determine their use for specific image interventions and as a result, they are received differently by readerships. The cultural theorist Stuart Hall (1973) examines the news photograph in the context of editorial publishing specifically, and culture more generally, through a socio-political lens. Hall believed that the cultural landscape was an environment of social action and intervention allowing a flux between power relations in newspaper publishing.

Hall posits the idea that media texts are encoded and decoded in his reception theory. A producer encodes messages and values that are subsequently decoded by the recipient. Decoding allows for multiple interpretations based on the experiences of the recipient which can alter the intentions originally prescribed by the creator. Hall asserts that audience members align themselves to one of three positions as they decode information:

Dominant (Preferred) Reading – The audience receives and decodes information true to the creators intention. This position is likely where audience members can decode messages clearly because they are of a similar age, or come from the same culture as the originator. Messages which have a simple, unambiguous narrative or that exhibit themes familiar and relevant to the audience also fall into this domain.

Oppositional Reading – The audience rejects part or all of the messaging and instead forms their own meaning. Examples might include messages that are structurally complex or difficult narratives, or themes which are unfamiliar and seemingly lack relevance to the audience. This difficult with receiving information can stem from differences in age or culture between the originator and the receiver.

Negotiated Reading – A midway position between Dominant and Oppositional Reading, where the audience is persuaded to accept part of the originators messaging, but will have discordant views too. Conditions that affect a negotiated reading position might be mixed. For example, the recipient could be of a similar age to the originator but from a diversely different cultural background. Equally, the recipient may enjoy the aesthetic of a subject but find the underlying narrative complicated or confusing.

Hall's reception theory recognizes the diversity of both the originator and the members of the audience and is therefore useful in application in an editorial illustration context. The reception theory model gathers the diversity of audience, whether described through age, ethnicity, gender or cultural association, but crucially, also recognizes that variables that are common in all of us, such as life experience and even variations in mood at the point of receiving information can make us accommodate or reject messages that are presented to us. Understanding that we, as recipients of messaging, can accommodate multiple positions depending on our experiences and mood explains why editorial illustration is in such demand and, by extension, why audiences have become so adept and sophisticated in decoding complex content so quickly and effortlessly.

Figure 3.6a–b
Blending time through image reconstruction is an effective method of reigniting memory of historical events and juxtaposing them against contemporary situations. Here, Doug Chayka makes an inert political point about the failings of the Nixon and Trump presidential administrations for *The Washington Post*. The images support cultural theorist Stuart Hall's reception theory examining how images are decoded differently through factors such as age and experience, but can also empower audiences to make connections through familiarity and causal linkages.

Theoretical positions

Editorial illustration is governed and shaped by how and why images are derived and constructed from text and when and where they are subsequently received by readerships. Different schools of thought inevitably exist about such relationships, depending on a number of contributing or contrasting philosophical theories that have emerged, gained traction and been debated since. These might include, but are certainly not limited to, the time that those theories were formed, or the parallel political, sociological and economic contextual surroundings of a particular age that has transformed, revisited and revised them.

Theories help make sense of developments in a subject, expand upon ideas either applied to illustration, or to the communication arts more generally, and on occasion influence the subject from neighbouring and connected fields including the social sciences, the physical sciences and other humanities. Theoretical applications makes the subject of illustration stronger as an identity in its own right and a valuable contributor to wider discourse about the history, development and future of communication design studies, both in terms of its conceptual communicative function and its physical graphic manifestation. Crucially, they signal the maturity of a subject and allow a position of recognition and respect. Conversely, cultural critics see the field of illustration generally as young and relatively inexperienced in originating and developing its own theoretical discourse. Equally, the subject of illustration is arguably inexperienced at receiving criticism and generating countering theoretical models of its own.

As a result, illustration has many theories applied to it that are misleading and worse, lack relevance. This places the subject perilously close to not being taken seriously as a cultural contributor and significant ambassador to future communication media development in arguably one of the most profound periods of change since the original Industrial Revolution. Creating a robust and defensible theoretical position of genuine, unique enquiry, where specific vocabulary and critically engaged discourse can be applied or assigned to aspects of illustration, will create a cohesive ecosystem that positions the subject with gravitas and conviction. The last twenty years have seen a concerted and determined effort to address this issue, with academic peer-reviewed journals dedicated specifically to illustration, academic institutions and professional bodies hosting conferences and symposia and a dedicated library of books released by major publishers that examine all facets of the subject.

Illustration is being taught under the ecosystem of integrated practice and theory that is relevant and pertinent to the subject and away from historic models that saw these two pillars of learning divided and misaligned. A greater number of highly educated graduates are available for hire with theories that are applied through the professional practice acquired in a fast-changing creative industry that is much more adept at signalling new trends, prototyping radical approaches and welcoming collaboration across age, ethnicity, gender and beliefs.

This section introduces some of the major theoretical discourse that students and developing professionals are likely to encounter. The following theoretical positions span the time that editorial illustration has existed. The introduction presents concepts related to visual beauty and aesthetic judgements of quality of art, and the rebalancing of craft as an integral part of a valued society that are championed by Immanuel Kant. The over-development and invasiveness of mass media and the resulting destabilizing effects on society is explored through the section on Marxism, whilst Walter Benjamin's output is investigated through the representation and potential politicization of subject matter and resulting speculation about the problematized relationship between creator and audience.

Moving forward, issues of representation through to important debates examining the misrepresentation of sexuality and gender in mass media are pursued through the writings of Laura Mulvey and Judith Butler. This section signposts areas where further exploration would be useful in an illustrator's pursuit of knowledge about the academic standing of editorial illustration and its cerebral connections to associated subjects for further study. Having a working knowledge of the underpinning theory is designed to give confidence to the process of explorative development. Serious enquiry is encouraged to equip professionals with the intellectual tools and connected production armoury to achieve a successful career that evolves and cements recognition for work produced.

Figure 3.7
Conceptualizing and rationalizing how human beings deal with out-of-body experiences requires the flexibility and the ambiguity of an editorial illustrator's approach. This example, commissioned by art director Michael Mrak for *Scientific American*, shows how American illustrator Brian Stauffer deals with articulating the human brain and its response to near-death experiences.

Kant: Definitions of beauty and judging aesthetics

Although Immanuel Kant's writings ceased by the beginning of the nineteenth century with his passing in 1804, his influence on what constituted a foundational aesthetic beauty in art was felt for many decades. The primary focus for some of his writings was centred on the spectre of aesthetic beauty and the judgement of quality in art. Kant's writings sought to prove and confirm a position where 'high art' artefacts such as individually produced paintings and sculpture were elevated above their mass-produced counterparts, including publishing and illustration. Kant's findings are repeatedly revisited by scholars and critics today, since his findings inevitably created hierarchies of quality that are both hotly debated and fiercely defended. Such tensions were – and, on occasion, are – played out as disciplines jostle for position within the cultural landscape.

Kant's writing has remained significant for three principle reasons. First, his work is grounded in a scientific method of categorization which emerges from the more rigorous study of subjects from the Enlightenment period. The 'academic' study of the big philosophical questions of the day, around what constituted beauty and how it could be accurately judged, occupied Kant and other thinkers, writers, philosophers and cultural critics. Each genuinely sought to apply a determined logical approach to collecting and analysis material and in Kant's case, sorting it into trusted hierarchies of information that removed the emphasis and prevalence of bias from more subjective judgements.

Specifically, Kant posited two kinds of truths, namely *a priori* and *a posteriori*, which he sought to defend rigorously through tangible, but definitive examples. *a priori* truths were mathematically based, reasoned calculations and propositions, such as the construction of paintings using linear perspective that were common and incontestable across a range of decoding processes. *a posteriori* truths, by contrast, were based upon subjective opinions and experiences which were dependent upon unknown or intangible knowledge of the viewer. These could not be logically determined nor proved and as such were unreliable and unsubstantiated pockets of knowledge that formed little more than a personal opinion. By setting this framework of oppositions, Kant places huge emphasis on a universally shared definition of beauty that elevates taste to be a recognized and accepted paradigm that allows certain artefacts to prosper whilst other forms are relegated.

Secondly, Kant's writing has maintained cultural weight as a result of this rigour and has subsequently been used politically to advantage certain artistic outputs over another, thus preserving 'high art' over emerging counterparts such as mass-produced printing. These Kantian principles of aesthetic appreciation of beauty and cultural judgement were primarily tested and reasoned in a pan-European context and did not therefore take account of works being produced in other parts of the world. Kant's writings neglect work produced by other cultural producers, such as indigenous peoples, or highly skilled makers from established cultural production of East Asia who operated under a different cultural

aesthetic. As a result, they are rightly contested as favouring European output as the dominant discourse in cultural production. In turn, this led to serious doubts about a robust universal system of measurement and authenticity of judgement due to the restrictiveness of the artefacts that this treatment were applied to.

Thirdly, his findings can then be used as the basis of a cultural barometer for developing cultural practices that were not present at the time of Kant's death, but have emerged from cultural advances in the social and technological production and reception since. Kant's work on the judgement of aesthetic beauty must be seen in the context of the time it was written. More than two hundred years have passed since his death and the representation and reception of published work have altered massively in the intervening period. For example, many argue that his observations are based on conventional fine art practice and the associated disciplines of printed matter were what could be surveyed at the time, and inevitably cannot take account of film, animation and computer graphics. For illustration application specifically, Kant's findings are problematic because functioning, communicative illustration is never seen as a visual standalone entity – it is contextualized through writing, surrounded by text and placed in a publishing format in print or on screen which delivers it to consumers. In the cross- and multidisciplinary field of twenty-first-century publishing, the unequivocal beliefs of Kant's writings seem distant and dislocated from ideas of low-brow art, kitsch or interactive layout.

Marx: Marxism and the rebalancing of society

Karl Marx's life was spanned by the Industrial Revolution and much of his theoretical position was placed firmly in opposition to industrialization, which brought inequality and imbalance to the lives of the majority of people. Marxism wholly rejected capitalism as a fundamental scourge on developing societies, dismissing the knowledge and skills built on traditional, time-honoured approaches to production. Instead, he was horrified by the steep increase in populations deserting the countryside where they had lived for centuries, for the filth and squalor of new overcrowded cities where they would experience a poor quality of life.

Resorting to work in appalling conditions and for little pay, Marx saw this new world order as a threat to the liberty and dignity of working-class people and what he considered to be their fundamental rights as active and contributory citizens in social relationships. As a result, many of the principles of Marxism can be seen in art movements of the latter nineteenth and twentieth centuries, including the Arts and Crafts movement which made no secret of the desire to return cultural production and appreciation to traditional, craft-based roots.

Marxism dismisses capitalist principles as nothing short of alienation, a term Marx himself repeatedly used to illustrate the connection between consumerist products and the debased workers who were forced to produce them as simply part of a larger production machine. Marx philosophized that the further workers saw themselves from the goods that they had a hand in producing and selling, the more they were merely objects on a conveyor belt contributing to the success and wealth of the few. This objectification was described as reification and formed the basis of political and philosophical thought for a range of thinkers including Barthes, Benjamin and Berger who expanded upon these theories in later years as the concern for cultural production being affiliated to and underpinned by economics grew.

Some illustrators remain deeply sceptical and uncomfortable about the power and control that major publishing houses have over the publication of content that they view politically advantageous and morally unsettling. By the same token, some accept that illustration has been positioned as a commercial enterprise which sits at odds with Marxist values and creates inevitable tensions that are played out in various forums by creators and critics establishing a tenable position for illustration as a subject to theoretically occupy and participate in the future.

Benjamin: The aura of art and issues of mass reproduction

The German philosopher and cultural theoretician Walter Benjamin was a Marxist thinker whose work in the first half of the twentieth century sought to expose the shortcomings of capitalism on the experience of authentically acquiring knowledge. At this time, the adoption of print-based reproduction processes such as halftone and rotogravure was extensive, and had revolutionized mass media newspaper and magazine journal production and dissemination. Benjamin's essay 'The Work of Art in the Age of Its Mechanical Reproducibility and Other Writings on Media' sets out a position where Benjamin believed the reproduction of artwork removes its *aura* of originality, authenticity and value.

This argument sets up a position about proximity and spectatorship which is important to illustrators as creators of original artwork and the relationship this artefact has through a passage of production where control is released before being viewed by the reader. Benjamin described this as a detachment and saw parallels with wider life where capitalism was, in his view, creating a state of estrangement from tangible and spiritual experiences. His belief that personal experience of artefacts and cultural objects offered a cerebral inner experience of belonging and collective ownership in wider society was threatened by what he saw as intrusive, Modernist approaches.

Inevitably, published illustration work has to be reproduced by some means, but the translation process that occurs between text and image, or between medium to medium, and between creator and receiver is steeped in imperfection. A direct translation is simply impossible because of the shift between the structural form of text and image, but also because the motivations of the author of the text will be different to the interpretation of the illustrator receiving that text. Benjamin's view of the process of translation was that whilst imperfection was inevitable, the process of translating and re-translating both lost and gained meaning and traversed a creatively productive process as a result.

What is foregrounded in Benjamin's thoughts on translation is the human relationship to content, where the need for implicit engagement and reaction to content is both needed and valued. This principle holds true to illustrators in a contemporary context where there are shifts in how editorial content is both presented and received.

Foucault: Power relationships and hierarchies

French philosopher and theoretician Michel Foucault was instrumental in forming and presenting a position which positioned societal organizations and institutions as arbiters of power relationships. Foucault believed that this top-down imposition and establishment of rules shaped people, by habitualizing their behaviour and thus defining their place and purpose in society. Rules were formed through a discourse that might be said to comprise imagery, text or even rituals that created a logical and corresponding system. Who or what determined these hierarchies of order could be traced back to the power relationships that existed in organizations and institutions. Inevitably, these were predominantly, if not exclusively, men and there was an established culture of privilege of access and nepotism which rooted these rules as the very socialization of society.

By extension, Foucault argued that previous history as recorded in books was biased by virtue of the fact that the authors who had unearthed and presented knowledge had done so from a privileged position. The exercising of power through social control had afforded opportunity for these historians not only to be given the chance to publish but had also affected what they presented and how they had published information in the public domain. Such publications, Foucault argued, were articles of bias by virtue of the fact that they included certain dominant subjects in particular orders while omitted others, thereby precluding or even preventing knowledge. In his book *The Order of Things* (1994), Foucault examines how information is organized into ordered taxonomies that preserve certain historical hierarchies as dominant over the other. For example, the classification of living beings places humans above other biological forms, separating out our relationship with other creatures into a dominant role which permits us to spectate on specimens. Foucault argues that this systemic categorization distances us from the obvious evolution that has taken place and which we have a spiritual and moral connection to.

The subject of illustration has a complex and knotted history with truth, and, in editorial illustration, the issue is heightened by what many see as the power of publishers to embellish, modify or obfuscate truth. Through the philosophizing of thinkers like Foucault, editorial illustrators need to exercise caution and awareness of both the accuracy and legitimacy of textual content and think robustly about the process of visually interpreting material for the needs of the audience. Editorial illustration, used well, should challenge presumptions and question associations to present alternative positions and offer paradigm shifts in structural thinking.

McLuhan: Theories of media development

Canadian cultural commentator and theorist Marshall McLuhan is a hugely important voice around editorial illustration, as his writings on communication mass media in connection with technological advances mean that his insight carries great weight across many cultural media studies fields. McLuhan foresaw the innovation and adoption of screen-based media as being significant to the way that future societies would be presented with, and eventually interact with, 'new media' during various mid-century critiques. These proclamations helped root developing accessibility and increasing familiarization with technology into a converging civilized domestic environment, as a rite of passage for modern societies to create and gain knowledge in equal measure.

McLuhan's 1964 publication *The Gutenberg Galaxy: The Making of Typographic Man* is an example of a seminal conceptual foundation prevalent in all forms of editorial illustration. McLuhan asserts that Gutenberg's moveable type effectively created the conditions for humankind to read from left to right and from front to back in what he describes as the 'linearization of print' in Western civilization. This observation aptly describes the culturing of the printed word away from its aural traditions of acts of shared storytelling, segmenting it as an entirely different, but not necessarily desirable, proposition for the reader. Printed source matter could be read and digested in isolation, but it created a lonesome experience to read and acquire knowledge that was unfulfilling and problematized. McLuhan argued that the resulting boundaries that manifested themselves in print-based work were in opposition to the multi-modality of the spoken word, allowing audiences to conjure interpretation and meaning that was steeped in diversity of background and experience.

This belief that McLuhan had in a democratization of thought, aided by the convergence of mass media communication with technological innovation, was a deep-rooted philosophical ideal of redressing and re-establishing the balance of peoples from what he saw as the enforced class separation of printed communication. The tradition of cultural elitism, supported by what he saw as entitlement and privilege afforded by print, could be offset by a revisionist society where the masses could reclaim cultural identity through mass media. The computer, McLuhan believed, offered significant opportunities for populations to take control of their own learning by suppling information in a format that made the machine a 'research and communication instrument'. Developments in the use of social media, where many argue that extended time spent interacting with a screen causes isolationist tendencies and real world withdrawal, create an interesting parallel argument that McLuhan both foresaw and warned of in his writings. This was countered by the argument that in making technology available, the masses would be freed to access information previously denied or unavailable to them and could make informed choices about their lives from a variety of perspectives.

McLuhan's next significant publication, *Understanding Media: The Extensions of Man* in 1964, provided an update on these perspectives through a system of coding based on active user interaction and experience. In the book, McLuhan sets out a hot to cold scale, where hot media are immersive and engage the viewer through an enveloping exposure to content. As media sources 'cool' they require greater investment from the audience to decode messages and understand content. Editorial illustration hypothetically falls into the cooler categories, depending on the level of decoding required to unlock meaning from an illustration. This theory also supported McLuhan's famous assertion that 'the medium is the message', which was a significant claim at the time and has had profound implications for illustration and communication design more broadly since. Positing such a theory determines that illustrations that are constructed from physical materials convey content-based messages differently to their digital counterparts and directly condition the audience response. Whilst hotly debated as a principle, the contemporary broad and diverse media landscape sees this theory played out addendum every day.

Derrida: The principles of deconstruction

Jacques Derrida is unquestionably one of the great thinkers and philosophers of modern times and follows a line of eminent world authorities from France (Deleuze, Foucault and Barthes) who were prolific in questioning and evaluating culture as a vital contributory factor to human kind. During his life (1930–2003) he was an extremely active observer and critic of a wide variety of subjects, but it is his work on deconstruction that is particularly pertinent to studies on the impact his work has on the subject of illustration generally. Living and writing in a postmodernist era, Derrida critically analysed sign-based systems such as imagery and text to understand and explained the foundations and formations of language, meaning and the transfer of information as progressive forms of knowledge.

Earlier in the twentieth century, Swiss linguist Ferdinand de Saussure had established a structuralist reading of signs as part of a strict rule system that dictated how signs were analysed and coded as signifiers, or how they were signified that were then connected and constituted as particular social behaviours. Derrida's work expanded upon Saussure's hypothesis by questioning whether communication and resulting meaning could be exactly extracted from specific signs. Instead, Derrida argued for a fluidity of meaning because, in a poststructuralist sense, signifiers 'float' and therefore express meaning momentarily. The complexity of imagery and words to create sophisticated meaning was enabled by this 'free play' between the sign and the signifier that could be 'indefinitely referred' as Derrida described it. In an editorial illustration context, Derrida's poststructuralist commentary is helpful and astute in considering the nuanced context that published output is both presented and then received.

Whilst an illustration may be originated and produced with a particular commissioned purpose for an audience, the context floats as that audience are composed of individuals with vastly differing experiences that affect the way they consume images and inbuilt messages. Consequently, the illustrator's ability, through their own licence or with cooperative consent from the person who has commissioned them, allows text and image to be interpreted by an expansive process of unlimited deconstruction and reconstruction of the illustration as it takes form and substance. In this context, a central spine of postmodernist thinking, namely that fluidity of interpretation must be open-ended and unobstructed is exulted through conceptual editorial illustration which relies on breathing space and shades of interpretation to imbue meaning for the reader.

Berger: Ways of seeing

Most students of illustration will be familiar with the writings of John Berger as a seminally important window into the communication design world. His output is culturally significant in Britain because of a 1970s television series, *Ways of Seeing*, which expanded knowledge of visual culture encompassing photography, visual communication and the visual arts for the general public and which became a catalyst for a global audience to find and appreciate his work. At the heart of this work was the notion that a viewer's cultural attachment to an image was massively important, as seeing occurs before reading and understanding. In editorial illustration, this observation is of crucial significance as a reader's eye is drawn to the image on a page or screen ahead of reading the headline or article that expands appreciation and enjoyment of the subject, emphasizing the importance of the illustration as arresting interest, setting a scene and evoking an atmosphere.

Berger's assertion that knowledge derived from images and words is in a continual state of flux depending on the social environment in which they are witnessed, perceived and understood distances the process from a mechanical construction of vision being a wholly scientific one built on objectivity and anatomical function. By default, an individual's perception is inextricably linked to their location, upbringing, life experiences and beliefs and so will be different from other viewers. Makers of culture, such as illustrators, photographers and artists, produce products for consumption that materialize into what he describes as 'species of information' by virtue of the fact that they are detached from their original studio setting. The resulting publication production process ensures that they pass through various hands, signifying ulterior motivations and concerns, are edited and removed from their original guise into an extrapolated context to reconstitute new meanings in published form.

Berger's work is seminal in visual cultural circles in helping understand imagery and associations and this work has been especially important in the development of gender studies and issues of stereotyping and bias. In *Ways of Seeing*, he examines the objectification of women through depictions of the female nude made over centuries of image production. Berger asserts that many of these historical products consciously expose women as objects of desire, conquest and belonging as they are contrived and represented by heterosexual male creators, who in turn control how female spectators

observe and quantify subjects, casting them into positions of passive submission. Using the context of advertising, Berger illustrates that stereotypical depictions of women condition strong architypes (for example, the perfect hostess or the voluptuous secretary) in a viewing public that then project those characteristics in a consumerist setting. Berger's work recognizes that despite individual male producers making the work, the debate needed to develop and recognize that gender bias was a conditioning principle of creators themselves by wider society both at the point of manufacture and in subsequent decades of critical reflection. Consequently, with strong connections to the wider philosophy of Marxism in Berger's work, many cultural commentators such as Laura Mulvey and Judith Butler have used Berger's observations to further their work on feminism and queer theory respectively.

Mulvey: Gender studies in film and moving image

Film theorist Laura Mulvey is a well-regarded authority on spectatorship and recognized for her pioneering work in analysing gender roles and assignment. Her work on the 'male gaze' is especially pertinent to illustration, and by extension, all forms of visual representation stemming from a patriarchal society. Drawing from Berger's earlier observations about the creative direction and depiction of men and women in visual culture, Mulvey's attention in a film context turned to films emanating from the big Hollywood studios which categorized and cast women as objects of spectacle through the lens of powerful, heterosexual men in positions of authority and influence.

The dominant Hollywood studio model of the 1920s was to cast leading male actors on huge salaries who would ensure viewing figures and develop business models for the industry to flourish. Successful audience engagement set up conditions for further projects and created a demand that kept the general public attentive and expectant. Mulvey argues that whilst the dominant male lead was increasingly portrayed as a heroic talisman, any female casting reinforced notions of them as objects of sexual desire and feats of conquest that interrupted action and created marginal distraction. The disproportionate treatment of men and women was enforced by a highly dominant and foreboding male production culture that created and preserved creative roles for men, whilst confining women to menial administrative or lowly support tasks that completely misrepresented their talent and their potential contribution to cultural motion products. Film crews on set were almost exclusively male, and the inevitable consequence of the lens lingering on female subjects was to objectify and sexualize them in ways that reinforced gendered societal norms of desire and repressive curtailment of their own identities.

Mulvey's work has ignited much critical analysis of the terms and conditions of employing female creators, establishing and promoting feminist modes of creative production and fairly representing women in the visual arts to address historical imbalances and provide alternative testimonies that are experienced and shared. In editorial illustration, the representation of women in stereotypical roles or in suggestive poses or situations has a history shaped by societal conventions and as such, acts as an interesting barometer of social history. For example, the compositional placement of women in magazines of the 1920s and 1930s as the subject of focus, whether through suggestive desire or ornamentation, has been replaced by more accurate portrayals of women as advocates of freedom and liberty, able to define their directions and be identified equally without prejudice. Greater numbers of professional female illustrators have entered the discipline since the 1950s, and the creative industries as a whole has seen a wider demographic influx of women from different cultural backgrounds, which has forced issues of representational equality to be addressed. The macho culture of 1960s and 1970s newspaper journalism, which did much to perpetuate these social myths, has been routed and overturned in a generation by a surge in bright female applicants to universities and talented, diverse graduates determined to make their mark in a fast-developing publishing world that offers flexible working opportunities.

Butler: Studying sexuality and gender

Judith Butler, the American philosopher, has spent her working career examining gender identity. Butler argues that gender is not a binary biological construction, but instead is shaped socially and culturally through repetitious actions that the body performs that reveal themselves in gendered identities. This position restricts personal expression because it forces people to inhabit personas and behave in ways that are acceptable to societies, by extension becoming masculine or feminine. Normalization in a societal context pigeonholes gender into neat, regulated groups that sit in opposition to natural situations, desires or nuanced identities. This normalization is so embedded in society, Butler argues, that it has become part of our everyday language, expression and expectation. As a result, we are steeped in a societal construct that prefers and perpetuates heterosexuality over other gendered identities.

Butler offers a more flexible model of gender in opposition to a simple binary choice. She proposes a fluid model of gendered identity that not only permits but supports potentially multiple changing stances depending on individual situation, mood and experience. This flexibility, she argues, better reflects a modern world where personal freedom and liberty is a prized and valued commodity by society and should therefore be applied to individual citizens, regardless of background. To do that successfully, there needs to be wider investigation into, and acceptance of, difference in multifaceted identities. Whilst editorial illustration has long been a discipline that welcomed and celebrated gendered difference in terms of professional identities of practitioners, the creative output produced disproportionately reflects this position as a survey of output.

Often subjects such as gender roles and identities, whether through subtly nuanced or overtly staged depiction, were considered taboo and risky and were not published. Some of this resistance can be traced to concerns about potentially expensive and damaging libel cases for publishing content that damaged reputations, or incorrectly exposed figures or scenes. In other instances, provocative content was seen as damaging to circulation figures or to advertising revenue, both of which were obvious and necessary financial lifelines. New approaches are needed to sensitively portray normalized gender identity within illustration. Some critics have argued that these depictions should be undertaken by artists who gender identify in non-binary ways as a fair and experienced way of empathizing with the issues. Others point to a wider profile of creators taking on these projects to better understand the codes and conditions of gender and to create new knowledge and understanding of what are clearly complex issues for many.

Barthes: Myths and meanings

French literary critic and theorist Roland Barthes is a much-cited scholar, whose work provides a contemporary critique on the structural semiotic writings of Saussure, specifically in relation to how they apply in a popular culture context. Barthes interventionist writings allow the rules and systems that Saussure introduced to the study of semiotic theory to be applied more widely across cultural subjects and artefacts. This permits illustration to be included as a vehicle that can demonstrate signs made of coded systems of signification.

Barthes book *Image, Music, Text* introduces the concept of the 'ideological worldview', where he argues that cultural outputs can be examined and systematically categorized to semiotically affect a viewer's reception and subsequent feelings about products and services. Barthes hypothesized that forms of cultural output – which he included as images, words, gestures and objects – all have ideological agendas intertwined into their production that skew how these reproductions of reality are rhetorically presented and absorbed by the viewing public. Such coded outputs directly affect the viewer as they are knowingly and specifically constructed to appeal to particular audience demographics. Their meaning thereby creates attitudinal shifts and changes in the viewer by denoting or connoting promoting certain segments of the market, or ascribing roles to gender identities.

Barthes's work considered the myth an important attribute in how we understand and comprehend the world around us. Myths lock certain expectations and assumptions about the semiotic reading of signs that is not directly ascribed, emphasizing that we have a shared understanding and acknowledgement of their meaning even though that meaning is implied and reality is intangible. The book provides an example of a *Paris Match* cover image depicting a young black man saluting France. The boy in the photo encapsulates the myth of nationalism and is chosen to promote the view that all colonial subjects are in servitude to their country. The

rhetoric surrounding the image suggests that a patriotic view is one of racial harmony between the races; a view that would be contested and questioned by many.

Perhaps most pertinent to contemporary illustrators working in editorial illustration is Barthes's studies on the theme of authorship. In his famous essay 'Death of the Author' (1967), Barthes challenges the view that an author or creator assumes control of content in published material through a solitary experience. Instead, he argues that readerships and audiences are imbued with other experiences that affect and shape their decoding of the semiotic images created by that text or image and can interpret that through many readings of meaning. The recipient brings the culmination of experiences to receiving information which enables their decoding to be highly personal and different to the next, which allows Bathes to claim that 'the true locus of writing is reading … the birth of the reader comes at the expense of the death of the author' (Barthes, in Dayton 1998: 383–6).

The authorial dimension to editorial illustration, in the context of Barthes's writing, therefore allows the formulation of a framework that sees an interesting exchange between the writer, illustrator, commissioner and readership emerge. The publication of content can be said to have mutated from its original form as a commissioned passage of text. Through the iterative musings of the writer who may have written and edited several versions, to the interpretation of the illustrator, possibly working with either the editor or writer, or both, through to the resulting placement on page or screen, content will have been shaped and directed, inferred and implied, and continually decoded and recoded before being witnessed by the reader or viewer. Barthes's writing allows subtle shifts around meaning, since his elevation of the reader to a position of equality also promotes the idea that readers may respond differently to the same content on account of mood, environment and immediate experience.

In a contemporary digital world where editorial illustration content is published and further edited in online editions, and where social media commentary on editorial positions is enabled to respond in real time, there are significant and profound consequences of Barthes writing in ways that now demand new, rigorous study.

Part Two

Content

With the context of why editorial illustration exists covered, the next part of this book explores the different types of editorial illustration used in newspapers, magazines and journals. From conceptual illustrations which challenge the reader, through to decorative images that serve the presentation of journalistic content, the typology of editorial illustration surveys historical and contemporary uses, drawing on internationally sourced examples of practice from some of the best exponents of the form.

Typology of Editorial Illustration

The range and scope of offerings serve to position editorial illustration as a flexible, fluid answer to changes in both production, dissemination and reception of journalistic content in textually supportive visual form. In so doing, the examples prove how conceptual editorial illustration can visually lead and act as a signifier for hard-hitting content, or how subjects can be interrogated through reporting on events and situations in the form of reportage illustration as visual essay. Depictions of subjects are explored through conceptual frameworks and practical descriptions of particular visual representations systems, such as the portrait or caricature, to reinforce the position that the content of editorial illustration deliberately and knowingly intertwines and interfaces between a subject's content and its construction. Some journalistic content requires deft editorial handling to heighten or accentuate information allowing approaches such as realism, hyperrealism or stylized realism to be employed by the illustrator. In other instances, careful depiction of complex batches of information requires clear linear depiction through diagrammatic or infographic specialism, allowing the reader to understand new or unfamiliar subjects in enlightening ways.

Figure 4.1
The financial bonds market is a conceptual editorial illustrator's playground with subject matter that is often elusively intangible and jargon-filled to all but the most serious, dedicated reader. Yet many readers have a vested interest in understanding what is happening to their investment, so a visual summary of complex, fact-filled and opinion heavy articles is required. Brian Stauffer grapples with the US bond market being a massive, unwieldly entity for *The Wall Street Journal*.

Figure 4.2
Joe Ciardiello's illustration commemorates seventy-five years of Columbia University seminars, featuring literary giants Margaret Mead, W. H. Auden, Kenneth Clark, Philip Johnson and Hannah Arendt. The illustration here places them in the same frame although they existed in different decades. Commissioned by Len Small for *Columbia Magazine*.

Types of editorial illustration

As an important form of visual commentary, editorial illustration has universal applications across a broad spectrum of subjects to educate, entertain and inform. Daily, weekly and monthly publication junctures allow the continual stream of content into the reader's consciousness. To encompass such diversity, editorial illustrations clearly must be conceptualized and constructed differently to suit particular purposes and relay information in ways that readerships will understand. An illustrated cover of a journal needs to arrest the reader by grabbing their attention, whilst an editorial double-page spread may invite closer scrutiny through dwelling and

musing on subjects in greater detail. A regular column or section may build up familiarity and rapport with a readership who look forward to the next instalment, whilst a spot illustration nestled in amongst text creates a brief interlude that enables the reader to pause and reflect, or enhances the mood and ambience of the surrounding text. The relationship between an editorial illustration and the readership therefore becomes intrinsically linked and bound, building emotional attachments and trusted confidences about the reporting of information.

Context, encoders, code and decoders – a brief overview

In the book *History of Illustration*, editors Susan Doyle, Jaleen Grove and Whitney Sherman posit a model of illustration connecting the image to the audience which considers *context*, *encoders*,

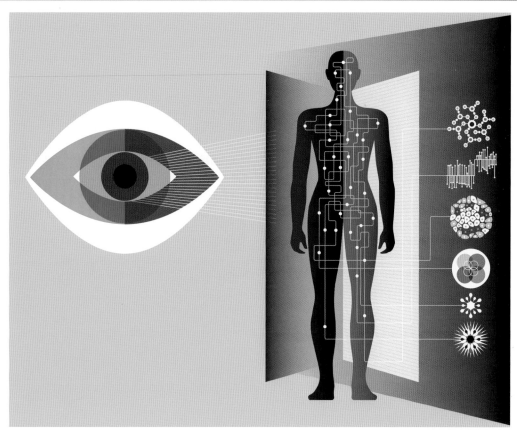

Figure 4.3 Paul Wearing uses clever compositional colour design in this illustration, 'Diagnose This. A Health Care Revolution in the Making', to connect the reader to the idea that the symbolic eye on the left of the image is observing and processing data about the human subject and their genetic construction, symbolized by the molecular structures on the right. Art directed by Dennis McLeod for the David Armario Design agency for client *Stanford Medicine* magazine.

code and *decoders*. This model is particularly helpful in the context of 'understanding producers' and consumers' motivations' (2019: Introduction, xviii) and 'what the social effects of illustrated media might be' in an editorial illustration setting, since it inevitably links to various established models of media communication theory.

The *History of Illustration* model recognizes that in a *context* phase, messages in communication theory must be sent as *code* which can include words and pictures. Creators of these assets are *encoders* and in the chain of message receivership, the recipients are therefore *decoders*. Sharing a knowledge of *codes* – what words and pictures might mean – is dependent on a degree of familiarity between the creator and recipient, and will be shaped by experience, environment and events. Inevitably, these will have geographical, political, religious or social biases and can be traced to a time that were created and consumed, hence why historical

reappropriation and re-enactment become possible by shifting contexts and consequences. In editorial illustration, the role of the *encoder* is not solely undertaken by the commissioned illustrator, since there is editorial input from various sources. These will include representatives of the publisher, the editor or art director for example, and possibly even the writer. The assets that accompany the illustration, including the headline, body text and pull quotes, and even accompanying information-based material in the printed matter or on screen that affects the readers field of vision, adds to the encoding experience.

Illustration *code* may be broken down into familiar components such as composition, colour, form and mode of production that contribute to, and convey, meaning. Doyle, Grove and Sherman define code under three headings: iconography, form and format. In this model, iconography is stipulated as being the subject matter and symbolism contained in the image(s), and form recognized by the way that those images are constructed as artificial representations through choices over composition, placement of elements and tangible marks, colours and tones employed. Format refers to the vehicles of communication delivery and dissemination to the consumer in print or on screen. *Decoders* of an illustration are intended recipients for whom the content was originally intended, such as the readership of a journal. However, published work is distributed into the public domain, opening up possibilities for greater consumption but also raising issues about receivership, intent and miscomprehension. As publishers open up more channels to communicate to existing and potential readerships, and audiences becoming increasingly more media aware and sophisticated in their consumption choices, so editorial illustrators find themselves in the centre of a vibrant and energetic debate about the meaning of images, their consequences and their influence on contemporary issues.

Some illustrators choose to work within specialist parts of the editorial field, such as caricature or reportage, whilst others wish to apply themselves more divergently across a range of genres. This section investigates the taxonomies of editorial illustration, how content is commissioned and handled, and why it serves a different function to the application of photography.

In order to understand the extraordinarily diverse and dizzying contemporary field of editorial illustration, it is necessary to pay homage and attention to its history. Much of what is now viewed as groundbreaking, original and innovative of today's work can be traced to the birth and development of the form, crucially in terms of both the visual construction and evolution of image-making, and to the wider contextual issues of depictions of content, including the forming of cultural identity, social history, political and philosophical stances, religious persuasion and national affiliation.

The synergy of greater literacy in the population, emerging technology to enable mass production and the growing popularity of consumption format gave rise to what we now recognize as the commercial artist – the illustrator - as a distinct and particular purveyor of communicative image-maker. The entertaining visual storyteller, the reporter of information, assuming a role of educator of the people. In a developing world where public education

was growing but still not a right for every citizen, illustration was landing in very fertile conditions for rapid growth and expansion of consumption on a scale never previously witnessed. The following sections break down the main types of editorial illustration and show examples of practice across print and digital publishing domains.

Narrative realism

By the 1840s, illustration in newspapers and magazines was capable of being reproduced and distributed widely. This coincided with perhaps the most turbulent and tumultuous period in the history of many civilizations. The Industrial Revolution transformed economic and social conditions, optimizing pioneering discoveries and developing nations into colonizing forces to populate and control other parts of the world. Pioneering these ventures was risky, adventurous and exciting. Results, discoveries and revelations had to be reported and celebrated, and the popular vehicle of illustration was used to convey the excitement and wonder of the new world through narrative realism. Illustrations were rooted in what might be termed a 'believable reality', characterized by conventionally proportioned figurative depictions in real-world settings, rendered using perspective and acknowledgement of scale and space, and usually lit by natural elements to reveal clear and unambiguous interpretations of scenes or events. The inclusion of detail provided evidence of truth and authenticity for the readership, although as constructed and fabricated forms, illustrations could only act as purveyors of this brand of reality.

As technology progressed, the wood engravings that characterized earlier works gave way to other reproduction methods which were aligned to the birth of photography. Early inventions such as the daguerreotype (1839) created a demand for celebrity photographic portraits, and many commercial studios opened in American cities. The general public flocked to see these new mechanically produced renditions of reality, fuelling a healthy appetite for personal keepsakes and a burgeoning interest in amateur photography. Illustrators responded by crafting output to match these expectations. Faithful and accurate imitations of life in visual form were produced, with an honesty and integrity about how figures were depicted, what they were shown to be dong and how they were dressed assuming major importance.

By the 1880s, the invention of continuous tone reproductions of photographic and illustrative imagery through halftone and rotogravure afforded a substantial shift in quality and the opportunity to render reproductions of images in full colour using multiplate processes. Initially used for magazine covers due to financial limitations, internal illustrations were limited to two or three colour reproductions, which inevitably affected how they were conceived and designed to benefit from those restrictions.

At the turn of the twentieth century, pioneering titles such as *Harper's Monthly, The Century Illustrated Monthly Magazine* and *Scribner's Monthly* were joined by lower-priced competitors including the *Saturday Evening Post, Collier's Weekly* and *Munsey's* in the United States. Competition grew, ignited by human-centred content as publishers realized that this format of communication presenting fact and fiction had mass appeal. Editorial and production quality rose in response, with authors and contributors keen to harness new approaches to collecting valuable information through investigative journalism, well-crafted fiction, epic natural photography and beautifully rendered illustrations. Editors fought to retain the services of accomplished illustrators who could guarantee circulation and brand identity. Quality content was underpinned by advertising revenue gleaned from product and service providers who had found a contemporary vehicle to peddle their wares. Rather than be confined to the latter pages of publications as classified advertising in regimented grid form, advertising was integrated into these developing editorial spreads, signalling a move that remains significant to this day and creating often paradoxical messaging in the minds of readerships.

Illustrators Howard Pyle and N. C. Wyeth, both American, are arguably the chief exponents of narrative realism, laying foundations for the likes of now-household names such as J. C. Leyendecker, Maxfield Parrish, Charles Dana Gibson and, later, Norman Rockwell. Their work captured and celebrated the theatricality of life, demonstrating an extraordinary sense of mastery in depicting figures in situations imbued with dramatic action, or quiet introspective reflection. The seeming familiarity of their work, depicting everyday situations reminiscent of readers' own

lives, provided both inspiration towards building the American Dream, and a reassurance of shared societal values of hard work, family bonds and wider community harmony as part of a wider national identity. The sheer versatility and consummate professionalism of their collective endeavours lifted illustration as a critically recognized form to new heights, defined as the Golden Age of illustration in printed form. In turn, their output gave credence and credibility to the pursuit of illustration as a commercial and professional discipline.

Central to much of this expansion and recognition were women as subjects, and later, lauded protagonists of work. Publishers recognized that many consumers of magazines and periodicals were women, but they were slower to understand that as arbiters of societal values, they were helping consign women to stereotypical roles linked to the home. Depictions of romanticized and idealized lifestyles initially sold well, imbuing a sense of domesticity, motherhood and unflinching service as homemakers, wives and moral custodians of the community. This depiction gave rise to the term 'woman's sphere' by cultural historians, who charted a woman's place as firmly rooted in domestic affairs. Many of the resulting women's focused publications, including *Godey's Lady's Book* and *Ladies Home Journal*, were born out of this conservative belief in preordaining women as matriarchically, and achieved colossal circulation figures.

However, the world was changing. More women were joining the workforce, earning their own wages and questioning the familiar rites of passage of marriage and motherhood. A new generation of reader demanded more contemporary content, including suffrage and equal rights, or physical education and leisure pursuits, and publishers realized that they had to meet these expectations. More and more female illustrators were hired for their contemporary lived experience and their critical insight into this newly focused audience's wishes, and to help realign values and beliefs towards an altogether more progressive and mobile demographic who were becoming highly educated and choosing their own distinct paths.

The fascination and appetite for stories of endeavour, discovery and conquest ensured that a flurry of assignments followed for those who had artistic flair and a talent for marshalling that into the construction of illustrations that could

Figure 4.4
Australian illustrator Guy Shield's sympathetic use of composition and colour evokes the adventurous spirit of travel in this cover, 'The Solo Traveler' for *AirBnB* magazine, reminiscent of the mood conveyed in Norman Rockwell's *The Saturday Evening Post* cover, 'The Runaway' from 20 September 1958.

communicate intent to the developing readership. That intent has subsequently become the discussion of much scrutiny and scholarly debate – are these images truthful and accurate renditions of events that occurred? Or are they rather a distorted reality, far removed by virtue of what they omit through editorial control, conscious and unconscious bias and revisionist agendas that purported to elevate the status of certain groups over others unjustly? The idealized depictions of life, livelihoods and community may not tell a complete story of the whole, but rather a segment of society that corresponded to the readership demographic publishers were striving to reach. Indeed, arguments extend now to whether this glorification of life has, in fact, entrenched and widened societal divides by stereotyping and characterizing figures of colour, gender and ethnicity into roles which have marginalized and alienated them from what might be considered mainstream society.

Narrative realism, as a bedrock and historic cornerstone of editorial illustration, clearly informs and perpetuates contemporary practice today. The work of illustrators such as Marc Buckhardt, Gérard DuBois and Anita Kunz draws heavily on narrative realism through depictions of recognizable celebrities or public figures for political or social comment on magazine covers and over columns of text. Works conform to structural compositional configurations and realistic logic, meaning that figures populate worlds which, although imagined, use elements such a proportionate scale, lighting and tonal contrast that imbues scenes with a degree of authenticity and familiarity. Within editorial narrative realism, however, it is possible to exaggerate both forms and actions in illustrations to make salient points about the subjects in question, drawing attention to aspects that would otherwise be obscured, or to make cutting satirical comment for the amusement of the reader.

Hyperrealism and stylized realism

The physical manufacture of image-based realism was influenced by wider cultural and creative influences outside illustration. As photography became more ubiquitous, it became cheaper to commission due to the burgeoning number of proponents keen to sell their images for commercial profit to publishers. Illustration risked being marginalized as it became more expensive by comparison, and beyond the highly accomplished producers, there were also a roster of less-artistically gifted artists scrapping for diminishing opportunities and returns. Illustrators

Figure 4.5
Marc Burckhardt's playful illustration for *Scientific American*
shows how narrative realism can be successfully employed to
deceive the reader's eye and make them do a double-take in this
editorial about shrinking animals.

instances adding detail to overemphasize and
highlight details or specific elements for editorial importance and significance. For example,
renditions of fresh fruit or vegetables could be
given a heightened sense of just being picked
by the addition of pearly dew drops catching
mythical highlights from sunbeams emanating
from the sun. Inevitably, advertising agencies
and their clients saw the immediate benefits of
this type of image rendition, but editorial illustration exponents such as Winslow Homer and
the other Sentimentalists also characterized this
approach until the 1950s, satisfying the reader's
curiosity by inviting them into deeper inspection
of subjects.

In the spirit of the pioneers who had explored
the Wild West and forged a healthy interest in
storytelling using narrative realism, the collective ambition of humankind to discover worlds
beyond our own, whether in the far reaches of
space, or deep under water, provided rich content
for illustrators during the 1960s and 1970s.
Coupled with a post-war explosion of fiction
that looked for signs of hope and the promise of
excitement about the future, editorial illustrators
were commissioned to imagine the possibilities
of these explorations and discoveries and render
them for eager readerships. These imaginary
worlds created a dilemma for illustrators who
needed on the one hand to show details that
were essential to understanding the composition
of environments, but were artificial constructions
imagined rather than exclusively drawn from
life or experience. As such, stylization offered
to blend reality with fantasy creating seemingly tangible scenes that were in fact wholly
imaginary.

Stylized realism became a way to achieve
a necessary level of detail that underpinned a
believable and authentic view of scenes and
events being portrayed, but allowed levels of
recognition between illustrators output to be
achieved. This visual style manifested itself in
increasingly diverse ways, through impressionistic handling of painted media to suggest the
lively interplay of light in scenes, or the exaggeration of scale and density of patterning on surfaces
to amplify beauty or quality of manufacture of an
artefact. The human figure also was stylized, both
in terms of elongating proportions to suggest
elegance and refinement or through suggestively
over-glamorizing appearance through rendering details such as make-up and hair with extra

needed to diversify and segment their offering
from photography as an enticing and valued
proposition. The development of hyperrealism
was a deliberate attempt to go beyond the photographic image. Rather than see photography's
limitation, these movements are perhaps better
characterized by illustrators imaginatively seeking opportunities to make images that evoked
awe and wonderment, but that also extended
the reach of what was imagined to be 'real' in an
analogue context.

Photography introduced audiences to new
paradigms of picture-making, including depth
of field within an image, where elements including figures and objects in the photographic
frame could appear in focus whilst other aspects
were blurred. This had the effect of guiding or
directing the viewer to particular parts of an
image, and creating ambiguity or uncertainty in
other blurred parts of the picture. By contrast,
hyperreality approaches enabled the illustrator
to construct images where every aspect of the
visual surface was at least in focus, in some

emphasis. Such stylization, whilst the visual manifestation of an idea, succeeded in reinforcing messages being communicated through the content of work.

In contemporary editorial illustration, hyperreality and stylized realism is proactively commissioned where emphasis and extra focus on subject matter is deemed desirable. Examples might include depiction in fashion-based illustration with overemphasis on the figure, clothes and accessories, or overtly introducing and displaying the quality of particular products being reviewed for special features. Ilustrations created digitally are especially subject to amplification through the myriad of tools and variants of effects available through software packages and associated plug-ins, allowing the illustrator an arsenal of custom-built options to really hone and define their work. Again, there are moral and ethical considerations embodied in producing work that is hyperreal or stylized. A good example is the recurrent debate about the 'Photoshopping' of images of human bodies to achieve an idealized perfection which, ironically, gains many column inches and has seen global debate about the misleading representation of often high-profile icons causing issues relating to mental health conditions and eating disorders. These images largely tend to be photographic in origin, but can be then rendered through digital software to masquerade as illustrations that a constructed interpretation of reality.

Conceptual

Arguably some of the most imaginative, vivid and memorable images produced in an editorial domain have been created as conceptual illustrations. Work produced by internationally famed illustrators such as Brad Holland, Pierre Le Tan, Javier Jaén, Guy Billout, Edel Rodriguez and Christoph Niemann provide powerful, thought-provoking encapsulations of subjects that jolt memories, provoke actions and incite responses. Their work is rightly celebrated and revered. Steven Heller, the renowned graphic design writer and one-time Art Director for the *New York Times'* Opinion Editorial page, explains that 'Conceptual illustration serves two purposes: it provides meaning – and commentary – and gives a publication its visual personality.'

The birth of conceptual illustration can be traced back to the rise in the use of photography in publications. As the photographic image, and

television programming and advertising more broadly, reduced demand for narrative illustration in the 1950s, illustrators had to shift their focus to creating new work for a decreasing number of publications. This demise of publishing, now competing with emerging lens-based technology, meant publishers and illustrators were often united in creating content that produced brand identity in publications such as *Fortune*, *Playboy* and the *Radio Times*. Here, illustration was increasingly conceptually driven, operating between the experimental and the documentary and often imbued with symbolism and intrigue. Culturally aware illustrators, such as R. O. Blechman and Saul Steinberg, referenced Surrealism and Dadaism in their expressive works which were heavily reliant on readerships awareness, curiosity and interest in contemporary issues. The increasing fascination with the role of the psychologist, or 'shrink', in society was a marker for wider issues surrounding the tolerance of alternative perspectives on life or lifestyles which promoted modest difference and acceptance.

Conceptual illustrators brought readerships pleasure and entertainment through sophisticated use of visual puns and metaphors, and a newly found passion for combing text and image to create allusion and communicate complex meanings. This movement attracted the well-educated reader who thrived on the intellectual challenge and engagement of this work, creating interest back into publications to the delight of publishers, and ensuring conceptual editorial illustration had a place reserved for its critical insight and thorough reflection. Illustration had found a way to offer something culturally, socially and politically relevant in a fast-paced world that was being bombarded with images on domestic television screens and through the rise of commercial advertising, set against a world beset by tensions, including Cold War nervousness, sexual revolution and family breakdown. In short, this movement established the credentials of illustration as a powerful and influential voice in publishing, and played a profound effect in the social upheaval being experienced in the neighbourhoods and suburbs of the 1960s.

To illustrate this connectedness between causes and effects driven by the wider world, the emergence of the 'Big Idea', a marketing trend born out of acute realizations about changing consumer interests and motivations utilized much of the conceptual thinking that was connecting to newspaper readerships during the 1960s. Advertisers and market-eers saw that products and services could be attractively presented through visual thinking, by fusing semiotic understanding with lively design to produce social meanings. Successful work became about making clever connections between the idealized product or service and the extension of the lifestyle it portrayed, rewarding the consumer by acknowledging their intellect in understanding the messaging on display. This focused and intelligent strategy of tantalizing and tempting the consumer shaped experiences of receiving text- and image-based communi-cation. The thinking that underpinned the Big Idea became a foundation stone that explains why audiences and readerships are so aware and capable of decoding sophisticated informa-tion today.

Conceptual editorial illustrations is commis-sioned where immediate interpretations of text are either not possible or undesirable, or where a particularly ambiguous subject needs to be given an editorial angle. This form of editorial illustra-tion places the illustrator in a potentially powerful position, as a key protagonist in constructing images that are non-didactic and non-literal from a personal point of view. Such illustrations privilege the voice of the editorial illustrator as a visual journalist, a purveyor of a particular editorial position and an arbiter of taste. In such instances, conceptual illustrations can imply or suggest meaning(s), without necessarily instructing them. As such they serve as a useful grammatical tool in the wider visual vocabulary of a publication; they might shock reminiscent of an exclamation mark if used as a cover; they might pause like a colon or semi colon between passages of information if used as an article header; or they might replicate a comma if used as a spot illustration surrounded by running text. Their placement can have a profound effect on the overall reading experience, rendering them as a vital component in the editorial design toolkit.

In his book *The Power and Influence of Illustration* (2019), author Alan Male provides a set of codes and conditions that define what he terms 'conceptual linguistics' which provide a useful prism to consider the function and effec-tiveness of editorial illustration communication, namely the mimetic, liminal, portal, intrusive and immersive. Mimetic concepts use realistic

and believable imagery to communicate to a readership through a series of conforming expec-tations. The mimicry of believable events – hence the mime – places trust in a reader's ability to recognize depictions of a reality through a lived or known experience. Liminal concepts balance a position that is ambiguous, oscillating between the real and the unexplained in an area that is transitional. Portal communications tempt the reader to uncover a subject but still leave much to the imagination and create a sense of intrigue and wonder.

Intrusive communication, by contrast, seeks to confront and overcome the readership by being deliberately provocative through both content and depiction. Finally, immersive communica-tion creates environments where the reader is knowingly wrapped into an experience, either conceptually or possibly physically depending on the platform of communication and is invited to share the thoughts of the image-maker. The choices open to conceptual editorial illustrators clearly reference the variety of subject matter and editorial viewpoint being portrayed, but also reference that the text is a carrier of informa-tion that must be read in conjunction with the image. They are interconnected through balance, consideration and deliberation.

Conceptual illustration may appear to have been made immediately and directly on first appearance, but its construction is complex and requires skill and aptitude to deliver a convinc-ing assignment. Successful outputs hinge on a conducive working partnership between the client and illustrator, requiring intellectual invest-ment, hard work and patience from both parties at all stages of the process. Groundbreaking concepts are hard fought and require many iter-ations of development to exact successful ideas. The successful conceptual editorial illustration will instantly communicate to the readership, but belies painstaking efforts to construct and execute an image that melds sophisticated think-ing with a mastery of crafting.

Line illustration

Originating from woodblock printing traditions, line illustration has been a staple of editorial output through the ages. A clear and concise way to present visual information, linear depic-tions of subjects have an immediacy and clarity that makes them suitable particularly for spot or vignettes to break up bodies of running text. Line

Figure 4.6a-b
Prospect magazine embraces the freeform
vignette edge of Michelle Thompson's illustration
in this sympathetic piece of editorial design that
deconstructs the traditional grid.

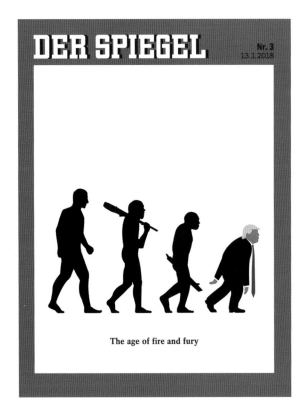

Figure 4.7
Edel Rodriguez uses existing tropes in the building of conceptual
illustrations. In this case, the 'Age of Fire and Fury' cover for
Der Spiegel magazine reverses the symbolic human evolution
timeline from ape to human, specifically former US president
Donald Trump, as an effective way of characterizing a perceived
demise of humanity under the Trump-led administration.
Illustration art direction by Svenja Kruse.

Figure 4.8
Lithuanian illustrator Eglė Plytnikaitė tackles the universal issue
of climate change in this image accompanying the article 'On
Climate, Biden Must Do More Than Undo Trump's Damage' for
Scientific American.

illustration falls into two broad sub-categories: clear line and calligraphic line.

Clear-line work maintains its proximity to early editorial woodblock images and often uses consistent weight of line, or lines, consecutively to delineate subjects. Outlines of objects are commonly represented in this way. Additional texture and depth is sometimes applied using a technique such as cross-hatching or dotting to give a variety to the forms being represented. Clear line can potentially be used in a technical or clinical capacity where it feels diagrammatic and informative. This gives subject matter a particular solemnity and gravitas. These illustrations can also carry very complex messages but present them in deceptively simple ways through the use of metaphor. Illustrators such as Saul Steinberg, André François and Pierre Le Tan are historically identified for taking the linear illustration to new critical heights with their blend of encapsulating wit and humour in their subjects.

By contrast, the calligraphic line expresses more exuberance and sensibility towards the forms being represented. The popularity of the approach owes much to the heritage of Japanese brush calligraphy that was highly influential for many artists and designers at the turn of the twentieth century. Chiefly employed as a style that was emotive and often flamboyant, the calligraphic line is historically associated with artist's like Henri Toulouse-Lautrec who influenced fashion illustrators such as Carl Erickson. The work can be simultaneously seen through the output of titles such as *Vogue*, *Harper's Bazaar* and *Vanity Fair* throughout the 1940s and 1950s. More recently, the calligraphic line has been used to cross boundaries into lifestyle illustration, and satirical political and social commentary as defined by Jean Jullien and Lauren Tamaki.

Figure 4.9
A comedic take on patient medical examination by Serge Bloch for *The Boston Globe*, using simplified forms and accentuated line to ambiguously conceal ethical details.

Figure 4.10
Jean Jullien's work is characterized by a sensibility and empathy towards subjects he is depicting, with a lyrical, calligraphic approach whether using a pen or brush.

Portraiture

Although photography might be considered the automatic choice for portraiture, there is clearly a rich history of portrait painting that precedes the camera and, in many instances, arguably gives greater insight into a subject. The lens of photography lends a particularly familiar veneer to imagery that readerships are used to, rendering many photographic images distant from their audience. By contrast, non-photo realistic depictions of figures create intrigue and suspense by virtue of the fact that they are constructed forms and can therefore extract personality and embellish their subjects beyond the surface of a form, allowing them to be seen and understood differently.

Illustrative portraiture can be incredibly intimate and revealing, penetrating the surface characteristics of the sitter and establishing points of visual and metaphorical interest through representations and constructed relationships of appearance, posture and environment. In an editorial setting, such discoveries and inspections are further invited through the inclusion and placement of headline and running text to enrich the content of the illustration. They also serve to allow artistic licence to render subject matter without the need for slavish reinforcement of recognizability.

Illustrative portraiture in this context can be used to examine figurative subjects that are beyond the reach of the general public, including royalty, politicians and celebrities. Given the universal expectation of photography being the ubiquitous mode of capturing portraits, the illustrated alternative offers some tantalizing merits of its own in an editorial context. The first is the element of surprise; we are used to seeing photographic renditions on the covers of periodicals and magazines that the illustrated equivalent, often seen on the cover of publications like *Rolling Stone* or *The Economist*, stand out from their competitors. In a media-rich world saturated by the photographic portrait, illustration can be employed to powerfully reimagine and redefine figures in fresh and often surprising ways, whether through poise, situation or artistic treatment.

For example, a photographic portrait may have a series of agreed restrictions prior to a shoot concerning distance between the photographer acting for a publication and the subject, or certain poses that are not permissible, or environments that may have suggestive connotations. Using illustration gives permission for alternative angles and vantage points to be considered, potentially draws the subject closer to the readership for closer inspection, or places them in unexpected situations to make them appear aloof, out of touch or unattainable. Readerships can therefore be represented with hitherto familiar subjects in surprising situations that may alter or question their preconceptions, casting illustration as the powerful and influential medium of choice.

In an ontological sense, illustration can be used to closely examine subjects in hyperreality, whilst phenomenologically, illustrations may draw key aspects of figurative subjects and present them in surprisingly obtuse but informed ways. In illustrative form, portraits of noble and grand subjects can be hyped and inflated to revere, or equally can be juxtaposed in unexpected environments to create socially charged and contentious statements that mock and belittle. By the same token, portraiture capturing Neolithic man allows us a powerful and fascinating historical insight into evolution. Crucially, illustrative portraiture

in an editorial setting does not need the sitter to exist in real time, enabling both renditions from history and projections of future forms with confidence and believability.

Having an acute understanding of figurative form, including an anatomical knowledge of how the body functions and behaves in particular situations, creates an underpinning confidence in handling portraits of the figure. Even if the visual language employed to depict the subject ultimately is stylized, understanding the construction of human form is vital to extrapolate and testify with conviction. Readerships exercise 'tacit' knowledge when receiving figurative information and are likely to find depictions ill-conceived and unconvincing if underlying research has not been thoroughly conducted. This problem is further exacerbated if the portrait is reproduced on a digital platform where it is permitted to move, as a lack of understanding about the human form expresses itself through motion will become pronounced.

Cartoons

The cartoon establishes a viewpoint on content using a visual language that is semi- or non-realistic and has a particular set of construction codes and conventions that define the form. In an editorial context, a successfully rendered and contextualized cartoon creates a different dialogue between the publication and readership and is used as a break between other content packages by the introduction of humour, irony and satire. Operating either as a single or multiple series of images in one or more picture panes, the cartoon format is able to offer a stylized, simplified rendition of events through a flexible mixture of still or sequential images and language interventions. Language is carried through devices such as speech and thought bubbles, typographic imagery or other types of graphic markers that suggest the passing of time. In a single pane image, often described as a 'gag' cartoon, it is common for the image to be accompanied by a contextualizing caption.

Caricatures and characterization

Beyond portraiture, figures can be further manipulated through caricature, cartoon and wider forms of characterization. Such formats are used frequently by publications when portraying situations where figures require more exaggerated

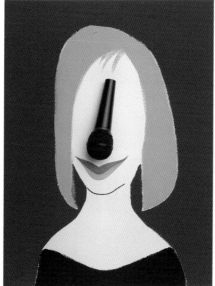

Figure 4.11
Hanoch Piven's witty portraits are iconic and have been widely commissioned by major newspapers for the insightful depictions of some of the world's most influential figures. Here, artist and activist Yoko Ono, singer and actor Barbra Streisand, singer and songwriter Bjork, scientist Professor Stephen Hawking, Rolling Stones guitarist Keith Richards and film director Woody Allen are depicted. Piven uses a mixture of found objects that relate to his specific subject and drawn elements, juxtaposed through collage into unforgettable illustrations.

and expressive depiction, or in environments and situations which are illusionary. These images will still be contextualized by text but are given wider licence to explore the unconventionality and obscurity of subjects or points of opinion, whilst still providing sufficient clues about their roots and origins. Political, social and economic commentary are favoured topics, although other subjects are not immune.

One of the central founding principles of editorial illustration has been as a stage to invite social and political commentary in the satirical form of the caricature. The art of characterizing personalities polemically and subversively, by poking fun, ridicule and distain through distorted and exaggerated depictions of human forms. Caricature manifests itself in often spectacular pieces of work that transcend editorial illustration and feature prominently in wider popular culture.

Historically, popular caricature has its roots in political commentary through the socially cutting works of William Hogarth in the early

Figure 4.12
Portraiture meets concept in this illustration by Anita Kunz
where former American singer-songwriter Ray Charles's
brilliant, charismatic, wide smile is replaced by the keys of his
beloved piano connecting his appearance to his larger than life
personality. Illustration commissioned by *The Dallas Times Herald*
and now in the permanent collection of the Library of Congress.

mockery of important national and international
events such as British political turmoil and the
Napoleonic wars, and by further socially sati-
rizing and parodying scandalous behaviours or
misdemeanours. Daumier's famous drawing *Les
Poires* (1831), a withering attack on monarchy
and government in France, became a national
symbol and was the source of many graffitied
marques left in towns and cities by disgruntled
citizens.

Acerbic observations were originally crafted
through the process of etching or engraving,
but the advent of lithography in 1798 revolutionized both production and greatly extended print
runs, allowing reproduction of images using a
reliable mass printing method for distribution
in pamphlets and news sheets, and these political and social images quickly became popular.
Helping create a link between politicians and the
general public, these cartoons provided much-
needed political and social accountability for a
world where social mobility was firmly controlled.
For the first time, these caricatured, often
grotesque manifestations of important figures
gave illiterate parts of the population an opportunity to participate in something that affected
their daily lives. The engravings and lithographs
etched into history views and opinions that
would have simply been impossible for ordinary
people to express to their elected representatives
and spread an opinionated view of life across
lands. Perhaps as a precursor to media interference that we are familiar with today, these

eighteenth century, although the English artist
ironically thought caricature frivolous. Other
exponents saw the opportunity to embrace
caricature, including Britons James Gillray,
Thomas Rowlandson, George Cruikshank and
later by French printmaker and caricaturist
Honoré Daumier. The British contingent made a

Figure 4.13
This simple vignette strip cartoon illustration by Tom Gauld captures the sentiment of many who work in the field of publishing, with a
witty observation captured through economical visual information that allows the joke to carry to the readership.

caricatures often involved financial patronage to enable their production to occur.

The caricature developed as an acerbic and vitriolic tool to lampoon and skewer unsuspecting subjects, moving from newspapers editorials to spawning its own particular set of publications, such as *Punch* which is still in circulation today. The covers and inside pages of established publications such as *Der Spiegel*, *The Economist*, *The New Statesman*, *The New Yorker*, *Private Eye*, *Rolling Stone*, *The Spectator* and *Time* represent a forum for topical subjects such as political opposition, media bias and propaganda to be exposed, humoured, critiqued and parodied. Illustrators such as Ronald Searle, Ralph Steadman, Gerald Scarfe, Joe Ciardiello, Steve Brodner, David Hughes and Ian Pollock cut their teeth on political and social caricature.

Given the nature of opinion-based content, caricatures are often produced quickly in hours or days. Such a rapid turnaround requires the illustrator to have a command of news analysis in addition to highly developed visual skills to manufacture images quickly. National newspapers employ in-house staff illustrators to create political cartoons and caricatures, working alongside journalists in the newsroom to synthesize observations and produce content for quick editorial comment.

Figure 4.15
Steve Brodner is internationally regarded as one of the best satirical illustrators working in the editorial field. His caricature of former Trump political advisor Steve Bannon shows an expressive style developed and honed over forty years of professional output without losing the capacity to skewer the most venal and controversial subjects.

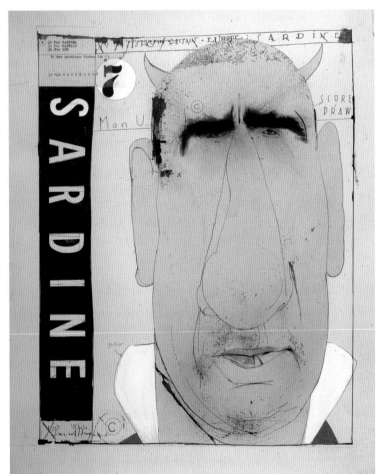

Figure 4.16
As a piece of cultural and social comment, this illustration by David Hughes for *The Times Saturday Review* caused controversy after French footballer Eric Cantona was reprimanded for attacking a fan in the stand at Crystal Palace. Cantona offered an apology of sorts with his immortal explanation of his conduct: 'When seagulls follow the trawler, it is because they think sardines will be thrown into the sea.' Despite continual baiting through the tabloid press, Cantona went on to be one of the most celebrated and revered footballers ever to wear the Manchester United shirt.

Figure 4.14
Instantly recognizable by his exaggerated and accentuated graphic language, Gerald Scarfe is a giant of illustration with a career spanning over sixty years. His caricatures of politicians, royalty and celebrities have adorned the pages of major publications and been seen on television, on postage stamps and in the theatre. He is famously connected to rock music giants Pink Floyd through their 1979 album *The Wall* and subsequent projects that came out of their global success, leading to images of other groups and superstars. Here, he takes a friendly swipe at the Rolling Stones from their Voodoo Lounge tour. Scarfe was sent by *The New Yorker* to make a drawing for the magazine in 1994.

Decorative

Decoration and ornamentation form one of the important roles of illustration more broadly and in an editorial guise, the depiction of content through decorative means can provide a welcome break and distraction to heavy content or powerful testament. Decoration is often used to establish and delineate patterns of content, introducing subject matter in a palatable and contained approach that seeks an emotive response from the reader. Setting the mood and refreshing the atmosphere allows decorative elements to thrive in an editorial context. Decoration can also act as an important visual triangulation and signposting tool to help find a favourite section of a publication, or to contain and navigate collected content.

Historically, the decoration and ornamenting of content can been traced to several historical sources. Illuminated religious manuscripts sought to guild and ornament as an homage to their subjects, whilst the Arts and Crafts movement sought to reinstate the decorative arts to the elevated positions of painting and sculpture by the 1880s by reviving traditional handicrafts and promoting exemplary design and print production. In parallel, the rise of Aestheticism as a movement across the arts, crafts and literature bound written and image-made form together in increasingly eclectic and decadent outputs. Exemplified by the work of Aubrey Beardsley, who along with Oscar Wilde, pushed Victorian conservative social and sexual limitations, decoration went far beyond merely ornamenting and became integrated content in its own right. Despite Beardsley's short life, his influence is far-reaching and can be seen both stylistically and ideologically in contemporary editorial illustration work through thoughtful exponents such as Olaf Hajek, Jody Hewgill, Jason Holley and Yuko Shimizu.

Another significant historical influence on decorative output is the poster movement which swept late nineteenth-century Paris. Many of the finest exponents, including Jules Chéret and Henri de Toulouse-Lautrec, combined exquisite, organic forms with decorative illustrative design to promote a myriad products and services. The influence of this poster explosion in France reverberated around the world and rocketed the status of the artform.

In doing so, it promoted commercial art in a way not previously seen and became influential in journals and through resulting exhibitions. The decorative form loomed in and out of popular conscience in the intervening decades, displaced by propogandist artworks reflecting the societal concerns of the day: Futurism and Constructivism and the Great War in the early part of the twentieth century, the Great Depression of the 1930s and the rise of Nazism, and the Cold War years.

The engulfing fear and paranoia was broken by the explosion of popular culture through Pop Art and the psychedelic movements of the 1960s, which saw decoration triumphantly return and become elevated to lurid and literally mind-bending levels of depiction. As wider popular culture reacted against seemingly meaningless and futile foreign wars, political manoeuvring and social immobility, through peaceful protest and rebellion against long-standing restrictions in pursuit of more profound freedoms, exponents of Pop Art and psychedelic-inspired editorial illustration saw opportunities to embolden editorial content.

Figure 4.17
The informal use of illustrated hand-drawn type is increasingly seen as a way of breaking conventions of traditional publishing grids, but also as a way of transitioning readers into digital platforms. This example by Lucy Truman for the Royal Horticultural Society contains countless transformational possibilities in the way it is constructed and in the organic subject matter being represented. The digital assets are each capable of being animated creating motion possibilities.

Figure 4.18a–d
German illustrator Olaf Hajek produces highly decorative illustrations mixing elements of abstraction with narrative realism that work well in a lifestyle editorial context.

Informative

The visualization of information offers terrific scope for editorial illustration as a platform to present data-based information in material form to elucidate, entertain and engage readerships. Historically, information has been contained and presented by the deployment of visual devices such as diagrams, charts and information graphics. In some instances these devices have been presented as visual signifiers in their own right, or as a piece of visual information used to succinctly contextualize headlines, sub-headings and supporting text.

In an increasingly globalized world, accelerated by the rise of the World Wide Web in the nineties and the proliferation of social networks that brought digitally accessible content immediately to consumers, the portrayal of data-based information visualization has become of significant interest to modern readerships. This generation of engaged readers have familiarity with computers, confidence with operating systems and increasing knowledge and awareness of how data is both collected and shared. This spread of interest is a cultural and social phenomenon, potentially connecting peoples beyond traditional divides of geographies and histories. Rather, it provides massive opportunities to read, absorb and share information, but also to pose fundamental questions and propose notional solutions based on the patterns emerging from the depiction of information.

Illustrative information can be designed and shared through recognized platforms such as bar, pie and line charts. These formats are immediately understandable, provide tangible comparisons and depict simple results. Such formats are best suited to like-for-like comparisons, such as political party performances in elections or segments of particular market share of consumables or services. Increasingly though, more complex data is able to be collected, requiring visual processing into formats that can be interpreted and interrogated by readerships. For example, rather than showing two-dimensional visualizations of data ('x' and 'y' axis), many data sets offer the prospect of creating three-dimensional images to illustrate the density of information (effectively a 'z' axis).

The sheer volume, variety and richness of data now dwarfs historical precedents, requiring information to be shared in more dimensions than traditional, representational models.

By default, this has had a profound effect on publishers. Rather than editorially decide on simplifying information, greater information sets demand detailed scrutiny, requiring ever more ingenious methods of depiction for audiences who are more curious about gaining greater statistical knowledge about subjects. The density of data affords real opportunities for designers and illustrators to be both imaginative and insightful. Statistics can be displayed as pleasing visual statements that explain accurate findings, suggesting a genuine connection between the arts and sciences over the 'aesthetic beauty' of data, while unique interpretations of information can be designed as systematic simulations of data in material form. The visualization of information clearly applies both to analogue and digital publishing outputs, but each have benefits and limitations. Physical published outputs have defined boundaries, with established sections of news content that navigate the reader and establish familiarity and trust.

However, published information is fixed and there are inevitable limitations on space that can be allocated to the illustration of information. Increasingly, digital platforms show their versatility for presenting visualizations of data in even greater abundance, where a dynamic and intuitive platform is able to host static and animated information across screens, linking to different content and providing a rounded view of content from multiple vantage points. Opportunities are being developed to enable user-participation to model different scenarios as part of a reading experience to create deeper learning zones, sometimes in conjunction with physical publications, or even with access to physical objects and spaces through the augmentation of information in a virtual or mixed reality. Digital platforms therefore potentially enable both visualizations to be depicted from alternative dimensions and can show build sequences or modelling that recognizes the user engaging with aspects of the data to create multifunctional and sensory experiences. The technology found in in-car displays of information for the connected driver is being developed by publishers to enhance future interactive reading experiences.

Depictions of complex information offer opportunities to extend beyond the clear and unambiguous demarcation of technical data representation, by creating opportunities to suggest or propose patterns in findings that elicit a visceral connection to readerships.

Visualizations may evoke emotive responses from a readership that allow new insights to be presented, and previous assumptions to be challenged by drawing on significant, reliable and mobilized data sets. In essence, complex information that is thoughtfully visually presented becomes a powerful supporting tool for individuals and groups to interrogate subjects, form cogent responses and draw together support as individuals or groups to pressure and persuade. In terms of shifts in patterns of content consumption, the potential power and influence of information in an editorial context is as significant as the introduction of mass printing, or the integration of photography was to editorial design.

Illustrators working with dense information need visual dexterity and an organized approach to filtering and sorting data to meet the needs and expectations of the reader. British illustrator Rod Hunt exemplifies such an approach and is well-known for his ability to concisely collect and represent often complex batches of information in a disarmingly clear way.

Fashion

The depiction of fashion illustration in the form of clothing and accessories often provides a welcome opportunity for playful exuberance, flamboyant celebration and joyful optimism in an editorial context. Images capture readers' attention through a mixture of acute reporting,

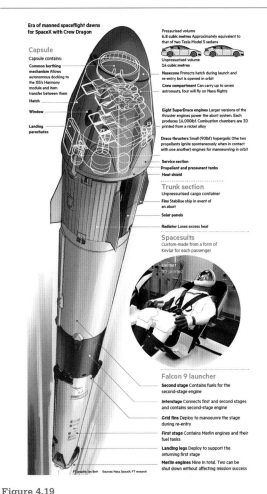

Figure 4.19
Ian Bott's Spacex infographic for the *Financial Times* is a very good example of how statistics and detailed factual information are distilled using a diagrammatic approach to technical subject matter. Bott is a scientific illustrator specializing in aviation.

Figure 4.20
Rod Hunt's rough shows the level of planning required to execute an editorial illustration of this level of detail and complexity. Illustration commissioned for 'Megacity 2050: Future Green City' for *Bloomberg Business Week*.

Figure 4.21
Rod Hunt creates very detailed illustrations that are information-heavy and require significant planning to communicate clearly to the reader. This illustration is a good example of the principle of penetration, where the illustrator permits the reader to see 'inside' the image – something that would not be possible with a photograph.

stylistic interpretation and attractive detailing. Fashion illustrators have heavily influenced and impacted readers understanding and appreciation of the form and, by extension, the times we live in. The subject enjoys an elevated level of popularity and status with readerships, partly due to public interest and curiosity about fashion as a major cultural signifier that punches socially and economically above its weight, but also by the increased fascination with the culture of global celebrity that inevitably intertwines it.

A useful historical and contemporary marker for the adaptability and versatility of editorial comment and communication as a whole, the depiction of fashion through illustration enables aspects of that industry to be exposed through the versatility of the form. For example, fashion illustration displays the latest cultural trends and reveals the next wave of fashion designers, but is increasingly subject to attention around wider societal issues including raw material

sustainability, worker exploitation and environmental concerns centred around waste and recycling. These issues grant fashion illustrations a place in sections of newspapers and magazines, or in internationally regarded supplements in their own right. They additionally propel stories about fashion into other serious sections of publications looking at the fashion merchandising economy through trend analysis, or the legislation around working environments and health and well-being sections that report on subjects as diverse as anorexia and associated physical and mental health conditions. Fashion thus becomes the gateway into subjects that are interconnected, but perhaps are more complicated to engage with. To understand this publishing diversity, it is worth investigating the roots of fashion illustration in editorial publications.

Fashion illustration, as we understand it today, emerged from historic depictions as costume and fashion plates. The highly detailed, etched prints of the early 1800s were pioneered by French illustrator Paul Iribe in collaboration with couturier Paul Poiret. Plates were often hand-coloured to give the dressmaker more guidance about recreating the designs as a garment, and to entice rich customers to place their orders. As a result, they become useful historical documents in charting both the fashion of the day, and the foundations for what we recognize today as global fashion empires. The single figure format, usually female, sought to showcase couture pieces in an elegant and sophisticated manner, accentuating features of the model by elongating limbs such as the neck, arms and legs. Such stylistic exaggeration is still employed by fashion illustrators to this day as an editorial tool to focus readers' attention on a specific piece, or combination of pieces, in a collection.

The evolution of plates also extolled social standing and presence in society, through fashion caricature and renditions of couture sophistication and etiquette. The couture culture of 1860s Paris spawned a wave of illustrators who would work in close proximity to couturiers and dressmakers to design clothing, and to represent finished garments for distinguished customers. This fledgling industry became one of the biggest industries in France and today, French fashion is rightly regarded as a key purveyor of sophistication and glamour. The rise of the specialist fashion journal can be traced to this upturn of interest and ensured that designs were shared in the major markets of Europe and North America.

The technical revolution of printing moving to rotary presses and enabling technologies such as halftone printing to be reliably employed created opportunities for fashion illustration to move away from its roots in faithful technical renditions of garment shapes and dressmaking details. The fashion plate gave way to fashion illustration and photography being adopted in new magazines and periodicals as a convenient hook for enticing more diversity in readerships. Fashion illustrators were able to capture and extoll fashionable dress as a socially exuberant and progressive form of display. Freed from the constraints of rendition, and charged by explorative artistic movements in other parts of artistic and cultural life, including Abstraction and Cubism, fashion illustrators enjoyed having traditional shackles removed

and introduced notions of stylized idealism and freedom of expression to readers. Despite two world wars, the rise of fashion can be attributed as a response to social changes and economic freedoms, and consumers took much of their knowledge about fashion from what was printed in newspapers where the role of fashion editor was established and flourished.

While undoubtedly there have been stylistic shifts in the depiction in fashion, with editorial photography being preferred to illustration on occasion, the adaptability of fashion illustration has meant it has found places to reside within publishing. For example, the American giants *Vogue* and *Harper's Bazaar* effectively withdrew fashion illustration from editorial spreads by the 1960s, favouring photography as a more immediate and socially relevant capture of those times. By contrast, weekend newspapers started to include colour supplements, creating space to include fashion illustration that coincided with consumers' disposable income to spend on high street fashion. The transference of couture fashion trends to the high street demanded attention and fashion illustrators were well placed to fill the gap.

Fashion illustration enjoyed a renaissance in the 1980s, partly as a rejection of the photographic form and partly pushed by cultural interest in celebrity culture – the covers of *Rolling Stone* being a good example. The interconnectedness of editorial fashion illustration to advertising and promotion is illustrated through the campaigns French fashion illustrator Jean Philippe Delhomme made with Barney's in the early 1990s, and these kind of collaborations propelled fashion illustration into the minds of commissioning editors.

The contemporary arena is filled with a myriad of fashion illustrators who are household names, both in terms of the mastery of their craft and their social media accounts that are often endorsed by influential fashion and celebrity followers. Illustrators such as Stina Persson, David Downton and Malika Favre lead the field as exponents of fashion house couture and ready-to-wear fashion. Their staggering diversity of output, rendered through gestural, fluid mark-making, highly accomplished digital silhouettes or sophisticated, hyperreal cross-disciplinary practice involving photography, typography and image manipulation, holds audiences and readerships in rapture and helps fuel demand.

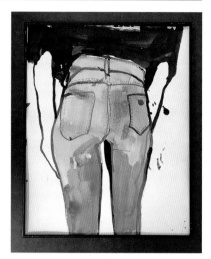
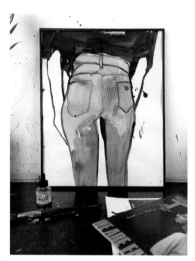

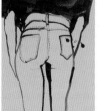

Figure 4.22
Swedish illustrator Stina Persson is widely
regarded as one of the best fashion illustrators
working in the contemporary arena. Her work is
full of energy and immediacy, characterized by
her imaginative, expressive use of media and
dynamic poses. Her working process reveals
an experimental approach to applying media,
collaging elements from other images and
continually cropping images to preserve the
energy of each piece.

Figure 4.23
Using striking colour and bold, geometric pattern, Malika Favre fashion illustrations creates a dynamic presence on page and screen.

Reportage and narrative essays

The strong journalistic roots of editorial illustration are abundantly preserved and celebrated through reportage illustration. The decision to use illustration to report on events as an eye witness creates a powerful and unique vantage point to bring a different perspective on news and current affairs content, opinions and authorship to readerships. All reportage assignments involve making judgements about the objectivity of the creator in responding both to the situation and to the editorial direction assigned by the commissioning publication and the conscious or unconscious bias that may be inferred. It is imperative that a balance is struck between the objectives of the assignment and the findings garnered from the experience of working in the field. Without this editorial control, the reporting on situations through illustrative imagery can give rise to accusations of propaganda or even dissent if recontextualized or reappropriated beyond their original intention.

The reportage illustrator might be sent on assignment to cover a wide variety of subjects, including wars, famines or protests that are of regional, national or international significance. However, not all situations need to be necessarily serious or life-changing. The reportage illustrator may instead be asked to report on more intimate and everyday occurrences, such as depicting specific people or groups, simple occupations and intimate environments away from zones of conflict, for example to accompany articles on travel writing or cataloguing aspects of social history. Unlike the intrusive lens of a camera producing photographs that inevitably capture a moment, reportage illustration is able to operate as a sophisticated, investigative tool. In the hands of a diligent and observant creator, reportage illustrators have the dexterity to provide blended output that stitches events together into a seamless whole image, or series of images, that can depict passages of time across a particular moment in time. The close proximity of illustrator to scene or event enables the opportunity to report on particular situations of capture, sometimes evidenced by embedded written notes or the presence of marks created in certain atmospheric conditions such as rain or humidity. Such proximity can have the effect of engendering and developing trust with subjects and can create more intimate and revealing visual insights for readerships.

The limitations of the camera, barred from recording sensitive events such as court cases, medical procedures or events that have particular rules governing image data protection in some countries, offer opportunities for reportage illustration to report events with conviction and a degree of accuracy, without compromising an individual's identity. They also permit editorial comment, by virtue of the fact that they can be constructed to edit and control certain pictorial elements. For example, vantage points can be aided through editorial direction to choose dynamic compositional choices, or unusual viewpoints to depict subject matter. Scale can be altered to emphasize certain points of focus of an unfolding drama, and colour, tone, texture can be contrasted or juxtaposed to navigate the viewers' eyes to a particular point of interest in an image. The activity of reportage illustration is dynamic, encompassing and total, with a clear synergy to work of a reporting journalist in the field.

Reportage illustration precedes the invention and utilization of the camera to record events. It was used as a way of reporting news back where visual content was required either to inform textual content in newspapers, or to supplement often important breaking news from points of conflict or trouble. Artists were sent to often dangerous and unpredictable events and situations to provide an authentic recording of proceedings to relay to readers often desperate for news of their loved ones. For example, Ronald Searle, the British illustrator, was a Japanese prisoner of war having been captured serving his country in 1941. His renditions of the tortured and brutal life as a POW remain as harrowing today as when they were first reported, having been created in secret and under extreme duress. At great risk to his own life, he covertly recorded scenes showing the squalid conditions of the camps and the brutality of the Japanese guards towards their captors on scraps of paper that were secreted under the mattresses of dying prisoners. The collected works serve as visual testimony both to the gruelling hardship and persecution that prisoners of war suffered, but also provided compelling evidence to implement changes of policy at international levels in the formation of treaties and adherence to international rules around human rights. Despite personal hardship and immense suffering, Searle covered the Nuremberg War Trails as a courtroom artist after his release.

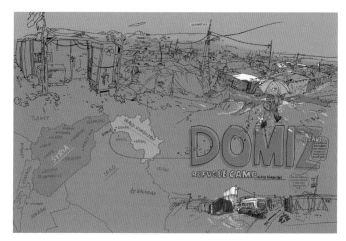

Figure 4.24
Olivier Kugler's reportage illustration work offers an insight into newsworthy stories that can be neglected or marginalized by mainstream news. His drive to tell stories and capture the testimonies of migrating people here through these set of images created from travels to Syria and the Calais Jungle Camp in France serve to show the true consequences of conflict, terror and displacement. Drawings by permission of the artist, first published in *Dem Krieg Entronnen* by Edition Moderne (2017).

The critical need for reportage in contemporary editorial illustration is arguably more required than ever. Despatching visual journalists to cover conflicts, election campaigns, famines and natural disasters raises awareness of global consequences of human actions, whether through religious tensions, political differences, taboos around healthcare and preventative medicine or our unquestionable contribution to climate change. Reportage illustration forces us to face our actions, presents situations that can illicit behaviour change in ourselves or our communities, or provoke us into campaigning for change with legislators and prosecutors. Illustrators such as Lucinda Rogers, Olivier Kugler and Caroline Tomlinson continue to uphold this tradition today.

Lifestyle

The rise of lifestyle editorial illustrations can be ascribed to readerships' greater focus, awareness and appreciation of leisure time opportunities. As a society, editorial illustration has invited and cultured us to value and appreciate our free time, whether that is the take up of new hobbies and interests, creating active lifestyle choices or taking pleasure and inspiration from seeing the exploits and achievements of others. Creating the time to enjoy, benefit from and value leisure experiences has not only made readerships more empowered and open to the possibilities of leisure, but has succeeded in growing new titles dedicated to such pursuits.

An increasing number of supplements to magazines and newspapers have sprung up to service this increasing interest. Specialist, niche interest pursuits are serviced by a seemingly burgeoning number of titles from a diverse range of subjects, disciplines and interests spanning all ages. Titles dedicated to servicing the needs of readerships looking to be inspired by stories of achievements, keeping abreast of the latest specialist news, comparing products and services or purchasing equipment can be found widely. It is a recipe that keeps publishers, readerships and advertisers hooked. For affluent societies, greater individual and collective wealth, and more diverse employment conditions, are undoubtedly contributary factors, but are not sole driving forces. Instead, we have come to recognize that a balance is needed between work and leisure that brings a different kind of reward, both for individuals, families and wider groups that sees a combination of using hard-earned free time and financial resources to attain betterment and fulfilment in their daily lives. In the much-maligned print-based publishing world, this leisure interest has been vital to finding new circulation routes and communities of interest.

The editorial illustrator working in a leisure environment will have a multitude of subjects to cover, ranging from outdoor activities such as camping and walking, through to home baking and crafting and into some highly specific areas such as fly-fishing or model railway engineering. Such examples not only serve to illustrate accessible and achievable pursuits that can be enjoyed relatively simply, with little financial investment or great prior knowledge, but that can create an immediate sense of enjoyment, betterment and health that can grow and develop with sustained and focused effort. Pursuits with family, or friends, or even finding new activities and interests to make new acquaintances is good for our physical and mental health.

Therefore, illustration work of this type is primarily about creating evocative and appealing images to create a combined sense of physical escapism and emotional investment, portraying an idealized environment that can be enjoyed singularly, or with friends and family. An article about healthy recipes could depict likely ingredients, or conversely, could evoke the mood created by engaging with well-being through depicting a scene where these new creations could be enjoyed in an imaginary, idealistic setting. In other instances, where readership awareness is already present, illustrations may

serve a more purposeful function and are more inclined towards the depiction of information, or a focus on more precise technical processes or capabilities. For example, perhaps the walkers now need more detailed maps or particular illustrated landmarks to identify on their hike, or the home baker needs to create three types of cakes using different ingredients and methods for the family picnic? Here, combining a decorative set of motifs or vignettes of landmarks with a coded information system of the pictorial landscape, including coloured roads, tracks and statistical details, still delivers a pleasing illustration that is imbued with helpful details.

The depiction of leisure pursuits through illustration performs several functions. It introduces opportunities and makes them inviting, often creating an idealized vision of the leisure pursuit being portrayed, as an enticement and temptation to find out more. Such images can promote inclusivity and diversity, by showcasing figures from different ethnic backgrounds participating and enjoying a mutually shared experience such as a bike ride, or by placing and privileging figures in situations which challenge gender stereotypes, such as a father playing games with

Figure 4.25
Using editorial illustration as a way to embellish and enliven product photography allows the evocation of a mood or atmosphere to be conjured up in the mind of the reader. Illustration by Lucy Truman for an article about trends in aromatherapy for *Better Homes and Gardens* magazine.

Figure 4.26
Food writing, including recipes and the health benefits of certain food types, is a growing feature in lifestyle sections of newspapers and dedicated publications specifically targeting home entertainment and cuisine have increased markedly in response to consumer demand. Illustrators offer an attractive alternative to photography, as in this impressionistic example by Lucy Truman which suggests the sense of achievement attained through cooking with simple, nutritious ingredients.

Figure 4.27
Lucy Truman's graphic language is highly versatile, here depicting an impression of a dining interior for *Better Homes and Gardens*.

a child. These gentle and subtle reinforcements of questioning orthodoxies and even encouraging changing behaviours can be hinted at through the dexterous and sophisticated use of illustration as a tool of deliberation and persuasion. In a similar manner, a leisure-based editorial illustration can explain certain activities, possibly through an image conveying information, perhaps as a cutaway or a labelled diagram, or through sequential images that provide a step-by-step explanation of a process. In this instance, enjoyment is prolonged through explanation, with a nervous or inexperienced baker guided through a complex process, or a feel-good factor is encouraged through the mastery of a process or technique that may have previously appeared unattainable.

Sequential

As a single image, an illustration already permits encompassing several situations within one compositional pane. Blending and blurring events by staging them together imaginatively is at the very heart of constructing illustration content, and juxtaposing visual elements can aid or alter an illustration's meaning, depending on how they are handled and for what editorial purpose. However, there are instances where the grouping together of two or more panes into a sequence permits the extension of an idea or narrative beyond the confines of the single image pane for entertainment, education or information purposes.

In editorial illustration, sequential images have historically manifested themselves through picture strips and comic panels in newspapers and specialist magazines, where multimodal forms of communication mixing image with text as an integrated expression are a recognized part of the form. More recently, illustrators producing this work in an editorial context have seen the expansion of their professional activity into parallel forms such as specialist comic book publishing, fanzines and graphic novels. With the growth of digital publishing platforms, the possibilities of sequential representation occurring in editorial illustration need to be revisited and defined. This is clearly an exciting and burgeoning area, not just for illustrators wanting to expand their artistic craft and their career development, but for publishers eager to explore ways of diversifying communication to readerships and new income streams.

Sequential image-making to tell a story or explain an idea is a foundation stone of the subject of illustration. The peoples of the Palaeolithic period sought to communicate by marking the walls of cave dwellings and hunting

Figure 4.28
Italian illustrator Camilla Falsini's graphic
language is perfectly suited to engaging
younger readers to care about their teeth in
this playful lifestyle cover and editorial spread
illustrations for *Uppa Magazine*.

grounds, whilst the ancient Egyptians merged
icons, symbols and picture-based alphabetical forms into hieroglyphics to be read in a
pre-ordained sequence. Later, the Bayeux tapestry reconstructed the Norman invasion of Britain
in 1066 as a near 70-metre sequential narrative
depicting and commentating on pivotal events,
as a sewn artefact of images and letterforms.
These were all forerunners of sequential work
in editorial form in that they depicted particular
facets of information and invited the spectator to
piece them together into a tangible narrative.

In an editorial publishing setting, sequential images constructed as cartoon strips have
enjoyed a long and prolific relationship with
readerships. Broadsheet newspaper editors
recognized the versatility of the form as the

perfect antidote to serious and stuffy political
and economic content, by allowing column
inches to be devoted to a considered and
more distanced commentary on events, or by
completely switching the mood with a funny or
satirical interpretation of an event or happening through sequential imagery. These cartoon
strips were popular and established a healthy
following amongst the reading public. Often, they
were able to carry content that was mischievous
and satirically sailed close to the boundaries of
common decency in a way that would seldom
have been permissible with text-based content.
Poking fun at establishment figures, or lampooning situations that were widely seen as absurd or
contentious, were likely targets for ridicule and
skulduggery.

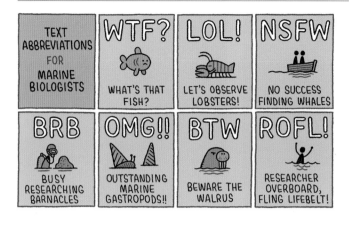

TOM GAULD for NEW SCIENTIST

TOM GAULD for NEW SCIENTIST

Figure 4.29
Tom Gauld's sequential running strip for *New Scientist* takes a whimsical view on scientific matters amongst articles reporting on serious, peer-reviewed and cutting-edge scientific discovery. The need for light relief needs to be paired with the intellectual expectation of the readership of this esteemed publication.

Regardless of the practical method of manufacture, the key to creating successful sequential images is that the images (modality of manufacture) express meaning through a recognizable system (a vocabulary) in an orderly way (a grammar). Much work has been undertaken to understand the theoretical and material construction of sequential images and their potential reach and significance to wider society through the cognitive function that these forms of communication have with their potential readership. Sequential imagery can have multiple layers of meaning which cut through as well as develop across the collective panes, raising possibilities to create either layers of connected narratives or parallel narrative structures which potentially have deeper and more profound significance. For example, a series of images may depict a chronological series of events in a day, but the underlying narrative may suggest clues about monotony, routine and entrapment. Crucially, the multimodal interface of sequential images

constructed of frameworks, images and text resonates with pre-existing experiences that we have experienced, stored and shared as liminal connections creating meaning.

For example, there are instances where single images reconfigured as a group help create an enhanced dynamism or intensity to editorial content, allowing a story or an idea to gain traction with a readership. Sequential illustrations in a static context might be formed of several smaller panes inside a strip or block of images, akin to comic conventions, that uncover, reveal and exploit dramatic situations or unfolding events. Working across panes can build narrative structures and develop trust amongst a readership to tackle potentially significant and challenging content.

Animation

Animated motion-based content creates an expanded and encompassing experience for the reader. On digital platforms, animated editorial

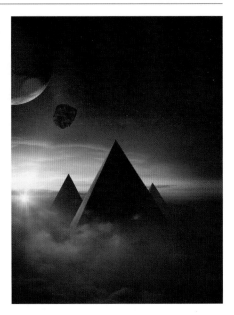

Figure 4.30
British illustrator Andy Potts's print and digital GIF illustrations for *BBC Science Focus* magazine show the exciting possibilities afforded through the seamless synergy of static and sequential platforms. The invitation to explore the galaxies and constellations is brought to life as we are permitted to travel through space and time in the sequence, bringing previously unattainable viewpoints of subject matter to life in an engaging, informative and entertaining way.

content is a developing arena for illustrators to experiment with facets of visual storytelling, explanation and promotion. Visuals permitted to move potentially allow subject matter to be penetrated, information to be condensed and messages to be embedded into the visual frame of a magazine cover or editorial spread. Publishers and cultural commentators widely view animated motion-based content as the next evolution in magazine publishing, with the necessary tools to dive deeper into content and offer an array of further presentation and communication opportunities than limited motion memes or GIFs. Instead of simply aping printed content, imaginative interpretation of why and how animation can be used to extend a narrative or amplify an idea is a source of potential exploration and employment in editorial markets in the future.

Animated covers were adopted into the mainstream publishing media around 2016 as a proactive approach to blend analogue and digital content into a seamless flow for the reader. Early attempts inevitably celebrated the possibilities of movement as a technical feat, but creators and publishers quickly saw that by marrying critical content to moving assets created intrigue, suspense and anticipation in the underlying narrative had some kind of pay-off. For example, if the visual clues lead the viewer to a memorable punchline or a visual pay-off, then the message is likely to resonate and stick in the mind of the reader. Illustrators such as Igor Bastidas and commercial outfits such as Studio Feixen are producing dynamic and innovative animated editorial content that challenges the traditional fixed image pane by suggesting objects popping out of the frame, or by generating characters who use the edges of a magazine cover to arrive in, or depart from, suggesting a world beyond the immediate composition.

The benefits of exploring animation for illustrators are obvious. Many visual languages lend themselves naturally to being animated, and many of the requisite skills needed in ideation, storyboarding and creating final frames are already established practices for many creators. Much of the software needed to create animation is readily available and cost effective as part of packages included on Adobe Creative Suites, and the opportunity of extending the reach of commercial work to create greater impact in new markets is an attractive proposition if you are prepared to invest time honing your skills in this exciting domain. The multimodal properties of editorial illustration's seminal link to text are given an extra dimension in animation through the possibilities of sound interacting with imagery.

GIFs

The GIF, or Graphic Interchange Format, is an animated series of images that are loped together to create a repetitive cycle of communicative content. GIFs offer additional animated content possibilities on digital publishing platforms. Released from the confines of print, these digitally constructed assets may be incidental, and sometimes accidental, in physical scale to other content they are paired with, but they have a tendency to punch well beyond their weight impactfully.

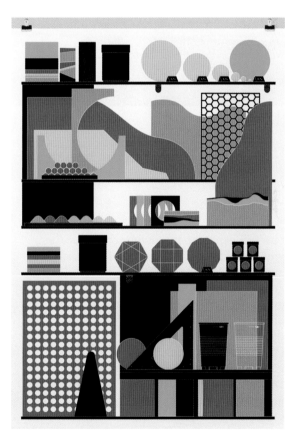

Figure 4.31
Swiss design team Studio Feixen's work for MIT The Engine is a great example of how print-based publications have been translated into assets for digital editions. This vector-based design works well as a sequential piece of editorial design in key frame form, but also has in-between assets that allow it to work as a piece of animation on screen. The client liked the illustration so much they even turned the designs into wall decals in the foyer of the lab.

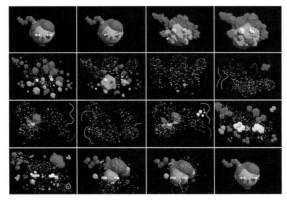

Figure 4.32a–b
Julian Glander's illustration for the article 'How to Help Teens Weather Their Emotional Storm' works across print and digital using an economical graphic language that is based on simplified shape-based forms and a complimentary colour palette. Art directed by Jaspal Riyait at *The New York Times*.

Figure 4.33
This piece of editorial design created by Studio Feixen for a feature article, 'What Lies Ahead', for *Wired Magazine* works across print and digital editions, here serving to bind editorial layout and animated typography through an illustrative identity.

The GIF may be silent or contain sound effects that add extra impetus to the communication with a multimodal approach. This potentially allows the GIF to function as a distanced asset amongst other editorial content and so raises questions about the proximity of textual content and the resulting connections that can be made by the reader or viewer. Similar to the benefits of employing sequential imagery, the GIF is able to introduce and create a timed release of information in the build-up to the telling of a visual joke, or to amplify incidental actions in the portrayal of a narrative. Equally, GIFs can be employed to create atmospheric interludes in longer-running passages of text to set a scene, establish the semblance of characters or drift anecdotal or additional visual information that supports the telling of a story or explains an idea. The single GIF, or multiple incidences of GIFs, placed amongst the editorial design on screen is also able to reinforce potentially complex and sophisticated or nuanced messages through simple, looped repetition that seeps into the reader's conscience.

GIFs ordinarily rely on strong graphic visual languages that are shape-orientated in their construction, as blocks of visual information are easier to manipulate than gradient-produced shading or colour or spindly line. Illustrators wanting to create these types of content need to be prepared to embrace motion design as part of their creative practice. It is likely that this decision will be well rewarded in the future as the expansion of these types of content looks set to continue. Thoughtful, eye catching GIFs on a looped, repeated cycle become almost mesmeric to watch and certainly grab a viewer's attention. Successful exponents include Christoph Niemann, Cécile Dormeau, Raúl Soria and Julian Glander, but many illustrators are recognizing that motion design opens up employment opportunities above and beyond editorial illustration.

Clever Thinking

Editorial illustrators enjoy the challenge of connecting and communicating with readers through clever thinking. Illustrations that arrest a reader's attention, engage them and enable them to understand received messages are both satisfying to create and addictive to keep producing. Creating the conditions for the transference of knowledge and information through observations, sensory perceptions and shared experiences is a skill. Using your intelligence to unlock articles and build illustrations that connect with the reader takes practice and perseverance, but is ultimately a key reason why editorial illustration is so satisfying to create and decipher.

Comedy is a well-known and well-trodden approach to clever thinking. It can be employed to connect and impart information, create a feel-good factor and generate an appetite for further stimulus. Editorial illustrators use visual gags and jokes as comic devices, including humour, puns, wit, parody, pastiche, satire, irony, innuendo and sarcasm to marshal their ideas. Such devices inflect content and draw responses from readerships that are quickly understood but may evoke deeper, more meaningful connections and reflection for days and weeks beyond their publication. The currency of clever thinking should not be understated and therefore understanding its purpose and application can give more opportunities to play with content for the benefit, enjoyment and future expectation of the reader.

Humour

As we have seen in Chapter 1 of this book, different art movements have accepted humour as being an intrinsic part of image-making to signify ideas. The Dadaists and Surrealists explored humour as an antidote to grave situations and used creative output as a way of escaping grim realities of the age. By contrast, Pop Art reflected the frivolity and frothy appeal of consumerism.

Humour manifests itself in many guises in editorial illustration, from the outwardly comedic funny visual statement through to black or gallows humour where readers are encouraged to find fun in situations that are pointedly bleak and hopeless. Clearly, readers all have senses of humour, but they are closely linked to their genetic code and their environmental conditions and are therefore magnificently different. Readers experience, use and appreciate humour differently based on their individual beliefs and concerns, and shaped by their cultural values, gender, ethnicity and identity as human beings.

However editorial illustrators choose to apply humour, it needs to match and embody the sentiments of the accompanying article, or the mandate of the publisher and be mindful of the audience it is intended to engage with. A provocative slapstick visual gag which gains a quick laugh will resonate quite differently from a joke imbued with biting sarcasm that is a withering commentary of its subject. Achieving a balance that hits home with an audience takes practice and patience. Often this balance is referred to as taste and readers judge humour according to whether they believe it is in good or bad taste.

Figure 5.1
Some subjects, such as finance, business strategy and pensions are difficult to originally depict and are prone to stereotypical imagery comprising hackneyed symbolism. This refreshing example by Malika Favre spotlights equities in a positive and innovative light by focusing on the tangible benefits that arise from investment. The client in this instance is Berenberg.

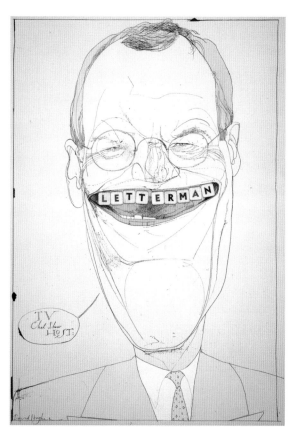

Figure 5.2
The clever use of illustration and typographic lettering in this portrait of the American entertainer David Letterman creates a humorous connection between physical appearance and his role as a talk show host. Illustration by David Hughes for *Entertainment Weekly*.

Visual puns

A visual pun is a play on images that can have multiple meanings. Visual puns have three stages of comprehension: the discovery that an image has a double meaning; an appreciation that the play on images is clever; the satisfaction that the reader gets the intended meaning. These stages set up the possibilities for recognition, connection and understanding. Whilst some might argue that puns are the lowest form of humour as they potentially insult human intelligence, handled successfully they can cut through content to create immediate visual statements that have a significant impact on the reader.

A good contemporary example of the use of the visual pun in editorial illustration is the work of Noma Bar. His work is deliberately visually paired down and simplified, but his choice of symbolic elements and their placement in the composition set up visual puns as jokes which

demand to be interrogated and decoded. For example, his portrait of Donald Trump wearing a yellow toupee in the bird-shape brand identity of Twitter cleverly implies that the former president should be characterized by his over-reliance on social media to portray a particular, controlled view of his political image that sits at odds with many opinions of him.

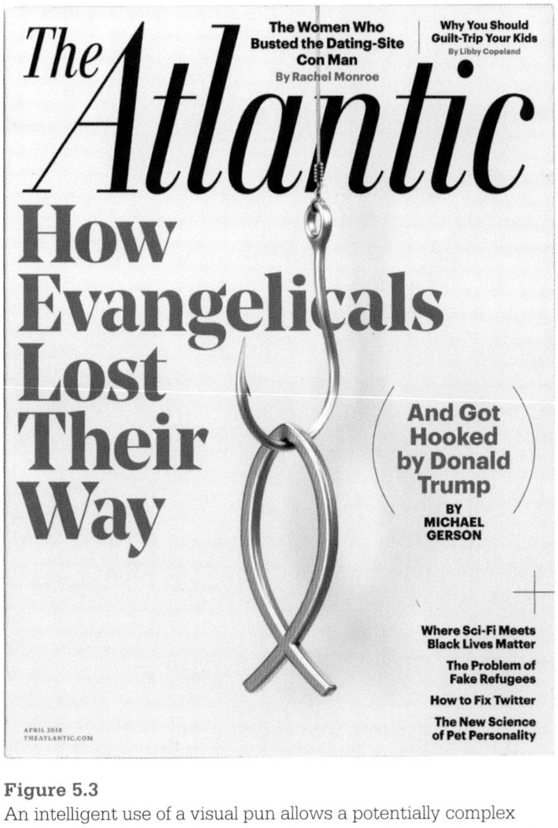

Wit

Unlike the pun which may evoke an eye roll or a sigh of exasperation, visual wit is widely recognized as a much more subtle and sophisticated way of imparting humour. Examples of visual wit are all around us and we see them daily – the hidden arrow in the FedEx logo, or the smiling arrow underscoring the Amazon logo that connects the capital 'A' to the 'Z' – but we don't always recognize them because they are so deftly constructed and applied. Their subtlety is the key to their success. *The Oxford Dictionary* definition of wit is 'a natural aptitude for using … ideas in a quick and inventive way to create humour'. For quick and inventive, read focused and intelligent. Wit relies on the reader picking up on subtle, playful and inventive clues in an illustration which create a positive connection in the mind of the recipient and reward their effort with a warm glow of satisfaction of how clever they have been in 'getting the joke'. By extension, the successful application and receipt of wit relies on a sophisticated emotional connection between creator and receiver.

On a sliding scale, wit could be argued to sit somewhere between seriousness and fun. It is therefore possible to evoke a witty response to a potentially dry topic by establishing conditions where a funny, surprising or unexpected angle is taken to load the image with hidden meaning that can be discovered. A good example is Paul Slater's illustration for *The Times* restaurant review where the illustrator depicts celebrity chef, Gordon Ramsey, sitting on a suitcase in an airport lounge. At the time of publication, Ramsey's restaurant empire was experiencing difficult trading conditions and the image wittily suggests his transient state without literally spelling out his financial difficulties. The application of wit requires a restrained lightness of visual touch in the construction and production of the illustration, allied to a clear understanding of the collective intelligence of the readership.

Figure 5.3
An intelligent use of a visual pun allows a potentially complex and delicate subject – in this case the potential manipulation of Evangelical religious believers by the Trump administration – to be covered without using specific visual material that may be contentious or even libellous. Illustration by Javier Jaén for *The Atlantic*.

Figure 5.4
Paul Slater's work often relies on comedic juxtaposition of compositions, or the playful relationship between scale of pictorial elements to poke gentle fun at his subjects.

Figure 5.5
Anita Kunz's satirical take on the film industry is played out in this illustration of American actors Quentin Tarantino (portrayed as Mister Brown from the film *Reservoir Dogs*) and Tom Hanks (portrayed as Forrest Gump), where notoriety seems to guarantee celebrity as much as talent and achievement.

Satire

Satire has its roots in ancient Greek or Roman plays and texts which delivered cynical commentaries on political or societal events of the day, but crucially encouraged constructive improvement in society at large. A satirical approach can be used to draw attention to subjects through scorn and ridicule and, ultimately, redress. Satirical expressions have been widely employed in editorial commentary, from the political cartoons and caricatures found in early newspapers, to devoted publications such as *Private Eye* today. Visual satire can work in single static illustrations, and is regularly seen in visual memes, GIFs and motion-based editorial content.

Satire is predominantly used across political and social contexts, poking fun at political misdemeanours and exposing foul play. For example, a piece of unpopular legislation may be satirically handled through editorial illustration which forces its proponents to question its motives or focus. But ultimately, satire also wants reflection and reappraisal of subjects to make society better. Juxtaposition of events or situations is used as a way of highlighting absurdities against normalities and, for that reason, satirical intentions often leave a serious aftertaste. It is important to note that not all satire is funny. Recognition of the situation or salient point being made, and creating conditions for the reader

to take action are key satirical drivers. To do this, satirical approaches use tools like parody, pastiche, irony, innuendo and sarcasm.

Parody

A parody is a creative work that plays on, sends up and intentionally mocks a subject through imitation. Parodies can reference all or part of original works of art, literature, film and theatre, but can also include real-life persons, events and movements. Essentially, a parody needs the audience to recognize the original from which the parody is drawn to understand and appreciate the resulting imitation. Parodies then allow a new satirical or ironic take on the subject in question by placing other characters in a similar situation, or by changing objects to signify an idea or belief, thereby forcing the reader to draw comparisons.

A particularly famous and often-exploited example is Grant Wood's *American Gothic* painting from 1930, which depicts a Iowan farmer holding a pitchfork and his daughter standing in front of a farmstead. The painting captures a sense of life in rural, depression-era America. The image has been reimagined on countless occasions, depicting different figures standing in the scene to mimic the two original figures, or to replace the farmstead with another building that uses similar architectural features. In these

Figure 5.6
Ben Challenor cleverly parodies Johannes Vermeer's *Girl with a Pearl Earring* for a healthy lifestyle article about an acceptable number of piercings for teenage daughters in *The Sunday Times*.

Figure 5.7
Jon Berkeley's cover, 'India Overheating' for *The Economist*, playfully pastiches the naïve, primitive style of Henri Rousseau.

examples, we might be invited to question the relationship between the figures, or perhaps query why they find themselves in such an unusual situation. Another example is Johannes Vermeer's much-loved painting *Girl with a Pearl Earring*, which has been parodied to endlessly make statements about how women are depicted in the media, or how societal changes have developed and altered in a contemporary context, as in the Ben Challenor illustration (featured).

Pastiche

A visual pastiche pays homage to an image by imitating or borrowing the style or character of the artist who created it. Visual pastiches aim to celebrate rather than mock in tone, which immediately sets them apart from parody. Their use is employed by the illustrator to provide a trusted visual source that the reader will understand the connection to. The aim is to create a warm, nostalgic feeling through resonance and familiarity with the original source. The pastiche is therefore usually a light-hearted, tongue in cheek, gentle ribbing rather than an outright assault on a subject. For example, Jon Berkeley's cover for *The Economist* takes strong visual inspiration from Henri Rousseau in both the composition and the detailed, wallpaper illustration style he employs to create the scene of the tiger with the burning tail to illustrate India's economy overheating.

It is important to say that there is a fine, but definite, line between visual pastiche and plagiarism, so the emphasis must be placed on imitation rather than copy. Using production methods,

compositions and depictions of events close to an original that mimic rather than directly lift content allow illustrators to recognize and show admiration for originals, rather than duplicate and profit from illegally acquired images. Borrowing and stealing are two markedly different things and transgressing copyright is a serious issue.

Irony

Visual irony is a rhetorical device that is used to illustrate a contrary situation. A seagull perched on a sign saying 'Please do not feed the Seagulls' is an example of visual irony. Again, the crucial ingredient to making irony work as a humorous device is the recognition of the joke between creator and audience that a situation or action is fundamentally wrong. For example, an illustration of a fire extinguisher throwing flames and setting a school ablaze is the very opposite of what the reader expects – it is ironic.

To work successfully, irony must be carefully planned and skilfully executed to draw maximum payback for both creator and reader. For example, the illustrator can privilege the reader by giving

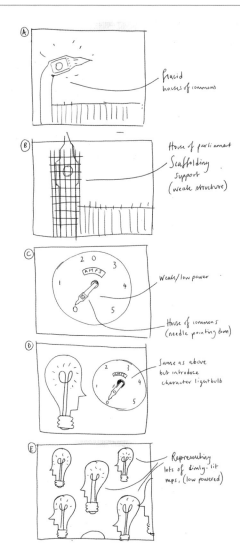

Figure 5.8
This illustration accompanies an article in the *LA Times* stating that there is no fixed profile of mass shooters, but also functions as a ironic social commentary given the availability of guns and weaponry in American society. Illustration by Doug Chayka.

advance warning of a situation that will happen through clues provided ahead of an event occurring. The depiction of a canoe carrying sightseers along a gentle river where a bend masks a huge waterfall creates the visual irony that a pleasant outing will ultimately end in the untimely and unfortunate deaths of the canoeists. When used well, irony is enjoyed and resonates for a long time with the reader and a sense of satisfaction in recognizing and appreciating the joke is felt.

Innuendo

Innuendo visually hints, insinuates and intimates at persons or objects in a derogatory or denigrating way. The reader is encouraged or invited to view seemingly innocent content with an awareness that something else is being implied through double meaning. Innuendo is employed to suggest something mean, risky or rude about the subject in question. It is often used to subconsciously draw attention to something that is of a sexual nature.

For example, two cupcakes topped by a cherries on a plate could reference a woman's

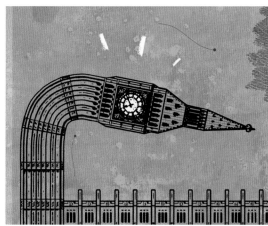

Figure 5.9
Frazer Hudson's early ideation process notes down ideas in simplified form for *The Guardian*'s article on weak government. He allows concepts to be gathered at pace and decisions made about which ideas to develop into preliminary roughs to show the client.

breasts. For such an image to work on that level, the creator need to construct the illustration in a way that credits the reader with being 'in on the joke' and that create an immediate and transitional recognition. The cupcakes not only visually symbolize their intended subject, but they also imply supporting sensory associations of the cupcakes (breasts) being soft and appealing. Innuendo can be skilfully employed in illustration to suggest things on a subtle level, but is also capable of causing maximum offence and upset if used rashly and inconsiderately.

Sarcasm

A more loaded and divisive form of humour, sarcasm is deliberately used to mock or undermine subjects in ways that are cutting or cruel. Visual sarcasm has an edge and bite to it that makes for uncomfortable viewing and is usually employed to cause discomfort and upset. It is often used to dismantle the foundations of beliefs or belittle viewpoints which are counter to mainstream views. The use of sarcasm as a tool to passively-aggressively attack a position or viewpoint can be very effective as a form of visual criticism, but it must be set up in the appropriate context.

For example, an illustration of commuters running for cover in a thunderstorm past a billboard advertising beach holidays is ironic. If one of the commuters is the weather presenter who had forecast sunshine that day that would be sarcastic because the intention is to belittle and criticize the job they had done in clearly getting the forecast wrong. The sarcasm relies on the reader expecting a weather presenter to be better scientifically trained and pouring scorn on their professional judgement.

Figure 5.10
The limited colour palette used here in the cover illustration titled 'Cornered' for *Time* magazine by Edel Rodriguez is effective in continuing a theme that underpins a number of sarcastic, biting images he has created in response to the Trump presidency. Rodriguez creates a graphic language to achieve brand recognition by continually using the colour orange as a way of parodying Donald Trump's hair. The repeated use of this device serves to reinforce the notion that beneath the veneer lurks a set of political ideologies that are not built on great substance nor conviction. Art Direction by D. W. Pine.

An Illustrative Dissection

In order to understand the enormous potential of communication in an editorial illustration, it is necessary to reveal the core structural attributes that serve to load images with meaning. This is especially necessary as editorial illustration transitions from print to digital platforms, combining our understanding of static communication theories with fields where limited and full motion is studied. Animation theoretician Paul Wells argues that a conceptual framework supports the creation and communication of an 'inner logic' in the mind of the reader (Wells 2006). Effectively, alternative realities are convincingly portrayed and their believability is accepted by the audience. This allows unbelievable environments, situations and actions to be rendered possible in an animated sequence.

If we accept that the principle of a key frame in animation acts as a significant plot marker – effectively a single illustrative image of a frame of action – then many of the principles that animation uses to structure and deliver content can be applied to editorial illustration in both print and motion-based form. These principles form a backbone and can indeed be likened to a spinal cord running through the illustration; part skeletal and part neural, allowing the reader to connect to the illustration through a process known as associative linking.

By peeling back the constructed layers of an illustration, it is possible to observe and identify the mechanisms editorial illustrators use to handle key content into a designated space economically and elaborately. Understanding structural parameters, and being able to utilize them confidently against tight deadlines, is crucial in developing a personal creative direction. It also establishes a strong foundation for producing editorial illustration consistently and effectively. Crucially, this level of understanding introduces, establishes and confers a necessary relationship between the creator and the reader.

To create an inner logic in the reader's mind, illustrators must use the principles of penetration, condensation, exaggeration, symbolism and metaphor to make content-heavy images readable and communicate effectively with their audience. Such principles permit the successful reception and decoding of images and are often used in combination with one another. The nature and extent of these principles vary; some instances are obvious, others not necessarily so tangible, but used successfully they provide further evidence of a metaphysical connection between creator and readership.

Penetration

The principle of penetration allows the reader to see beyond the surface into the inner being of a subject. Illustrating difficult concepts or complicated structures, processes and systems can be more successfully realized through penetration. For example, penetration permits access to the subject matter such as internal architecture and functions of the human body, tiny micro-organisms in the deepest oceans or what lies at the heart of a nuclear reactor.

Penetrative editorial illustration can also be seen to have spatial qualities. Ideas can be communicated beyond the containing parameters of the surface of an image, to connect contextually to other modes of thinking. Additionally, penetration permits and enables deeper thinking to become possible in the image itself; as viewers we are permitted to explore into, through and around a subject. This allows us to understand how vital organs interconnect, or understand the food chain of life in the ocean, or how nuclear plants are kept safe and cool.

The possibility of communicating visceral or unexperienced ideas is exposed and enlightened by the editorial illustrator. Using a penetrative approach, it becomes possible to bring sense to the unimaginable. Penetration establishes an order and logic to what would otherwise have to be imagined by a reader, without access to determined knowledge.

Figure 6.1
French illustrator Matthieu Bourel draws inspiration from Dadaism and his deceptively simple images are often complex in layers of meaning through an exploration of 'Data-rism'. Bourel is interested in the assault on the senses from the bombardment of information in our everyday lives, here for an article titled 'The Psychiatrist Who Believed People Could Tell the Future' by Sam Knight, published in *The New Yorker*. Art Director: Aviva Michaelov.

Figure 6.2
Spanish illustrator Sergio García Sánchez's take on the Covid-19
lockdown life that many people have been forced into for *The
New Yorker*. The illustration was rejected, but Sánchez was
later commissioned to create his 'Tribute to Eustace Tilley' for
the publication, continuing a long tradition of cover illustrators
reimagining the publication's dandy mascot.

Condensation

Condensation refers to the compression of
content through ideological concepts or visual
depiction, or both, in an illustration. Collapsing
events creates concise, economical and concen-
trated statements. Condensation permits the
construction of illustrations that bear no relation to a realistic time frame of real events. This
liberates the illustrator from a pre-specified chro-
nology, opening up possibilities for re-imaging
interpretations of events through still or sequential images. This then allows the reader to see
and respond to visual clues deliberately determined by the creator.

The condensation of time and space in
particular is frequently explored by editorial

illustrators. Depictions of time and space can
be altered by cutting out superfluous information, and highlighting moments in a story where
key actions occur. This creates a specific and
pronounced focus to a story. Similarly, merging
events together warps passages of time and
space, altering their length and amplifying their
focus, but also concentrating their meaning.
For example, the image of a murdered body
may be part-seen through a blood-stained hand
representing the victim rather than showing the
whole figure. The illustrator then creates the back
story of the murder by condensing events in the
unfolding drama to explain the events leading
up to the killing. Using the principle of condensation builds on previously acquired knowledge
the readership has in decoding and interpreting
visual material. The staging of conflicting events
in unison becomes an intriguing possibility in
the art of retelling a story to create drama and
intrigue. This principle is often used in Western
films where a newcomer enters a bar and drink-
ers stare. Their emotions are condensed into
shortened images of faces in the bar making
eye contact with the stranger, the swinging bar
doors or close ups of hands slowly reaching for
handguns.

The separation and reconciliation of events
can create new conceptual and narrative

Figure 6.3
In recent years,
race relations
in Western
democracies
including the
United States
of America
have sadly seen
situations and
events which
inevitably draw
comparisons with
the original Civil
Rights movement
of the 1960s. Here,
Brian Stauffer
is employed to
condense and
capture those
tensions in his
illustration 'Black
Shooting' for the
Dallas Observer.

structures, and will offer innovative approaches to engaging readers. For example, illustrators utilize condensation to summarize knowledge and information collected to reward readers. Visualizing editorial content into a synthesized and processed image allows the set-up and delivery of particular visual gags, from a puns to a satirical observation by editing unnecessary and conflicting information out. Staging content through the process of condensation is a useful exercise using pictorial elements imaginatively to convey illicit meanings and developing visual literacy.

Exaggeration

Editorial illustrators use exaggeration to alter both the perception of subjects and focus of ideas in the mind of the viewer. The projection of particular subjective attributes can enable the eye and the mind to focus on key signifiers in an image that overtly pushes a particular idea to the forefront of a reader's consciousness. In the visual arts, the caricature is a useful example in this sense, where selected scaled elements of figures are exaggerated for comedic effect to exemplify and denote attributes of their perceived character.

Figure 6.4
American illustrator Joe Ciardiello is a prolific editorial creator and internationally recognized artist. His work often profiles and skewers subjects in the public eye, in this instance an acerbic profiling of former US President Donald Trump in royal robes.

Making a political figure's nose larger than other parts of their face creates the focal point for a visual joke. It symbolically suggests that the politician is recognized as nosey for interfering with events that are beyond their brief. Exaggeration can occur in other constructions not limited to the scale of features or objects. For example, the intensity or the overt use of colour can draw the reader's eye to signify a set of emotive ideas like exaggerating the colour of toes too close to an open fire. Altering the tonal contrast between objects and their environments can act as a focal point for the expression of emotive power and contextual effect. The editorial illustrator must strive to achieve an ideological and compositional balance between exaggerated and ordinary components in an image to create maximum impact. Gross exaggerations can result in images not being believed, or being read in unintentional ways that dilute the original potency of the message being conveyed.

Symbolism

A symbol is a mark, sign or object that indicates, signifies or represents ideas, qualities or relationships. Editorial illustrators use symbolic imagery to both suggest and extend meanings, create associations and develop relationships between content. The use of symbolism can enrich and project meaning beyond a depicted subject to infer other connotations and meanings. The substitution of literal representation for a symbolic object can both signify and heighten meaning and can also enable other complex, abstract ideas to emerge. For example, the image of a clenched fist can replace the depiction of a large crowd of protestors that is particularly suited to an editorial illustrator's need to condense information visually. As the medium of illustration is constructed, reimagining the meaning of signs allows new identities and meanings to be built into compositions. Symbolism is therefore a crucial part of an illustrator's image vocabulary.

A well-known example of symbolism in illustration is the heart symbol employed by Milton Glaser in his now infamous 1977 'I♥NY' logo. This piece of work has been parodied and copied by other cities, organizations and institutions globally, revealing the global understanding and resonance of the work. The use and re-use of symbolism enables the symbol or sign to be unlocked from historical or material associations

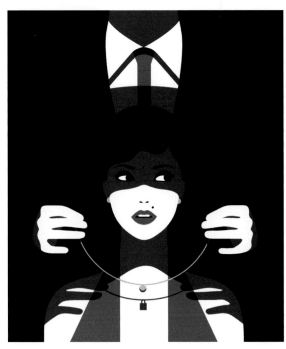

Figure 6.5
A clever use of symbolism in this editorial illustration by Malika Favre for *The New York Times* creates a tension for the reader between a supposed reality and an underlying suggestion about truth. Freedom is depicted by the gift of a necklace; the padlock in shadow suggests a different fate.

and be reappropriated for the evocation or allusion of a constructed narrative. Inevitably, the success of understanding the often subtle or underplayed use of symbolism requires the audience having sufficient prior knowledge of the event signified by the symbol. This requires an investment of experience, knowledge and intelligence from the readership who make visceral connections to conjure up a complete picture in the mind. It is worth stating that symbolism is not merely restricted to elements within the image, but that the work as a whole may be symbolic of greater ideas and beliefs. These are not always intentioned and are created in part in response to how the work is received, through its contextual location on a page or screen, headlines and captions and by its associated surrounding content.

Metaphor

A metaphor is a figure of speech that is applied to words, phrases, objects and actions that are not alike but have something in common. Metaphors are not literally true but support an idea or a belief. For example, an illustration of a rhino representing a jeep is a visual metaphor for a tough, rugged beast that can overcome obstacles in its path because of its size and power. Many editorial illustrators use metaphors as an important visual comparative device to reinforce symbolism with a deliberate but open appeal to a readership. The use of metaphors invites interpretation from a reader over and above obvious literal depictions to consider greater symbolic associations.

Historically, visual metaphors in illustration have been used as an inventive way of rising above censorship and provoking wider debate. For example, John Heartfield, who escaped Nazi persecution, made posters as visual graphic statements against the extremist totalitarian regime in 1930s Germany. Using photomontage as a method, Heartfield's works employed metaphors to introduce ideas that criticized the Nazi regime, and allowed viewers to developed thoughts and sensory perceptions that would encourage different perspectives. Contemporary editorial illustrators such as Edel Rodriguez have used visual metaphors to capture the divisiveness policies of Donald Trump's presidency. Rodriguez suggests perceived associations with the extremist Klu Klux Klan organization through his depiction of the former president wearing a peaked white hood as an icon of hatred and bigotry. Similarly, Canadian illustrator Gary Taxali metaphorically denotes the end of the Trump presidency by depicting the former president's facial profile as the folds and creases of a trash bag of rubbish left alone on the street. Indeed, the Argentinian novelist Jorges Luis Borges remarked that 'Censorship is the mother to metaphor' (Manea 1992: 30), implying that metaphor has been used as a creative tool of choice to response to acts of suppression for many years.

A visual metaphor can therefore be said to represent a system and hierarchy of ideas to preside over and be pervasive of its readership. The use of single or multiple visual metaphors can be read as parallel narrative devices to other actions taking place within an image. Editorial illustrators routinely mix metaphorical association by including symbols and realistic depiction in the same image space to develop, enhance and embolden meaning. This recognition and processing of the metaphor as being loaded with symbolic meaning is known as associative linking. The reader is subconsciously encouraged to both analyse and empathize with depicted content to make connections and form attachments in the image. But associative linking is also effective on levels beyond the portrayal in the illustration itself. In a wider context, it connects the reader to a writer or a publication, giving them brand loyalty through a targeted emotional or spiritual investment.

Figure 6.6
Canadian illustrator Gary Taxali satirically dumps former US President Donald Trump; a deceptively simple image that embodies the complexities and the contradictions of that period.

Fabrication

For some editorial illustrators, the construction of ideas to aid meaning can be further enhanced using particular materials and processes. Using production materials to fabricate their ideas can extend, enhance and explain meaning. This is especially true where illustrators choose to use production methods such as collage or create and photograph three-dimensional artefacts as a part or whole of the image. The sensory properties of materials can allow readers to make visceral connections to the materials being used and create emotional connections to the images.

For example, a figure created from cut-paper may be perceived as being malleable or controllable depending on the grade, colour and texture of paper used. A dog created by carving a three-dimensional form out of wood could

Figure 6.7
One of the most powerful and memorable images of the last few years, the *Der Spiegel* cover 'Das wahre Gesicht des Donald Trump' (The Real Face of Donald Trump) provoked significant controversy and debate on its publication in August 2017. Art directed by Svenja Kruse, the illustration starkly portrays Trump as a reputed Klu Klux Klan sympathizer, a clear statement about his perceived bias towards race relations in the United States of America.

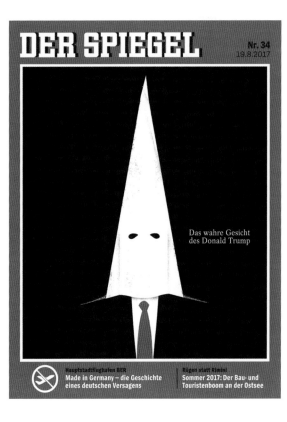

Figure 6.8
Mid-construction for one of Michelle Thompson's illustrations, utilizing finds from old prints and woven book covers. The image is a good example of the principle of fabrication, where the material an illustration is created with has a connection that the reader can identify with the subject matter, giving potential emotional depth and layers of implied meaning to the subject.

suggest a long-lasting friendship implied by the warmth of wood grains, or an environment built of porcelain clay might suggest fragility. All of these examples could exist in a box frame that collects seemingly disparate objects, but places them together for the reader to make connections and draw conclusions. These examples show the thoughtful and considered use of materials can create a 'meta-reality' as they are reimagined beyond their singular material existence.

Associative relations

The concept of associative relations involves building a relationship between unconnected and disparate images. These images can that belong to differing 'image families', despite having related or connected semantic properties. For example, a boat and a ship are interchangeable, yet a 'boat' is a specific vessel; a ship is an informal grouping of vessels. Their connection in a composition becomes logical and informed through their juxtaposition, meaning that seemingly incongruous forms and figures are married together convincingly in the mind of the reader. This can lead to a new narrative or conceptual focus through the imagining of the consequential relationship between the images in the same frame. The editorial illustrator's ability to marry seemingly disparate image components that are unconnected or disenfranchised from each other into forms that suggest or confer logical allusion is known as a process of associative relations.

Understanding and mastering these conceptual constructs enables editorial illustrators to accept briefs with subject matter where they have limited experience and knowledge. They are able to draw deep on a reservoir of conceptual knowledge and personal research to create striking, communicative and successful imagery for their commissioner. The conceptual constructions discussed are utilized in differing degrees by creators in the same illustration to concoct a visual message that connects the original concept to the reader. This allows the successful depiction of ideas that is often referred to as the 'magic' of illustration.

Whilst understanding that mastering these conceptual constructs are important, it is worth stating that they are not in themselves a recipe for producing consistently exemplary outputs. Editorial illustrators must allow for visual play, experimentation and adaption in their work, both in their open-mindedness of depicting subjective content, and in expressing ideas and opinions that will be successfully decoded and understood by readers.

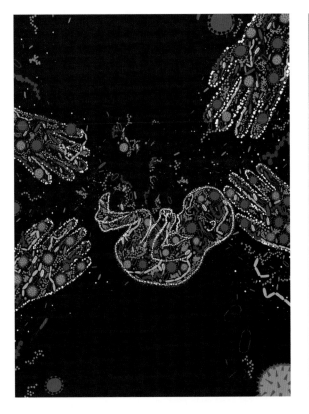

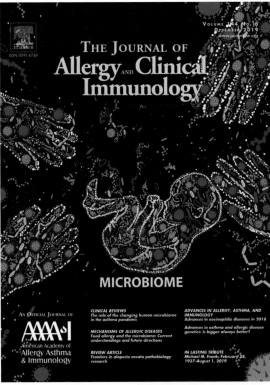

Figure 6.9
An example of associative relations, the baby made up of cell matter represents humankind being formed by celestial hands in a universal laboratory to suggest that scientific discovery is manipulating the biosphere. Illustration by Andrew Selby for the *Journal of Allergy and Clinical Immunology*.

Visual Language

A successful illustrator needs to have command of visual language theory and practice to develop their own work over a career that could span many decades. Having the authority and confidence to utilize visual language to convey ideas, narrate stories or express emotions is a fundamental requirement to producing successful editorial illustrations. Importantly, it also forms a lifelong learning journey as a creative practitioner to evolve a method of working that is flexible and accommodating as the practice of editorial illustration unfolds.

It is important to unwrap the term 'visual language' since its use is widespread but its interpretation is not universally shared, and is certainly open to debate. For example, the term can be used differently by creative and cultural practitioners to their cognitive and linguistic scientists counterparts, and whilst there are undeniably areas of overlap, there are also significant points of departure or dispute. In large part, our understanding of the possibilities of communicating through visual language are still forming, particularly with the burgeoning transition from print to digital platforms which have huge implications for cultural reception and acceptance of modes of visual communication.

On a basic level, the formation of a visual language must involve three core cognitive attributes: modality, structure and meaning. The modality of visual language refers to the individual components – units of graphic code – that can be constructed together to create a representation of a particular element in an image. The structural ordering of these codes presents tangible and coherent visual systems of representation. Meaning is derived from the visual morphemes, or smallest elements of meaning in language, that are pieced together through a structure as an experienced or remembered visual morphology. The more experienced we become at receiving and interpreting visual languages, the more our visual vocabulary grows as we store this information, retrieve it and apply it to new visual encounters.

An introduction to visual language

Visual language, like its spoken and written counterparts, is a nurtured, educational activity that is developed and enhanced through lived and shared experiences. In an illustration context, a visual language composed of graphic code operating in an ordered system combines with text to create *multimodal* interactions that suggest or imply meaning. A parallel would be spoken language being delivered in combination with gestures that amplify our understanding of a subject. Over centuries, we have become educated in and comfortable with using multimodal communication to deliver information in nuanced and sophisticated ways that blend conceptual information into whole messages. Crucially, this finessing of implication and emphasis in visual language is vital to illustration as being a fundamental part of a wider visual communication contribution. The discourse historically – and in the contemporary arena – is important in building up our understanding and appreciation of the power and influence visual language can have in communicating to a readership or audience.

Neil Cohn, the cognitive linguistic scientist and critic, argues that 'humans are built with one expressive system that manifests conceptual information in three complimentary modalities, each of which has its own properties and structures' (Cohn 2016: 3). This helps explain that visual languages are not universally externalized but instead are reliant upon dominant and leading cultural contexts specific to regions of the world. We know that the combination of utilizing graphic code and systems to convey

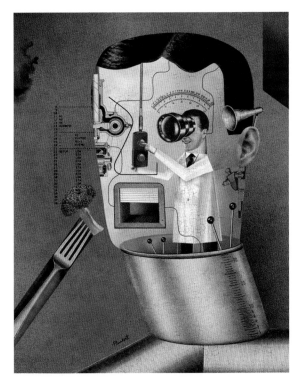

Figure 7.1
David Plunkert's graphic language is chosen here to represent the blur between the science and the ambiguity of human choice in this article titled 'Why We Like What We Like' for *National Geographic*. The blend of scientific signs and symbols such as measurements and scientists wearing white coats contrasts with the arbitrary nature of the broccoli floret on the fork seemingly appearing at random. Plunkert's limited colour palette aids the surprise of the broccoli with the green of the vegetable contrasting with the red background.

Figure 7.2
Creating successful editorial illustrations relies on combining multiple skills under pressure. Editorial assignments are challenging, absorbing and fulfilling, so developing the skills to unlock the requirements of the assignment, collect visual research and build a visual response that answers the brief consistently requires patience and perseverance. Here, Jean Jullien's simple graphic language disguises a complicated feat – how to convey emotion and sensibility in a singular image.

meaning produce a myriad of illustrative outputs that can radically alter meaning. Creators control how these attributes are permitted to function in synergy with each other for the reader through the process of making artwork, or writing passages of text or composing music, through a developing vocabulary. We also know that readers will bring their own cultural experiences to the reception and decoding of these visual languages, written text or pieces of music.

Given that we are seeing the start of an explosion into cross-platform versions of editorial publishing, such cultural experiences will only broaden, flourish and be shared by readerships, raising further issues for debate in the cognitive sciences, linguistics and social anthropology fields that consider illustration as one of the subjects that use graphic code as the very DNA of representation.

Graphic code

Put simply, a piece of graphic code is a unit, or mark, made by a creator that is constructed with other codes into an image. The combination of graphic codes are interpreted by the recipient as representing something on a spectrum from realism through to abstraction. For example, four

equal lines drawn at right angles from each other's end point would form a square, where each line is a separate piece of graphic code. By the same measure, each pixel on screen is a unit of graphic code, or each individual painted brush mark. As a parallel, in written text, each piece of graphic code is a letterform, numeral or punctuation mark. Or in written music, graphic code is represented by different musical note value, key and time signature. Graphic code is the basic building block by which images, words and sounds are derived.

As a singular item, a piece of code has minimal meaning but when combined together, the creator can control and execute the manner in which an output is manufactured. By taking a drawn line as an example of graphic code, the type of line, its size, width, length and colour can all be described as variants of that code. Multiple codes, expressed for instance through the frequency of lines drawn on a surface, and their proportionate or disproportionate space from other corresponding lines, can create areas of rhythm or spikes of intensity. As a parallel, in written text, written code placed in a particular order in lines makes words, sentences and paragraphs.

A single letterform teaches children the alphabet, and simple combinations of letterforms make short words that are the building blocks of a child mastering language. Complex constructions of text that truly reflect the dichotomy and expressive power of language connect with our soul to transform or mood and emotionally connect on a deep sensory level. Similarly in music, combinations of coded notes placed in a particular order can allow a musician to play a simple nursery

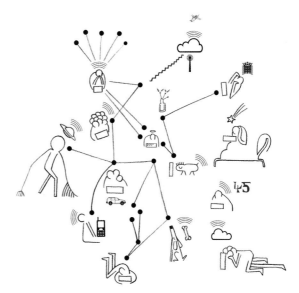

Figure 7.3
Frazer Hudson's 'Six Degrees of Separation' explores the need for staying digitally connected through periods of lockdown induced by the Covid-19 pandemic. The illustration is a good example of graphic coding where the reader has to decode and narrativize meaning based on the pictorial clues provided.

rhyme, or a concert orchestra to play a complex symphonic score depending on the compositional frequency of written notes as combinations of graphic code. All of these examples need more that an outpouring of code. They must be dictated by some kind of structural framework, lexicon and vocabulary that aligns to a set of predetermined rules. These vary in terms of their regimented or free-form approach depending on the needs of the creator.

Structure

By juxtaposing collections of graphic code together into a composition, a system is formed which is governed by a set of conditions determining how graphic codes can operate and how content can be understood. In an illustration, the orchestration of visual elements is controlled by the creator to form an image containing visual clues that help a reader to understand a concept, unlock the parameters of a story or rationally explain information. Physical visual structure is imposed by employing graphic code in particular and deliberate ways to create a framework that can be controlled and regulated by the creator. For example, controlling the scale, colour, contrasting hues or texture within a compositional structure can intensify or calm the delivery of particular messages, depending on the needs of the image content and the creative intent of the illustrator.

To use the parallels of writing or music again, textual compositions are formed through bodies of running text operating as vignettes, sentences and paragraphs that help frame and compose the writer's thoughts into bodies of information, or passages of description, or steps that explain information cogently. Such sections are structurally grouped to become chapters in books or articles in newspapers and magazines. In music, structuring code is achieved by applying notes into bars, lines and sections that may be verses and choruses in popular or choral music, or movements in classical music. Ordering a structure helps readers, viewers and listeners form clues about content that aid meaning, but, by default, extends their growing vocabulary and makes visual, reading and listening experiences more pleasurable as their residual knowledge grows and matures.

In illustration, the most obvious physical structural device is the edges of an image that contain content. However, not all structural

devices are so immediately visibly tangible. Within an illustration, various intangible visual systems are present and in operation to enable images to be successfully decoded. These systems direct the reader's eye around the image, hunting for visual clues that can be pieced together to form a cogent and cohesive understanding of the content being expressed. For example, using perspective in an illustration creates a framework that is widely understood and accepted as a visual device for ordering pictorial elements in a composition. These elements can be brought into the foreground of an illustration to emphasize their importance or to amplify their meaning through scale when seen in conjunction with other elements. Other elements might be proportionately smaller, being deliberately diminished to suggest that while present because they are still relevant, their purpose is to support the main subject of the work. Pictorial elements may act as additional clues for the main body of information contained in the illustration. In this example, the perspective structure is invisible on the image surface but is playing an important role structurally to control the ordered visual readability and content of the image for the reader.

On other occasions, some pictorial systems are openly employed as part of the image. Indeed, the display of pictorial systems is an integral and necessary part of the illustration and become additional elements of graphic code in their own right. For example, diagrams may have intrinsic visual code built in to them to decipher or explain meaning, such as numbers or letters. Such alphanumeric codes may additionally be colour-coded to add an extra layer of informative meaning and may even have a key panel to explain their particular function. Graphic visual devices, like maps, may have specialized built-in structures such as grid lines to help the reader navigate accurately, or have arrows or dotted lines to indicate direction or mode of transport respectively. All of these systems must be designed to correspond with and complement other visual systems in synergy or the image will fail to communicate.

These examples mirror structural use in text and music. Punctuation, sentences and paragraphs allows text to be ordered by collecting, separating and emphasizing into meaningful content for readers on a basic level. The use of a tangible structural device like a punctuation mark allows writers to draw attention in a body of text by placing emphasis that creates tension or builds drama through to employment of certain words or phrases. It establishes control of the text, allows motifs to be introduced – or re-enacted – and directs readers to connect ideas, understand situations or gives permission to explore alternative narrative avenues. Sentences form natural pockets of information, describe stories or contain salient information to piece together to form a holistic view on a subject. Paragraphs group adjoining sentences together to extend and amplify meaning. Likewise in music, notes are punctuated by particular signs and symbols which break the music score by controlling the pace and flow of the piece, whilst they are separated by verses and choruses or by movements, depending on genre.

Interpretations and applications of structure inevitably invoke questions about formality and informality. Formal structures tie in with expected paradigms that readers, viewers and listeners will have seen before. By contrast, informal structures permit play and the blurring of traditional boundaries, creating unorthodox approaches to expression of content through innovative and surprising structural choices. For example, an illustration accompanying an article about a serious topical issue might need to be tightly controlled to ensure that no ambiguity is present in the image. The resulting picture plane will be governed by a set of rules that clearly establish the parameters of compositing the pictorial elements clearly in the image, emphasized perhaps by using limited colour to convey a striking message. On other occasions, articles that celebrate an event or person in an abstracted way, or through contrasting points of view, might be more expressively handled. This allows greater freedom to be given to the composition of elements, and perhaps encourages a frivolous method of manufacture and bright, or contrasting pops of colour or texture.

In parallel, unstructured written text might be a piece of automatic writing often found in poetry, or a piece of experimental music that moves away from orthodox models of composition to explore the fringes of a genre. Rules are there to be interpreted, so while road signs contain deliberately simplified visual iconography in limited colours to clearly instruct road users,

Figure 7.4
Sergio García Sánchez's take on *The New Yorker* dandy Eustace Tilley uses the famous monocled figure as a motif to condense several narratives into one illustrative structure by suggesting a contextual thematic relationship with each other. In this example, everyday activities are played out against a contrasting colour palette emphasizing 'the city that never sleeps'.

ambiguous expression may involve a myriad of symbols, colours and textures to invite much wider interpretations where there is time to ponder such motifs. At the end of the process, there may not be a firm answer. Structure permits control, but it can also be successfully utilized to invite open interpretation.

Meaning

An illustration's meaning is derived from decoding the enclosed visual information and deciphering the accompanying text into a combined holistic statement contextualized by our existing visual memory. Selecting the type of code and placing these units together in a structured composition forms a perception of the diegetic world of the illustration. This is then subject to the cultural and critical judgement of both the creator and the reader. The myriad of possible meanings contained in illustration owes much to this bank of knowledge that readers have acquired through encountering and participating in visual communication as a shared, cultured experience.

Meaning can be directed and unambiguous such as an instruction. Equally, meaning can be implied without explicitly being cited, or can be embedded or intwined to suggest something. This is often used to imply or infer an editorial view, without firmly stating it. It is obviously possible to build up many layers of meaning using this approach. Directing where meaning can be found and what it represents is crucial for an illustrator to comprehend and action in their work, as it permits control of the content of an image and can greatly influence its reception by the readership. Exercising control over meaning can underplay the significance of elements within the composition to understate content, or alternatively, can amplify and force the reader to confront a subject or create a surprising and unexpected view of content that questions or even shifts opinion. In music, lyrics and musical score combined and performed together form a similar function through descriptive narration or metaphorical association.

In a structured illustration full of graphic code, meaning absolutely relies on a connection between the contained visual information, accompanying text and the process of reception, recognition and acceptance by the reader. Human beings store and retrieve vast swathes of visual information from their long-term memories and use this as the basis of their visual vocabulary to decode images and unlock meaning. Such memories are stored as retrievable schematic patterns that resemble familiar and recognizable structures of code. They effectively act as shortcuts or shorthand approaches to condensing and imparting information.

For example, a child's drawing of a house may comprise a door, windows, a pointed roof and

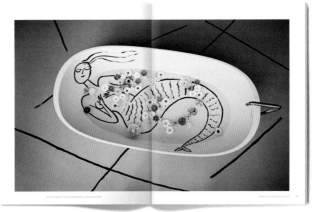

Figure 7.5
These spreads for *Süddeutsche Zeitung Magazine* show Serge Bloch in a playful mood, in homage to the work of illustration greats such as Saul Steinberg and André François who themselves had fun with the same subject matter. His lyrical, expressive line work is reminiscent of those two great exponents of expressive, joyful work.

accompanying chimney stack as a learnt visual schema, or pattern, of elements for a house built from visual memories. That iconographic interpretation may not be the same for a resident of an apartment whose door is hidden within the structure of a building, or who does not have a fireplace and therefore requires no chimney stack. Nevertheless, readers will have enough familiarity with this combination of structural graphic code to recognize a house. Learning and retrieving visual patterns in a visual memory unlocks meaning almost instantaneously which explains why we are so adept at receiving and decoding visual information quickly and concisely. Such patterns often manifest themselves through recognizable graphic stylistic expressions as an integral part of collecting this information into memorable schemas. In the same way that we develop a linguistic vocabulary, our visual lexicon becomes more and more sophisticated as we are exposed to more and more visual imagery. How, what and why we store images should interest every illustrator, drive their future output and make them strive to understand how their creations affect readerships and audiences.

Graphic styles

In the visual arts, graphic styles allow the visual expression of content in a particular manner. The creator's personal mark of expression might be an extension of their personality, or signify a strong conviction or connection with the underlying thrust of the subject matter on display. In parallel, writers develop and employ written styles in a similar manner that helps distinguish their output from that of other writers, while musicians interpret songwriters and composers scores through musical styles that can see the same piece of music interpreted radically differently. Stylistic interpretation permits personal expression of content, whether that be exuberant, careful, detailed, flourish, fresh, mesmerizing or economical interpretations of content to be communicated to the audience.

These stylistic interpretations extend the graphic code, test the structure and expand the meaning of subject matter, imbuing it with personality that enriches its identity. In turn, the recipient of that content connects with the visual, textual or musical information and makes cognitive connections through highly developed nodes that are finely tuned to decode complex content into meaningful statements. Our brains process this information in nano-seconds giving credence to the phrase 'a picture is worth a thousand words'. As noted in Chapter 1, the history of graphic style development and display aligns to wider artistic and cultural output of various ages, cultures and traditions. The visual flamboyance of particular periods have a unequivocal connection to perceptions of the political, societal and economic mood of the time – like the expressive, vibrant Parisian poster artists of the 1930s, who revelled in the relative stability of French life between the world wars. By contrast, the Constructivists pursued a graphic style that was directional, functional and commanding in communicating a communist manifesto to the newly liberated Russian population following the Revolution in 1917.

To that end, many contemporary illustrators reference, reinvent and reappropriate visual imagery in new, innovative and surprising ways. The British illustrator Michelle Thompson is clearly influenced by the Pop Art movement in her use of collaged pictorial elements and compositions, but her work plays with ambiguous structural deviances in the form of brightly coloured accidental graphic devices, like scanned ink spots and scribbles, that also reference Abstract Expressionism. Thompson's output utilizes scrapbook finds, photomontage and a highly personalized colour palette to distinguish herself from other illustrators who form illustrations through collage and montage. Her work is unmistakable for its signature graphic style and has been nurtured to be applied to a wide range of editorial outputs for clients such as *The New Statesman*, *New Scientist* and *The Guardian*.

The employment of a specific graphic style can help to create, display and solidify the brand identity of a particular illustrator. Recognition is massively important in the world of editorial illustration, and many illustrators have highly identifiable output that has taken time to develop, helps mark their work out from competitors and gives them a strong presence in the market. On one level, employing and mastering a graphic style might be used to build audience trust through brand confidence built on quality of work and ability to work to deadlines. Publications benefit from using work of this kind to create both visual recognition and editorial positioning that creates loyalty with readerships.

Equally, showcasing a strong graphic style allows the illustrator's work to be recognized through association with a quality client roster that helps promote quality and reliability, thereby driving up an illustrator's commercial worth. Illustration agents often point to a reliable graphic identity as being one of the key attributes to gaining commissions, but this applies less in editorial markets than in advertising and helps explain why editorial illustration is often seen as a good launch pad for aspiring illustrators. Editorial illustration is often seen as a good place to foster and shape creative modes of expression and nurture raw talent.

Other illustrators prefer not to be bound by what they see as the constraints of style and work across different image systems, even on occasion working deliberately to pastiche or parody other visual approaches to suit particular assignments. A career in editorial illustration relies heavily on the illustrator knowing the currency of their visual output, and currency fluctuates depending on factors beyond an illustrators control. Fashion, cultural significance, over-exposure and new technological developments are just some of the factors that affect how illustrators fall in and out of favour with clients and commissioners.

Winning assignments can be dependent on whether work is deemed fitting and relevant for particular assignments, so having a degree of flexibility is often part of a successful development strategy to ensure continuity of work and remain relevant in a contemporary market. By extension, some graphic styles are not suited to the move from static to animated editorial image which has forced some illustrators to consider their output and reinvent their approach in the commercial marketplace. In other instances, an illustrator working partially in editorial illustration but with a portfolio of work that extends through publishing and into other commercial activity needs to consider the application and frequency of such work to satisfy those commercial demands. This is a complex area that is not simply reliant on content, but also affects the choices an illustrator has in relation to production and presentation of their creative output.

Sequential multimodality

Sequential work has been an important vehicle in communicating particular ideas in printed editorial illustration, through cartoon strips or short sequential narrative panels. Increasingly, publisher's digital platforms have developed opportunities to explore and exploit animated content to entice readers and retain interest by presenting content in imaginative and compelling ways. The transition from print to digital platforms affords massive opportunities for illustrators to be imaginative and progressive about organizing graphic code and structure into expressive meaning. New sequential opportunities also raise some important questions about the structure and reach of multimodal sequential communication. In turn, they pose some interesting options for creators, publishers and readerships alike in charting a future that takes advantage of the opportunities digital platforms present.

In traditional sequential work there are some important additional considerations that need to be understood and employed when thinking about code, structure and meaning. Any combination of images sequences must be ordered, creating a grammar that is understood by creator and reader as representing something. Neil Cohn (2013) notes that a grammatical system for sequences must therefore encompass all aspects of their structural framework. This will include how they are graphically presented, how space in each image is depicted, how their conceptual content resonates with the reader through the narrative structure and how the individual frames are navigated in the correct sequence.

Presenting sequential content is often achieved using a combination visual and textual graphic code. Images and text are linked in the same pane and have some kind of planned interplay with one another. This interlinked code is correspondent to the conceptual information supplied in a single panel. This allows image and text to be content load-bearing but not depict the same content, so the action depicted in an image will not use text as a description. Instead text may add another layer of narrative meaning that provides other detail about events depicted in the image. Extra layers can provide specificity, or conversely, can be used to inject ambiguity into our understanding of content. Additionally, if icons and symbols are employed, they become additional systems of communication used within illustrated panels, enabling meaning in their own right which further shapes and communicates their content. Graphic representation across image, text, symbols and icons offers

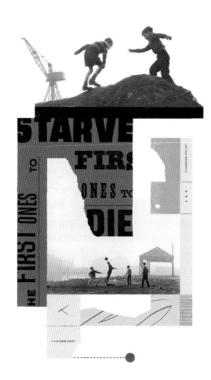

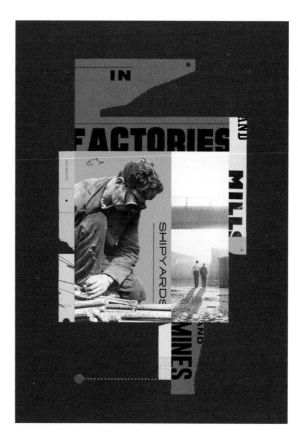

Figure 7.6
Matthew
Hancock's
Workers Song
illustration set for
Fare Magazine
evokes strong
thematic and
visual connections
with the
Constructivist
movement.

the illustrator a host of options to communicate meaning.

Meaning can also be derived, aided and enhanced from the depiction of space between objects and situations articulated by graphic representation. For example, in certain panes, the creator can privilege a certain viewpoint to present and impart information in close up, or draw attention to elements in the individual image by the use of scale or placement. Corresponding panes in the sequence can then use this previously gleaned information to develop alternative perspectives. The reader collects this sequential unfolding of more information into contextualized scenes by fusing information offered by different viewpoints and angles the creator has used. The presentation of content triggers and enables the reader to decode information through their stored, memorized visual morphology, unlocking conceptual content as meaning.

Planning a narrative structure is vital to present information across a sequence of panels. Creating an accessible point of entry and then allowing events to develop requires panels to be planned to relate to each other towards a satisfactory conclusion. In a simple step-by-step sequence, information can be imparted in a chronological order. A logic exists about why panels are sequenced in a particular order. But in sequences that are created to emphasize or highlight aspects of a story, or deliver a impactful punchline, the overall narrative flow of the sequence can change pace. This allows the reader greater time to spend studying a panel that can amplify the narrative and concentrate meaning. Equally, repeating a scene or event over panels with little narrative development slows the pace and suggests a pause in action, permitting the reader to contemplate the aftermath of a previous action or build to the next event. Controlling pace through a grammatical understanding of narrative provides the creator with conceptual possibilities about structuring the narrative, and gives the reader a rounded, cohesive view of the subject.

The reader is invited to read methodically from one panel to the next in a guided sequence through a grammatical understanding of navigation. This is dependent on cultural variance. In Western countries, sequences are read left to right, top to bottom, whilst in Arabic and Eastern cultures, the opposite navigational path applies. A reader could be faced with an equally proportioned grid of panels. Equally panels can be presented in a grid that permits differently sized panels, or be separated by spaces. It is also permissible for panels to overlap or be staggered, thus creating different navigational options for creator and reader. Sequential images can be a useful structural feature when space in a layout is limited, or when dense information needs to be condensed.

Understanding grammatical structure not only unlocks meaning through decoding, but just like our verbal communication, permits us to understand deeper, richer and more sophisticated concepts. We develop a fluency with sequential decoding of content and meaning to apply to other communication mediums. Successfully navigating a sequence not only builds an ordered understanding of content but extracts meaning into a developing vocabulary that can be applied to future sequences. This can enable readers to understand cultural variation in visual languages and remain open to emerging variations offered by digital sequential possibilities, in turn creating a world of new opportunities for editorial illustrators to invest in.

How sequential work develops from print to digital platforms is an exciting, unfolding development for creators and readerships. A sequence of digital content can offer much more than simple two-frame GIFs. For example, it may develop by encompassing both static and motion-based graphic representation in the same sequence. There is the possibility of embedding motion-based headlines in a sequence, or by pulling sub-headings or body text from an article into an integrated image and text motion piece. There are extended possibilities for utilizing the spoken word, musical accompaniment or sound effects on digital platforms as part of the multimodal experience that completely envelops content and reader as an immersive experience. Further still, the experiential possibilities of using augmented, virtual and mixed-reality opportunities between print and digital platforms offers exciting possibilities to enable human expression through a 'live' relationship with corresponding content.

Figure 7.7
Tom Gauld often creates illustrations that play with the blurring boundaries between reality and imagination which can create interesting juxtapositions between time and space. In this example, the reader is afforded the chance to see the innermost thinking of the characters depicted in the scene, creating their own mini scenes.

Part Three

Creation

The creation of an editorial illustration is both challenging and rewarding on many levels. The joy of seeing your first piece of published work, or your first cover printed on a newsstand or in a digital edition, is difficult to express as it is usually the culmination of a hard-fought education and training to that point. For every success, there's also a string of failed commissions that never saw the light of day, or ideas for illustrations that were rejected, or working relationships that ended as commissioners moved into new roles.

Whilst editorial illustration undoubtedly places the work of successful illustrators in the sightline of commissioners and the general public who read publications, it does not guarantee consistency of work or economic security. The editorial illustration domain continues to see change on an epic scale. Many illustrators look beyond newspapers, magazines and journals to other related markets such as publishing, advertising and design agency work to support their editorial endeavours.

On one level, editorial illustration is the welcoming entry point into a career for newly qualified or fledgling illustrators as the exposure to risk is less financially and reputationally cumbersome for the publisher. At the other end of the spectrum, seasoned and experienced editorial illustrators can be relied on to deliver high-quality work, often aided by highly pressurized working conditions where decisiveness and clear thinking are critically and financially rewarded. The field of editorial illustration has historically welcomed both camps as a way of blooding the new and savouring the experienced and creating a competitive environment for others engrossed in this fascinating field to fight and scrap for the assignments that might be career changing and life enhancing.

Promotion

Successful editorial illustrators must balance the flow of work to keep busy but also allow sufficient space to take on new work, develop personal projects and concentrate on administrative tasks away from their creative time. There are often a highly individualized set of circumstances that surround career decisions – financial considerations, job sharing, family responsibilities and caring roles shape many illustrators' daily existences – and that will make advice about practising feel incomplete. Above all, a balanced enthusiastic and responsive attitude is key to building the foundations of a relationship with a client.

The following guidance is based on surveying illustrators at different moments of their careers and should be seen in the round as a guide rather than the rule.

Figure 8.1
Lasse Skarbøvik's illustration output is used as a successful device in promoting his professional output in both printed format and on digital platforms. The vector-based illustrations can be translated into handmade paintings and prints, and Skarbøvik also creates a range of stationery-based materials that form a considered and targeted promotional platform.

Figure 8.2
French illustrator Malika Favre has a highly distinctive, bold, minimal Pop Art meets OpArt style that is defined by colour and the imaginative use of positive and negative space. Her vibrant images ensure she is in continual demand as an editorial illustrator – here for *Brummell* exploring new horizons. Favre's work is consistent, bold and professional – all key traits for commissioners of editorial illustration.

Curating a portfolio

There is a clear art to portfolio building in analogue and digital form, but the key attribute in common is a visual flow and pace that allows illustrations to be seen as a unified, coherent body of completed work. Composing this flow relies on a constant process of arranging and rearranging imagery and the process should be given the time and effort it deserves in presenting a cogent professional face for your work. A sense of order and logic needs to be present as an underlying anchor to the work that is presented. That could be through the visual tone of voice that ensures work has a consistency of approach and execution. Many illustrators have a personalized colour palette which instantly defines their work. Others may have a diversity of applications across areas such as fashion, lifestyle, pastimes and hobbies, but their work has a familiarity of stylized execution that seamlessly binds any differences together through a personalized visual language. Like handwriting or speech, there are personalized and individualized markers that signify and characterize an illustrator's output.

A traditional editorial illustration portfolio served a historical vital function as the passport to new clients and assignments. It was the single most important presentation item in an editorial illustrators arsenal in forging a career in the discipline. Ranging in size and finish, the portfolio usually comprised ring-bound or loose-leafed sleeves containing finished artwork pasted or printed on inserts that could be changed and updated as new work was published. This kept the portfolio alive as an evolving set of works that showcased the talent, output and versatility of the illustrator.

Traditional portfolio building also created a job in devising an approach, maintaining consistency over content and experimenting with ordering sleeves to build a story that was memorable and convincing. Varying the scale of illustrations and their placement on the sleeve inserts created visual drama and a sense of surprise as the pages were turned. Giving illustrations captions created opportunities for the client to ask questions of the illustrator and offered chances to break away from a formulaic style of presenting. Trying out different running orders gave important feedback opportunities for clients to express preferences which some illustrators then used to create speculative self-promotional work. The managed ecosystem of maintaining the traditional portfolio to a high professional standard was a time-consuming but vital and potentially very rewarding experience in building an editorial illustrator's professional profile and career aspirations.

Sadly, traditional physical portfolios are swiftly declining in popularity. The reasons are obvious and are mostly linked to changes in people's working practices, especially around time and availability of both illustrator and publisher. Taking a portfolio to a publisher was often seen as welcome respite from the studio for many freelance illustrators, but a tortuous experience for others who preferred the isolation of their desk. The experience certainly provided opportunities for face-to-face engagement with a commissioner or client which could be useful for presenting work, receiving important feedback and gaining interest and recognition where new clients were concerned. Physical visits allowed relationships to be built and, indeed, many illustrators remain on strong professional terms with clients after successful assignments born out of face-to-face meetings. In well-organized visits, clients could be wowed by an illustration portfolio as a visual spectacle and taken through a mesmerizing array of work that guaranteed both exposure and plaudits and would often lead to paid assignments and promises of future work that could last weeks, months and in some cases, years.

For illustrators less confident about their physical presentation skills, the arduous process of having to present work to clients, speak about fees and licensing and answer challenging questions that they were themselves trying to fathom answers to forced many to question whether this career was for them. They are certainly better served by opportunities to

showcase their work in a digital realm. However, the age-old process of nurturing illustration talent through art direction and editorial incubation has undoubtedly diminished, which is unfortunate. Time pressures have simply made face-to-face meetings rare. The practical difficulties of living within reasonable commuting distances, and the associated costs of travel and taking time out of the working day, has also been a challenge for many.

The digital portfolio has undoubtedly assumed far more popularity in recent years for obvious reasons. For the creator, digital portfolios can be shown on websites which have greater reach and potential significance in attracting global interest. They can be set up relatively quickly and easily and some organizations have been adept at creating beautiful templates that promote cool typefaces, large image templates and full customization interfaces to satisfy the pickiest. Companies like Squarespace and Wix offer pricing plans that are very competitive for hosting a professional-looking site, with a series of price points that correspond to the main and support services on offer. Many offer special deals and contracts which can be spread over affordable monthly payments, with ranges of customization that bring in other services such as online store options, technical support and affiliated marketing services to help grow your brand.

Having the ability to customize and detail the layout across different parts of a website helps control the pace that visitors experience your work. A portfolio grid full of images undoubtedly provides a visual impact, but perhaps some form of magnification or a new pop-up window is needed to inspect the detail of finely detailed work. Alternatively, providing a slideshow of images through animated screens or transitions can also positively affect the pace by which work is seen. It is important not to let the technical aspects of the site dictate the content of the work, and fussy transitions can negatively affect seeing imagery, especially if your viewer has limitations on bandwidth. By the same token, a carefully crafted and thoughtful biography about you is a really important part of introducing yourself. This text should allow an insight into your interests, your professional background, experience that is relevant and perhaps some of your professional accolades or achievements.

Figure 8.3
Maintaining consistency and creating a body of work that
showcases a curated range of outputs is important in building
commissioner confidence. Here, the late British scientist and
cosmologist Professor Stephen Hawking is sympathetically
caricatured in this gentle illustration by Anita Kunz, with the
circular rims of his spectacles thoughtfully repeated as atoms in a
perpetual universe. Kunz's work brings conceptual ideas together
with her ability to caricature through portraits that work well
across political, entertainment and cultural subjects.

Web presence

A personal website is an absolute necessity for
an independent editorial illustrator. Websites
must be appealing, functional and easy to
navigate, but they must also sympathetically
show off illustration work to the best advantage.
Increasingly, providers such as Squarespace
and Wix offer bespoke design solutions that are
elegantly proportioned and use digital-friendly
fonts that illustrators can customize to fit their
work. Paying a small subscription fee to avoid
pop-up banner advertising will pay dividends
for cleaner, unfettered access to creative work.
These providers also have sophisticated search
engine optimization (SEO) settings that allow
websites to be easily found by major search
engines, promote the quantity and quality of user
visits and push websites higher up the rankings,
aiding visibility. Sophisticated SEO functionality
allows illustrators to track analytics about who
is looking at their work, the frequency of which
images are being viewed and the order in which
visitors click between pages of information. This
data-based insight is helpful when considering
uploading newly published work, or creating
personal projects that can potentially lead to
desired commissions in specific areas. In short,
more control is placed back in the illustrator's
hands which is vital when developing a career in
the field.

A landing page should introduce the illustrator and their work to potential clients. As a
shop window for talent, it is import that this
page strikes the correct visual tone of voice.
Functionality, simplicity and visual impact should
be key achievement goals on any landing page.
A clear menu that can be quickly identified and
allows the visitor to navigate to a portfolio of
work needs to also appear on the landing page.
Some illustrators also include client testimonials
or sketchbook work, but only if space allows.
An uncluttered landing page works best for
maximum visual impact. Some illustrators use
an animated one as a way of showing a range
of work and creating a strong visual dynamic.
Creating visual links to associated social media
platforms that showcase work is an important
consideration too, and using their embedded
icons is a way of saving space and letting the
work stand out.

Details about the illustrator should be kept
professionally concise but well written, as the
search engines use factual details in this text
as specific search terms. Spending time introducing yourself, by selecting words and phrases
that have poignancy and reach is worth it, so
a 'conceptual editorial illustrator' will generate
more specific enquiries for your services that
the general term 'illustrator'. Using a dictionary
or thesaurus to craft your biography can really
help to marshal and focus your commentary. Ask
friends and family to objectively read the copy for
accuracy and to suggest improvements. Content
could include educational attainments, previous
experience or commentary from trusted clients
that have already commissioned work. Many
illustrators like to explain their creative process or
modes of production with corresponding visuals

DAVID PLUNKERT

Figure 8.4
An impactful
landing page
for a website
is an absolute
priority. It should
be well ordered,
easy to navigate
and demonstrate
instantaneously
the brand values
of the illustrator.
David Plunkert's
website is a
fine example;
impactful,
engaging and
enticing the
viewer to discover
more.

which can be useful for new clients and can aid an understanding of the motivations, interests and potential points of collaboration behind the work. This information could be introduced in the biography and then continued as another link on the website to showcase this process in more detail. A client list is very helpful as this breeds confidence and reassurance in potential clients that your work is consistently of a high quality and able to be produced within professional deadlines.

Similarly, some illustrators like to use a website to create an essence of what inspires, motivates and gives them pleasure. To that end, links that showcase their creative environment, their collections, hobbies or interests and links to connected content are all worth considering. Websites are like coral reefs – constantly changing their appearance to stay alive – an adage well worth adhering to for frequent visitors who will be expecting updates and developments. Web maintenance, if only to check site analytics, is a daily habit to get into that will prevent updates from being a substantial and unedifying job.

Websites alone are not a guarantee of visitors, nor commissions, and thought should be given about how to publicize their existence.

Integrating print or social media into a personal marketing strategy will generate interest and traffic, but careful consideration is required about the type of information and frequency being used in an analogue and digital context. Postcards, or single image tear sheets, are a recognized way of instantly promoting websites. They perform the function of signposting a viewer to a site, are relatively cheap to produce and easy to send. Equally, some illustrators devise short run editions of work that can be printed as collectable sets. Key to deciding the best approach is always focusing on what will ultimately benefit the illustrator's next batch of work and their broader career aspirations. For example, if a limited set of well-crafted and professionally produced cards unlocks several commissions that lead to regular work, the investment will have earnt its return handsomely.

Social media presence

It is important to develop a strategy for what you want social media to do and how this affects the overall communication strategy that you have as a pioneering creative. There is little doubt that strongly curated and quick-paced social media channels can be a way of keeping your work in the public eye, introducing talent and furthering exposure. But social media is fluid as an entity and this needs to be factored into the equation when forming a strategy. Different channels have different attributes and, by extension, different demographics that they are aimed at. Professionally engineered social media platforms can gain rapid and unexpected exposure to many new clients and interested parties and it is worth the effort to maintain and promote the platforms that you operate from.

There are many social media exponents that are worth investigating for their different motivations and methods of bringing work to public attention. For some illustrators, the platform to showcase new work is a popular reason to use social media and inevitably creates excitement and interest. Others use social media to tell the story behind the creation of the work, or introduce new approaches to production or dissemination that they have been experimenting with. This route can be attractive to established followers who have an invested interest in your work. This approach also works by linking your accounts to associated posts from like-minded individual creatives or organizations that provide context or extended exposure to your own work. An example might be an independent bookstore showcasing the work of a particular illustrator, or a publisher who has decided to post your illustration on their feed. Social media is also a useful way of highlighting external recognition and accolades for your work, including awards and prizes or client testimonials that are designed to fit the respective platforms.

Social media channels should work in tandem with a website as a collective visual communication strategy. For example, Behance, Instagram and Dribble are all designed to promote visual content but they have nuances that make their style and manner of presentation and interaction different. Building such customization into your strategy helps achieve continuity between platforms and minimizes contradictions which is important in maintaining an authoritative professional voice. However, do not underestimate the time and effort it takes to maintain such a proposition. Generating new content is time-consuming and requires an approach that is sustainable. Finding a rhythm to maintaining social media platforms is an individual choice, but it should be enjoyable rather than onerous.

Figure 8.5
With nearly two hundred thousand followers on Instagram, Gary Baseman has a serious digital profile that consistently needs feeding and managing new content. Central to his success is providing characterful and inspiring insight not only into his professional illustrative output, but the influences and expectations that drive his creative hunger and passion. Baseman's work covers publishing, broadcast and product lines, but his social media presence is cleverly curated to also show snippets of his home life, including his inspirational partners Blackie the Cat and Bosko that often make cameo appearances in his work.

Figure 8.6
A well-curated social media feed can be an active promotional tool in landing assignments when time is tight. Here, a piece of topical political conceptual commentary by Simoul Alva for the *MIT Technology Review*, rendered in 3D works across print and digital platforms.

Facebook

The ultimate 'granddaddy' social media site has evolved over two decades to connect a hefty proportion of the world's population and has become an economic and social colossus on the world stage. Fans of Facebook as a business marketing tool point to its simplicity as a social media platform for introducing and maintaining contact with fellow users who are familiar with the platform. However, it was not primarily developed to showcase visual content and many find its user interface clumsy and dated.

The accelerated growth of Facebook causes many users anxiety over how private information is used, particularly in relation to their personal privacy and how this is used to generate targeted advertising. For example, the Facebook acquisitions of technology firms WhatsApp, Instagram, Giphy and Oculus VR has fuelled a growing sense of unease amongst some users. Critics point to the organization as being a publisher of content in its own right, which fundamentally affects its place and responsibilities on a global stage, particularly in regard to charges of influence and interference at national governmental levels. However, or perhaps in response to these criticisms, advertisers have backed Facebook, with more than 3 million active accounts in 2016. Advertisers actively use harvested information supplied by users to skilfully direct and target their messaging.

Illustrators are more likely to use Facebook as a blog-type platform to update followers on their activity, rather than a portfolio-style social tool of choice. Other illustrators use Facebook as a virtual signpost to other social media channels or to go 'behind the scenes' on projects as a retrospective look at a particular process after an illustration is published. This can include audio visual documentary-style excerpts that provide a richer user experience and potentially speak to interested parties about creative direction choices or specific production processes.

Figure 8.7
Editorial illustration becomes cultural commentary as Javier Jaén explores the problematic position of Facebook in a democratic society. The print and GIF versions accompanied an article titled 'Can Mark Zuckerberg Fix Facebook Before It Breaks Democracy?' for *The New Yorker*.

Instagram

Founded in 2009, Instagram began life as an app that allowed users to place filters over photographs. Since its acquisition by Facebook in 2012, Instagram has exploded in popularity to become the illustrators app of choice to promote visual content. The grid platform format allows an immediate summative picture of output for visitors that establishes a strong tone of voice about the work and the intentions of the creator. The ability to click and examine posts individually, and to post and reply to comments also allows opportunities to develop your profile by showing your professional approach to the subject. The seemingly universal social media etiquette of having a follow policy allows a network of like-minded interests to build and creates a form of critical engagement with your audience. It is also a good way of encouraging more work as a way of generating decent quality content for your site – but in moderation. A curated presence is much more appealing than a blanket-wide approach and the aim should always be on quality posting that will enhance and further interest in your work.

Instagram is now recognized as *the* lifestyle platform, graced by celebrity posters and influencers creating mass hysteria and excitement over new content, or product endorsements. In the wider context, users are genuinely interested

Figure 8.8
Illustrator Doug Chayka evokes the scientific principle of multiplying cells in this illustration accompanying an article about Instagram's phenomenal growth rate, for *The New York Times*.

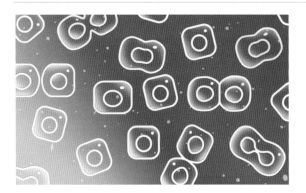

to see behind the scenes into the world that content creators inhabit. For the illustrator, that might include individual workspaces and studio environments, influences and inspiration that you use in your work, or contextualizing posts that perhaps show where you last exhibited or where your work has been seen in context in the environment. Curation is key but the authorial voice behind the work will allow content to grow with a creative communication strategy in place.

Behance

A platform dedicated to showing visual work, Behance is part of the suite of offerings from Adobe, who have a long-standing professional association with illustrators and designers. Providing bespoke tools and platforms to produce and showcase work, the Behance app has recently been joined by Adobe Portfolio as the company recognizes its legacy in the self-promotion market. Behance is a recognized and trusted platform for illustrators and helpfully allows images to be grouped together as projects.

It is therefore possible to show iterative stages of projects, including initial sketches, reference material, compositional development and final artwork in the same neat project space. This can be a good way of explaining your creative process if you are new, or useful if your approach to creating artwork has taken a new and exciting twist.

Pinterest

Launched in 2010, Pinterest is a social media platform that allows collections to be captured and curated on virtual pinboards. A sizeable proportion of its historical content is dedicated to fashion and lifestyle collections, where images from other parts of the internet can be pinned together. As the platform developed, visual creatives saw the possibilities

Figure 8.9
Janne Iivonen has a strong presence on Behance. Here, he tackles the perennial topical subject of preparing for changes to our climate for *The New York Times*. Iivonen's graphic style is well chosen to provide some clarity to this subject which has markedly different interpretations by some commentators.

Figure 8.10
Pinterest has become a favoured digital tool to collect and manage sources of inspiration, both for illustrators who are constantly looking for material to supplement their visual research, but also for commissioners of illustration. Having a dedicated archive of 'found' and 'interesting' illustrators is a valuable asset when matching a creative to an assignment, and for seeking out new talent for upcoming projects.

of collecting visual reference, inspiration and posting their own creations to subject-specific boards. In turn, these images were re-pinned to other users boards, including those of publishing houses and art directors and editors who formed their own collections of favourite illustrators.

The platform acts as a neat and convenient way to keep interesting images together and sort them into different collections by keyword search for ease of retrieval. For illustrators, if offers yet another shop widow to display online content and to give permission for work to be shared with interested parties.

Twitter

Primarily a social media platform for pithy and well-timed comment, Twitter developed visual content capabilities for posting images, GIFs and memes in 2017 At the same time, it raised its character count from 140 to 280 characters which some argue has reduced the creativity of posters to be inventive within the original 140-character limit. Twitter has become increasingly polarized in terms of followers and motives, but there is little doubt that as a barometer for political and social comment, it has an engaged following who value well-considered and thoughtful content. Using Twitter can expand the pool of recipients of your work globally with some dedicated, curated content and accompanying commentary.

There is an increasing school of thought that also sees Twitter as a largely self-fulfilling echo chamber of prophecy and that only like-minded followers see the content in your posts. If you are working with existing clients or have an established base of followers who know your work, then Twitter still represents a good medium to keep them abreast of your developments. If you are looking to Twitter to provide meaningful and constructive criticism of new approaches or developing new production methods, then take any resulting commentary with a large pinch of salt. Motivations for providing commentary vary massively, have inevitable cultural variance and are quite often taken out of original context. Fundamentally, your strategy should be to maintain the platform to support and develop your creative endeavour, not undermine your confidence by taking every last piece of criticism to heart.

Figure 8.11
Twitter has become a social media platform that illustrators use to promote work and stories about professional and personal ventures since static and sequential images were enabled. Illustration by Doug Chayka for *The New York Times*.

LinkedIn

The power of LinkedIn is more of a professional networking tool that enables users to maintain a serious industry presence. Its search engine capabilities are powerful, both in attracting interest and filtering out poor quality enquiries. LinkedIn uses front of stage tools such as posts to help illustrators publicize new work or provide commentary about content that is of professional interest to them. This creates a professional and public front which can be very useful in projecting an air of authority around your experience, interests and employment offer. LinkedIn groups offer chances to further these dialogues with like-minded professionals.

Private networking is more of a private backstage activity but is a massively useful tool in making vital connections with high-quality, respected potential clients and collaborators. The networking algorithms work overtime to ensure that connections that you may make beyond your field are relevant and considered – a far cry from the cold calling services that purported to represent illustrators' best interests in the past. New collaborators can lead to new opportunities for creating work in unison, especially if an illustrator can pair up with a coder, user interface designer or animator to genuinely expand the portfolio of skills to a wider user group.

Publishing presence

The publication of editorial illustration works themselves are an important form of self-promotion. Publishing etiquette would dictate that all illustrators, photographers and

Figure 8.12
British illustrator Andy Robert Davies cleverly combines a topical news story about the Covid-19 pandemic into a diagrammatic map, emphasizing the immediate threat of the virus on everyday life. The illustration accompanied an article titled 'Where the Streets Have No Name' for the *FT Weekend Magazine*, art directed by Namyoung An. Promoting work through LinkedIn ensures a professional tone and guarantees that the audience are invested in finding new talent, which is perhaps different to some of the more leisure-based social media platforms.

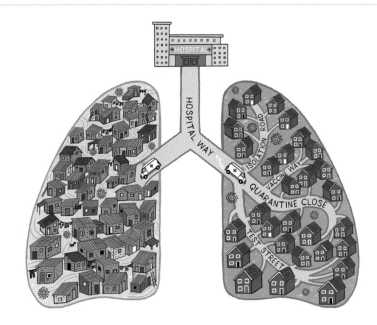

writers should be credited for the work that they have produced. Sadly, this is not always the case. Make sure this is part of the agreement that you have with a commissioner or publisher from the outset – it establishes a professional working practice and hopefully a mutual set of expectations. Some illustrators place a discreet credit in the image pane to ensure that their work is recognized.

There is little better self-publicity than published work. It demonstrates an acknowledgement of your professional quality output, your ability to work in a team dynamic and to have produced an outcome to a deadline successfully. Having work on the cover, an inside spread or website of a published newspaper, magazine or journal is tremendous free publicity. Illustrators see their work as an overall product of consumption, rather than a standalone image, and the work is often elevated in terms of quality by its contextualization and by the accompanying work that surrounds it. Many illustrators have enjoyed successfully riding off the publicity caused by another illustrator's work, and the company that your work keeps can elevate it to a position of visibility and assurance that it would not receive if published individually.

Collecting and utilizing this work needs to be part of the marketing strategy to generate new enquiries. In times past, illustrators might use these contextualized printed outputs in a

Figure 8.13
The best form of self-publicity is published work. Developing a visual language that easily translates between single and sequential images is increasingly required in modern editorial illustration as digital editions gain traction with readers. Malika Favre's clever silhouette illustration of Bob Dylan works as a striking static image, but has flexibility to be animated as a digital GIF too for *The New Yorker* online edition.

traditional portfolio as a way of convincing new clients to employ them. Printed images used in this way must be the very best quality possible. The arrival and adoption of social media allows a more creative and directed approach to be adopted, with bespoke product shots being captured on the illustration in situ, with the possibility of an accompanying sequential narrative as a post, or with a voiceover as an Instagram video story. In both instances, the production quality is again key to delivering the right message and tone of voice.

Illustration annuals

Self-promotion through annuals remains a contentious topic for illustrators, with questions arising about their effectiveness for generating work and their cost-effectiveness against other publicity routes. Digital resources have certainly helped propel this argument to another level, but there are some merits to printed annuals that allow them to retain their place in the self-promotion market. Some commissioners of illustration like the familiarity and reassurance of an annual that allows work to be printed as high-quality reproductions and has a presence on the book shelf.

Annuals fall into broadly two different types: the jury-selected competitive annual and the source annual catalogued index of contributors. The first is aspirational and highly valued by illustrators and clients alike. Publication in a substantially recognized annual like the *Society of Illustrators* (Society of Illustrators of New York), *American Illustration* or the *World Illustration Awards* (Association of Illustrators) is rightly recognized as a prestigious moment in an illustrators career. Inclusion is a feather in the cap that can generate much publicity and interest. The accompanying physical exhibition of works is a further chance for local commissioners to see the work, and annuals are moving to a position of having the substantial added benefit of an online archive of selected and chosen works that display quality works. Jury-selection by peers and industry professionals is a guarantor of quality to other commissioners of illustration. These annuals are extremely competitive to enter, but in terms of cost effectiveness, they offer the promise of lucrative commissions for relatively little outlay beyond entry and publication fees. They are also

proven to have a shelf life that sees commissions continue to roll in years after original publication, furthering their cost-effectiveness still further. Selecting the right images to beat the competition requires serious time and effort. Choose illustrations that you are proud of and will capture the type of future commissions you are looking for.

Figure 8.14
Illustrator Victo Ngai is much in demand for her beautiful conceptual illustrations and exquisite narrative sensibility. Her work has been consistently recognized by award juries including the Society of Illustrators, 3x3 and American Illustration. She was recognized as a Forbes 30 Under (Art and Style) honouree, showing her substantial impact beyond her discipline.

Indexed catalogue-style annuals use publication fees from contributors to fund production and dissemination of annuals to potential clients. Without editorial control over the quality of content, some images may not be to the same professional standard to others, so choose your publisher carefully. Equally, the distribution of annuals relies heavily on an up-to-date database on recipients who will commission work. Given the frequency that editorial commissioning roles change hands between organizations, maintaining a current database is a regular activity requiring consistent updating. Check that the annual has the capacity to do this. It is worth noting that whilst editorial job roles change, annuals have a lifespan that sees either the annual move to a new home of potential commissioning, or a new incumbent who can use the annual to seek new contributors. The broad scatter gun marketing approach can leave some illustrators feeling they have little accountability for where annuals are sent, but there is a counter argument to be made that recognizes that new clients can be reached through this method of publicity that the illustrator may not have reached previously. Another advantage of this type of annual are the run-on tear sheets of your individual published page which can be used for self-promotional activity.

Self-publishing

Creating self-published samples for potential clients can be a potential marketing route. This approach needs to be thought about with care and attention, both in terms of production values and when those pieces land on a client's desk for maximum exposure. There is definite merit to creating self-published marketing material, with the caveat that it must be well designed and produced. Clever, well-thought-out and desirable limited edition prints, or cards made as limited editioned boxed sets are well regarded and likely to catch an art director's eye. Some illustrators use self-publicity stickers or decorated envelopes to make their marketing stand out. Displaying the work in a carefully considered context with excellent production values, including legible contact details, is worth the time and effort needed to construct and disseminate these marketing products. The golden rule is that the material should lift the commissioners mood and create a 'feel-good' reaction.

Marketing gimmicks don't work, so it is best to avoid odd-sized samples or unusual folding mechanisms, as they have a propensity to be damaged. Similarly, samples that require construction are unlikely to be made due to time constraints. Seasonal-inspired cards and prints run the risk of mass competition from other creatives at points of the year such as Christmas, New Year and Easter. Avoiding these bottlenecks will pay dividends to at least getting the work seen in a receptive light.

Most illustrators have moved to an online system of sending work to clients, mindful of time constraints and limited space for recipients to store samples. Creating a miniature PDF portfolio is probably the most effective way of doing this, as this can be customized to the exact needs of particular clients. The PDF can be attached

Figure 8.15
Peter Allen is an illustrator who enjoys creating self-published projects that get his work seen by commissioners of illustration. *The Radio Times* has long been a supporter of editorial illustration, using imagery to adorn its covers, inside features and radio and television listings. Here, Allen produces an illustration to promote the BBC's 500 Word competition aimed at inspiring young creators to write a five-hundred-word story for publication and broadcast.

to an email which allows the illustrator to intro-duce themselves and explain the content of the attachment. It also offers opportunities to explain the approach, which may have been generated through working for a client through recommen-dation, or through a competitor.

A PDF portfolio can be generated with pre-existing page layouts that allow the work to be shown to the best possible degree. It is worth including details of title, date and medium together with some brief information about the illustration to help provide a context. Details of client and commissioner are also useful as a further reassurance about the authenticity and professionalism of the work. Some illustra-tors faintly watermark the images to safeguard against copyright issues, or lock the PDF with password protection.

The Commissioning Process

The best examples of editorial illustration are created by a successful partnership between the illustrator and their commissioning editor or art director. A common misconception is that editorial illustration is a solitary, lonely experience. Nearly every illustrator interviewed for this book or providing illustrations to accompany the text says the exact opposite. Whilst work may be produced and crafted independently, much of the initial exchange of ideas for approaching and dissecting the assignment are best achieved through dialogue. Successful work is often built on empathy and trust, gained over time and through the careful nurturing of ideas formed from interpretations of content. Many illustrators work with clients long after they have left one publication and in many instances, illustrators credit particular publications, art directors and editors as being pivotal to their professional success.

The process of finding the right illustrator for the right publication, or the right assignment, is therefore critical. Historically, the days of showing physical portfolios to commissioners of illustration are sadly diminishing through time and accessibility constraints, but where the practice remains, it should be cherished and valued. Other alternatives such as online meetings exist, but as we continually discover, reducing interaction to a digital visual and aural exchange misses the nuances of many meetings. In an increasingly global world, the professionalism shown in meeting clients, negotiating the details of the assignment and maintaining clear, consistent lines of communication can grow a creative business immensely and can lead to some surprising and pleasantly unexpected collaborations.

Figure 9.1
Illustrated political commentary on the Covid-19 pandemic has been instrumental in making the public aware of the debates and the conflicting viewpoints in the biggest universal story of our lifetime. Here, Edel Rodriguez illustrates the *Time* magazine cover in May 2020, suggesting that removing health-based restrictions on political grounds was unwise. Commissioning the right illustrator who can handle the pressure and convey the seriousness of content is crucial. Rodriguez has proven himself a reliable supplier of powerful visual criticism.

Fit and relevance

For fledgling illustrators starting out, editorial illustration offers terrific opportunities for exposure and for experiment. The trade-off between getting published work from a reputable source that can prove a professional ambition, and the risk of taking on someone untried and untested characterizes many experiences of contributors to this book. New exponents of editorial illustration are often still wrestling with the synergy and balance between their creative pursuits and forming this into a viable and desirable commercial offering. Doubts reside over how to approach clients, how commissions should be negotiated and accepted, how workflows should be handled

and how the relationship between the commissioner and creative can be developed into a meaningful partnership that can secure future work. These doubts do not necessarily diminish over time, but knowledge about how to manage them becomes more rounded and nuanced and a perspective emerges. Through the experience of making, publishing and adapting to feedback received about positively and negatively received work, a successful and sustainable career in the field is possible and worth pushing for.

Clearly, not every illustrator will be suitable for every assignment. Understanding the application of your work is a time-consuming and sometimes bewildering business and finding a truly objective vantage point is almost impossible. Having critical friends whose opinions you value can be very helpful, but trusting your own judgement is important as you look to navigate your way through your career. Finding your range, or frequency, is helpful in both targeting the work you want, but also creating boundaries about where your work does not fit. For example, if your illustrations are not witty or satirical in nature, then approaching newspapers or satirically orientated magazines is a waste of effort. If your images are more open and experimental in nature, it is unlikely that you will be commissioned to illustrate dense pockets of technical information as an illustrative cutaway piece of artwork.

These editorial application category boundaries themselves are blurred, hence using the term frequency to explain the scope of an illustrators potential fields of expertise. Editorial illustration is a broad church and welcomes new, diverse and experimental approaches to generating interest in content through unorthodox means, so fit and relevance to particular assignments should be viewed as an evolving process. As we see an increase in digital publishing, it is inevitable that more illustrators will want to see how their work can either move or work across narrative or ideological sequences, so future fit and relevance will automatically need to be questioned and adjusted.

Having successfully commissioned work in a portfolio breeds confidence and generates a hunger for more opportunities and challenges. A published set of editorial illustrations shows an illustrator that they have marketable and desirable products that are competitive and appealing, through a process of gaining trust with commissioners who have seen the possibilities and benefits of using their work to communicate, entertain or inform readerships. Commissioned work goes some way to dispel personal doubts about whether an illustrator feels good enough about their collective output. A significant part of the creative process hinges on confidence in one's own ability to perform, and editorial illustration acts as a good barometer. It shows how the illustrator is able to respond to time constraints and professional pressures of quality and reliability to produce solutions that are of consistent publishable quality. From a commissioner's perspective, trustworthy output and clear communication channels are the two attributes that are consistently raised as key skills for new editorial illustrators to possess, exhibit and develop in these fledgling relationships.

Figure 9.2
David Hughes's acerbic wit is evident in this illustration of Sylvester Stalone for *The Times*. Stallone's desire to be seen as a serious actor provides the perfect invitation for Hughes's anarchic genius to be triggered with his trademark rapier-like pen and ink graphic language emphasizing his cutting cynicism.

Figure 9.3
Illustrator Jianan Liu's highly decorative illustration is a playful, engaging accompaniment to an article about cultural capital(ism) for *IPPR Progressive Review*. Here the brief demanded a more upbeat and light-hearted interpretation of the text by Liu. The dense composition and vibrant colour palette leap off the page, bringing an information-heavy article to life for the reader.

Meeting the client

Approaching prospective clients can be daunt-ing experience, forcing issues of self-confidence about work and contributing to possible low self-esteem that the illustrator may feel when describing their work. The thoughtful preparation of work for viewing by a client can do wonders for making the illustrator feel more confident about how to strategically approach how they present work. Show work that you feel proud of and can talk knowledgeably about. This might include details of how it was made and under what particular working conditions. If the work was produced to a tight deadline, or to an exacting brief, then it is wise to use this information to contextualize your output.

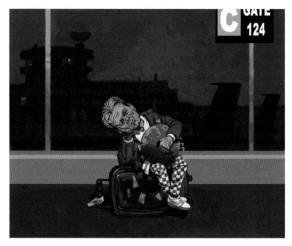

Figure 9.5
Paul Slater is a master of characterizing famous faces and parodying their situations with a satirical sense of humour. Here, his target is celebrity chef Gordon Ramsey's new restaurant Pétrus, for a restaurant review column authored by critic Giles Coren in *The Times*. Slater has proven himself the perfect choice for food review illustrations, with his summative illustrations often acting as a palatable way of disguising – or amplifying – the food critic's findings.

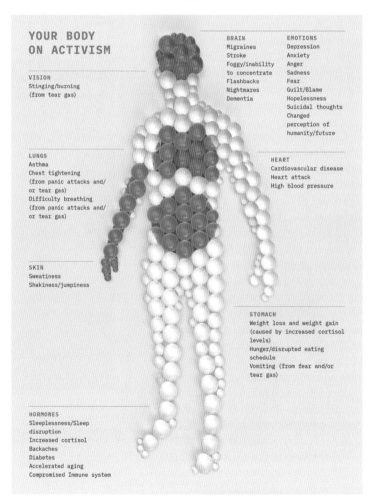

Figure 9.4
A diagrammatic approach to explaining an article about the effects of activism on the human body, created by Simoul Alva for American news aggregator, *HuffPost* (formerly *The Huffington Post*).

Figure 9.7
Conjuring up impressions of locations and experiences is a central use of editorial illustration in some lifestyle sections of weekend newspaper supplements and magazines, allowing readers to allow their imagination to drift and place themselves in inviting situations and memorable moments. This expressive illustration by Christopher Corr is full of energy and vibrancy, attributed to many hours of observing and recording in his sketchbook.

Figure 9.6
Brian Stauffer uses a mixture of hand-drawn and computer-generated imagery to create impactful visual responses to highly charged subjects, such as gay rights, prison reform and political interference. His illustration 'Patriot Predator' for the *Phoenix New Times* shows how his economical use of simple, shape-based motifs combined with strong, graphic editing can create an immediate and impactful journalistic voice to publications.

Figure 9.8
Ben Challenor creates collaged illustrations that create a mood or atmosphere, using visual elements set in compatibility with, or opposition to, other subject matter to force the reader to interpret and engage. This ambiguity is well commissioned in this piece on farming for *The Sunday Times*.

Figure 9.9
The economy and expressiveness of Joe Ciardiello's line use makes him a popular illustrator who can turn assignments around quickly but always delivers on quality insights of his subjects.

Similarly, if the work was created and then modified through changes requested by the client, that information suggests that you are open-minded to receiving suggestions to improve the communicative quality of the work. By contrast, work that doesn't live up to the standards you have set yourself should be omitted. Trying to defend a piece of work in your portfolio when you are unsure of its merits places doubt in the mind of a commissioner and can harm the professional demeanour you are building. On occasion, this might be the final artwork that has been created, or it might be the design of the page that the illustration appears on. If the former, then you can resurrect the final artwork as a standalone piece of illustration in its own right, provided that you feel confident describing its merits. Presentation skills require constant practice. Getting used to seeing your work from the objective position of a client or commissioner requires preparation, so practise by experimenting with different layouts in an analogue portfolio, or on your website or through designing a custom-built PDF. Practicing verbalizing the reasons behind why the illustration was executed in a particular way can also show clients that you are in command of a brief and are brimming with ideas.

Hi Fei,

Thank you for your sketch. We'll keep it for a next cover for Monsieur, maybe for September issue.

Because now the issue has a little bit evolved, the main theme is **well-being**, more than shoes finally. Good in body, good in mind. Move, eat better, sleep well, green life, nature, zen spirit. There, some key words.

Hope it will inspire you !

Have a nice afternoon

Thu-Huyen Hoang
Monsieur / Montres Magazine
Directrice Artistique

Figure 9.10
A typical example of an editorial brief received by Fei Wang, the illustrator known as Mr Slowboy. The brief for the cover of Monocle magazine is loose due to a prior working relationship between illustrator and art director, with room for interpretation by the illustrator.

Taking the assignment

Editorial illustration assignments are notorious for changing shape due to the fluid nature of a busy newsroom or editorial content being regularly updated. The illustrator needs to be flexible and accommodating to adapt to these shifts, but there are some common ground rules that determine a briefing, and the illustrator should be alert to asking for this information at the point of initial enquiry. Some assignments are formulated and written in advance, but increasingly through a digitally based editorial office, many are emailed or phoned through to the illustrator to save time. It is entirely routine, although not necessarily desirable, to be sent the body copy of an article as 'the assignment' and be asked to interpret it. Some illustrators enjoy the freedom and spontaneity of this approach, whilst others understandably want more clarity and direction to understand the feel and nature of the accompanying written content. The golden rule is to ask the right questions from the outset and use a friendly but professional approach which builds confidence and trust between commissioner and creative.

Firstly, the practical elements should be established:

What size and resolution are the required illustration?
Where will it be placed – on the page or screen?
What is the deadline for rough sketch or visual for approval?
What is the deadline for artwork?
What is the fee?

Size dimensions are supplied in horizontal and vertical measurements. Historically, the horizontal measurement is supplied first, followed by the vertical, but it is always best to check whether the orientation is portrait or landscape with the commissioner. Illustrations can be made in proportion, or 'in pro', to the final size. Some illustrators prefer to work in proportion by scaling up their artwork for practical media handling reasons, so that it will look crisper and sharper when reduced to published size.

Illustrations need to conform to particular resolution sizes for print and digital publishing. A printed version of artwork will normally be 300dpi (dots per inch) to maintain visual clarity through the printing process. An illustration for a digital online platform can be reproduced at 72dpi. If this information has not be supplied, then clarify with the commissioner before proceeding. Publications with print and digital platforms often want higher resolution artwork so that they can scale to suit the platform. Some illustrators like to send locked digital files so that certain actions like cropping or more savage edits can be prevented. Due to the fluid nature of the editorial spread, it is better to send unlocked files and to try and build a more positive rapport between creator and commissioner that sees them respect the artwork as being crafted for a particular space. Many illustrators have taken issue in the past with designers who have slapped headlines over part of their image, or who have laid artwork out in a manner which is unsympathetic to the work that has been created, but for the most part, good will to try and produce the most effective pieces of communication is a shared aim between illustrators and their commissioners.

Deadlines in editorial illustration are tight, with little room for manoeuvre. Always ask for the deadline for initial sketches to show an idea, as well as when final artwork will be required. It is fundamental that the illustrator understands their working practice enough to know if they can manage a job in the allotted time. For example, some broadsheet newspapers have been known to commission jobs that have a 24-hour turnaround. Such commissions are reserved for illustrators who have a track record of proving themselves to be capable of turning in quality work to such exacting deadlines. Most editorial illustration commissions are spread over days or a week, sometimes longer, but rarely extend beyond two weeks. Editorial illustrators normally have honed their creative approach to take account of both production capability and financial reimbursement.

Figure 9.11
The front cover of the *FT Weekend Magazine* by Janne Iivonen, with accompanying internal illustrations, takes a humorous look at why major corporations struggle to embrace new opportunities and leave gaps for pushy start-ups to occupy, for an article titled 'Why Good Ideas get Stuck' by Tim Harford. Iivonen's simplified graphic style creates the blueprint for how the article headline and typographic grid are handled by the editorial designers.

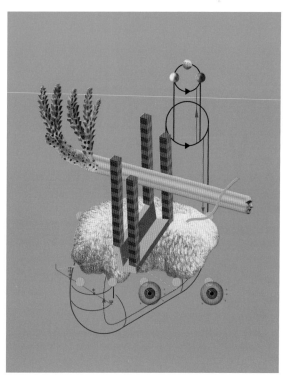

Figure 9.12
Matthew Richardson's illustration 'No Narrative' for the Association of Illustrators' *Varoom Magazine* shows his clear interest in Folk Art representation, forged out of a perpetual interest in collecting postcards, curios and knick-knacks to aid his playful working process.

Fees in editorial illustration vary greatly. Whilst it is certainly true that illustrators working in advertising command much higher fees, some editorial illustration jobs can be prestigious and well rewarded. Equally they can be frugal. Much coverage has been devoted to stagnation of illustration fees in general, and this has disproportionately centred on editorial illustration in recent decades. Some of this scrutiny is well justified because factual information exists to support the argument that fees have not kept in line with inflation, or of that with similarly intellectually crafted products such as photography. By contrast, fees for advertising jobs have been more elusive to pin down, partly due to a lack of transparency in the commissioning process and the reluctance of agents of advertising clients to disclose the full disposable budget for these types of jobs.

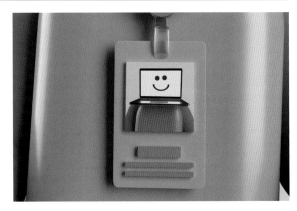

Figure 9.13
Editorial illustration is often used as a reflective pause in an ongoing debate. Here, Simoul Ava's illustration for an article about not being defined by job title, but rather for personal principles and beliefs, needs to balance a generic, welcoming approach for readers from different backgrounds and identities against a sense of being able to determine individual paths. Commissioned by *The New York Times*.

Figure 9.14a–b
Serge Bloch is commissioned by *The Boston Globe* to illustrate articles that on one level are serious, topical issues where there are polarized views. His visual approach is chosen to ease readers into the article and be more accepting of the content to see the opposing point of view in context.

Since at least the arrival of digital production and dissemination processes, editorial illustration has had to deal with some fairly substantial and unprecedented changes to the professional operating landscape. Issues such as digital paywalls, stock illustration and the thorny, persistent problem of creator rights and the licensing and ownership of artwork have dogged some of the development of the field and made the process of fair and reasonable negotiation difficult. Publishers needing financial returns on their product have constructed paywalls for digital content which has directly affected suppliers and compressed fees. Stock illustration can be re-licensed by agencies, or direct through some illustrators, and undercuts the value and appeal of custom-made illustrations for specific content. Licensing and ownership can appear to be a minefield for the independent illustrator when faced with the might of a multinational publishing media group. This sense of scale of issues to the relative impact an individual illustrator can make is a cause that has been championed by organizations such as the Association of Illustrators (AOI) and the Illustrators Partnership of America (IPA) looking to turn the tide and represent a coherent, combined creators voice.

Some of the issues can be attributed to major shifts in working conditions resulting from increasingly digital workflows. The perceived efficiency of digital communication, production and dissemination has squeezed production and resulted in shorter deadlines. The suppression of fees is also partially an economic response to an increased supply and demand for work. Editorial illustration has historically been an entry point for young creatives aiming to carve a professional career and who are prepared to work for reduced

Figure 9.15
Illustration is often commissioned for subjects where empathy and compassion are required in support of an editorial article. In this instance, Eva Bee uses a mixture of realism and symbolism to foreground the danger of child abduction. Commissioned by *The Observer Life & Style Magazine*.

fees to secure published outcomes to build a portfolio. But there is still high regard for professionals at the top of their game and publishers will pay for brand recognition and exposure with strong editorial content. Additionally, new digital publishing streams demand a diversity of content and greater innovation both in terms of how illustrations are technically produced and presented, and how they are cognitively received. In this spirit, editorial illustration has a healthy and bright future.

Creative Environments

Creating the right environment to produce professional work is essential. Offering a checklist of what that would entail for each illustrator would be impractical. By definition, illustrators are highly individualistic in their interests, output and environments and their needs differ greatly.

This section instead highlights considerations that should be taken into account when making choices about the right environment for you to successfully operate in, specifically the physical environment, and then considering essential analogue and digital tools to make great work and build your professional standing.

Physical environments

A solid physical environment is an absolute priority for working professionally. Most illustrators contributing to this book try to keep their professional practice separate from their private lives, and a designated studio space to work in is a clear preference. Having control over work and leisure time is increasingly important. Recent events have taught us to be grateful for working spaces but have also highlighted operational problems that perhaps force us to view our surroundings differently. A studio space that is demarcated as a distinct working area with control over light and sound is worth hunting for and investing in. Some illustrators like having this as part of their domestic environment for flexibility and easy access. Others prefer to commute to work away from their homes as part of their professional discipline, and as a way of leaving work physically and mentally behind when they return.

Solo occupation of a studio obviously brings control and peace of mind around things like setting a professional working environment free from noise pollution, other people's annoying habits and access arrangements. A single occupancy space means control without compromise. Spaces can be set up to benefit the individual including location and size of desk, layout of studio equipment, storage options and optimum heating and lighting conditions. There is no queue for any shared facility, nor any fight over internet bandwidth. Phone calls can be made and received in peace and confidential discussions about fees and licensing of artwork can discreetly happen without interference. There is clear accountability for time spent on projects and the cost of utilities needed to support production and dissemination of artwork.

Other illustrators prefer to share a space that brings comradery, shared facilities and a creative buzz. They are willing to sacrifice their personal requirements for the sake of the creative endeavours of the whole group sharing the space. Much of these considerations depend on personal idiosyncrasies, but factor in financial

Figure 10.1
Inspiring surroundings can help trigger ideas, encourage new approaches and act as reminders of quality output in creative spaces. Michelle Thompson's studio is a treasure trove of finds sourced from all over the world.

considerations and personal mental well-being and the outlook may alter considerably from an individual perspective. Sharing a studio space can help develop talent, create important networks and pool together money for more targeted and professionally produced marketing campaigns. Using the residual knowledge of shared studio inhabitants can also open new opportunities for collaborations, learning new skills, experimenting with creative processes and getting constructive, critical feedback. Higher-quality equipment, such as iMacs with larger screens, drawing tablets or digital cameras with high-quality lenses and professional lighting, are less burdensome if shared amongst the working studio of professionals. New equipment such as high quality 3D printers and video production equipment may be within the reach of a group with combined purchasing power and some will open these facilities to individual creatives for a fee. The rule of thumb is to invest in the very best environment and equipment you can afford – this is your livelihood. Your working set-up needs to feel welcoming, comfortable and capable of sustaining you for long periods of time for your productivity and well-being.

An illustrator's studio desk needs to be chosen dependent on the type of work they produce. Historically, that may have comprised a tilting, cantilevered drawing table, but more contemporary set-ups need space for both analogue and digital production. As such, a desk that is deep and wide enough to support flexible working is probably the most sensible choice. Having space to work on jobs simultaneously is advantageous and creating dedicated space for practical and electronic production means that activities can be kept separate. Good lighting sources are a must when analogue working, so consideration should be given to installing daylight simulation bulbs or halogen spots that deliver cool tones to working environments to aid productivity, no matter what time of day. It is advisable to plan where cabling will go to minimize any trip hazards and maintain safe working conditions. Digital production also needs plentiful electrical supply so always have more sockets at your disposal than you need. Be mindful to bunch cabling together to keep power supplies neat and tidy, but do not overload the local supply in case of fire. Some companies will offer PAT testing for a small fee which gives great peace of mind and can be required by some insurers.

Labelling cables is always good practice so that no supply is adversely disrupted by being disconnected suddenly. Ensure that your working position is set away from any monitors, at a height and distance that is comfortable and does not place any strain on eyes or body posture after extended use.

Many illustrators who have contributed have reported adopting a workflow throughout the day where they force themselves to move around their studio spaces for their physical and mental health. Ergonomically informed production space will differ from a communication or accountancy space as a way of helping complete the particular task in hand. Some illustrators prefer to stand at a desk to work, whilst others need to sit. Being active within the workspace is good practice – if nothing else, a change of scenery keeps the mind and body active and forces a different perspective. To encourage this type of working, considering places to work, rest and relax is important when planning a studio space and a choice of chairs should be considered. Making an investment in ergonomically designed desk chairs is well worth it, as they can last many years if well cared for and maintained. A height-adjustable chair with lumbar support is ideal. Choosing a mesh fabric will allow air flow in summer and can be covered with a blanket in winter to provide extra warmth. Many of these chairs have a swivel and tilt mechanism that can see them double up as a more comfortable chair, especially if on castors, which allows them to be moved near a window or a quiet corner. Other fixed chairs can offer alternative working or relaxing possibilities and choosing a stackable design saves on space if you need to entertain clients or work collaboratively. If you can fit it in, a small sofa or easy chair is a great place to take a well-earned break, get inspiration from the bookshelf or social media, or mentally map out what's next.

Analogue tools

All illustrators use analogue tools at some point in their creative journey. Through the educational development, trial and error or recommendation, an illustrator's studio is a treasure trove of surfaces, preparation and production tools and presentation materials. Paper, card, boards and grounds come in a myriad of weights, thicknesses, colours and finishes. Studio equipment including pencils, pens, brushes, palettes, scissors, knives,

Figure 10.2a–d
A professional studio space should be inviting, comfortable and organized. Not everyone can afford a dedicated studio, but scaling a space to your needs and ensuring that it is maintained will create the necessary environment to make professional level work. This beautiful space, complete with large trestle table, plentiful storage and amazing natural light is home to British illustrator, Michelle Thompson and graphic designer, Gareth Wild.

cutting mats and glues are offered to suit every need and budget. Mediums such as paints, pastels and inks offer well-developed and tested shades and hues that cater for every eventuality an illustrator could come across, segmented by factors such as professional quality of pigments used, their coverage and capabilities of remaining lightfast for archival purposes. Portfolios, sleeves and mounts are offered in variety of styles, sizes and finishes, again dependent on budget and quality of materials used to ensure years of service and performance.

Analogue suppliers have a tough job competing as physical store locations as they are expected to hold a wide variety of stock for the discerning customer, but operate with little wriggle room on overheads offering merchandise that is already expensive from the manufacturer. Margins are tight, but nothing can compete with the experience of shopping for studio supplies

at stores like Blick in New York City or Tokyo Hands in Shinjuku which have floor upon floor of high-end equipment for even the most discerning customer. The alternative to this model of practice is the online material suppliers who offer quality stock, a sympathetic – if somewhat complicated – browsing experience, compensated by ease of payment options and the speedy delivery of purchases. The physical experience certainly wins out if you want to try materials before you buy. No YouTube video can ever compensate for being able to get your hands on equipment firsthand. However, not everyone has access to larger suppliers and so online offers the convenience and guarantee of quality equipment regardless of how isolated a delivery location is. This factor has allowed illustrators to work in areas that are non-metropolitan, greatly increasing lifestyle options whilst maintaining quality clients.

Figure 10.3
David Hughes' love of etching is apparent in this satirical portrait of singer, songwriter and musician Hank Williams, where the subject's features are almost carved and scored into the surface. The tactility of Hughes' ground and material choices are a hallmark of his work and testament to hours of painstaking drawing to develop a highly personalized visual language that is instantly recognizable.

Figure 10.4
Caroline Tomlinson's impressionistic illustration for *Geo Magazine* shows the freedom and frivolity of skaters in New York City's Central Park evoking the sensibility of reportage immediacy while illustrating leisure possibilities in a large city. Created using fluid ink and wash, the illustration also has elements such as the figure skaters that need to be capable of being animated. These considerations can often affect the choice of production materials and visual language approach adopted.

Figure 10.5
British illustrator Christopher
Corr's work is well suited to
lifestyle editorial illustration
assignments like this enticing
travel map of Europe. Corr
works in a painterly graphic
language that is seductively
evocative and emotionally
charged. His colour palette
here is distinctive and used
to enhance the political
geography need to delineate
countries in this kind of work.

The rule of thumb about buying materials and equipment lies in investing in what you can afford for the long term. Well-considered, researched decisions will reward you for many years and will maintain their quality if well cared for and valued accordingly.

Digital tools

Investing in digital tools is a complex business, made more pressurized by choice of brands, products and suppliers, and the continued technological advancements in both hardware and software over the last two decades. Unlike the advice to invest in quality analogue equipment, one of the key decisions with digital tools is whether to make large-scale purchases, or possibly look at alternative financing plans such as leasing. Flexibility can often compensate for technical advances and ensures that obsolete equipment doesn't end up cluttering up storage spaces. However, flexibility costs and many prefer to see the fruits of their labour in tangible assets that can be offset against taxable expenses. Many hardware and software companies offer new versions of their products, so peripherals can be traded for later models and software can be updated for the latest versions to work seamlessly with operating systems. Decisions need to follow work you are already making but should consider work you would like to make in the future as investing in your future is a key decision point in

planning around core digital tools: a computer, tablet, mobile phone and external peripherals such as scanners, cameras and printers.

The decision about whether to choose a desktop computer, laptop or tablet is somewhat reliant on established or developing working environment choices. Options around brand, size of processor, memory, screen size and connectivity become prominent considerations dependent on need and budget. Working on a desktop affords the possibility of running simultaneous displays which can massively aid productivity as many windows can be kept open to toggle between jobs. A laptop or tablet offers more flexibility if you need more portability, with the latter able to function as a drawing surface with a stylus. Many illustrators have more than one device, encompassing the production and presentation of work, so compatibility for these devices to connect and function is an important consideration. For example, Apple's Sidecar functionality allows an iPad to be used as a second screen that can house palettes, clearing more space for the digital surface on a main screen, and also offering both fixed and flexible work options. A tablet can show web-based work if you are called into a presentation meeting, so fulfilling the function previously performed by a traditional portfolio can be covered using this approach.

Many illustrators need the option of image-grabbing peripherals, so scanners, cameras and tablets or phones with cameras are also important considerations. The scanner is a versatile piece of kit that can get heavily used, especially where hand-drawn or montaged works are being made and then translated into digital assets. An A3 scanner offers the best flexibility if you have space for it and consider one made by one of the brands associated with photography and imaging as the technology will be more robust. Clean the glass surface with a lint-free cloth to prevent scratches and unsightly marks. Many scanners connect smartly to your core device through Wi-Fi which removes the need for cabling.

Increasingly, illustrators are seeing the advantage of having a more flexible set-up and a digital SLR camera with interchangeable lenses offers many options and has the distinct advantage of being portable. It therefore earns it stripes as being an important production and post-production tool, allowing images to be captured as direct or indirect reference as well as recording professional quality copies

of artwork, and even capturing content for all-important social media posts. Many DSLR cameras have video capability too, so the realm of videos, vlogs and images that can be manipulated into motion becomes a distinct and attractive possibility. Most illustrators invest in the best camera body they can, and then build up a collection of lenses and lighting as they can afford to do so. There is a strong second-hand market for quality DSLR lenses, so expect to upgrade as needed and don't be put off by purchasing second-ownership lenses which will be entirely serviceable at a fraction of the price of a new model. A good quality tripod, together with height and direction-adjustable LED lighting, complete a professional set-up.

Over the last few years, the technology harnessed within phones and tablets for taking pictures has seen significant advances, to the point where lower-end digital cameras have been largely replaced by smaller, more powerful devices that can take exceptional images and

Figure.10.6a–d
This series of portraits for *CN Traveler* created by Lucy Truman break the conventions of portrait photography by disabling the forensic examination of the subject that real-life likeness can permit, and instead creating a more relaxed mood for the readers expecting a sense of freedom and escapism from the publication. Although seemingly analogue in appearance, they are created digitally but retain their sensitive drawn roots by being created on a tablet. This series includes portraits of Jenny Han, Jermaine Clement, Lupita Nyongo and Rosario Dawson.

Figure 10.7
Simoul Alva's illustration style has a versatility and adaptability that makes it eminently suitable for accompanying lifestyle articles where readers are encouraged to reflect on their own experiences by projecting themselves into the space that is created between an article and the illustration. Creating this space for pause, reflection and accustomization is one of the key benefits of using illustration over photography. This illustration is titled '5 Ways to Get Structure Back Into Your Kids' Lives' for *The New York Times*.

also disseminate them in a matter of seconds. Many illustrators use the high-definition functionality to collect research material, photograph items of inspirational interest and even use images as part of their production process by digitally manipulating source material through programmes such as Photoshop. The power to literally point and shoot at high-enough resolution to be capable of reproduction is an amazing asset and informs every stage of an illustrator's pre-production and production process. Of course, it still functions as a communication device, so having the flexibility of receiving commissions when on the move, or talking through projects or posting in progress work through social media channels are routine operations for smart phones and cellular-enabled tablets.

Peripheral devices such as external hard drives complete the essential digital tools an illustrator should consider. Technology is evolving to the extent that we still don't know whether archived work saved on devices will be retrievable in the future but having a strategy of back-up at least offers some peace of mind and accountability. Many illustrators archive work using a cloud internet service to back-up work, as part of a package supplied by a broadband supplier, but will also use external hard drives as a secondary means of back-up to ensure their work is recorded and preserved. Portable drives with rubber bumpers are a good option if you need the flexibility and can be a godsend if one is

accidentally dropped on the ground. Most reputable manufacturers include a service for retrieving files if a hard drive fails as part of the retail price of the item. Try to purchase the biggest amount of memory you can afford and keep your hard drive in a dry, cool position for optimum performance. Backing-up work is a routine many find tedious, but it is a necessary part of the day-to-day administrative side of running a professional creative business.

In researching this book, the one item of equipment that is quickly becoming obsolete is the desktop printer. Once a staple of illustration studios, increased digital workflow in both production and presentation of artwork, and indeed the electronic filing of invoices and contracts, has rather consigned the printer to the margins of studio life. General concerns over the environmental cost of printers and local recycling difficulties of sustainably managing the correct disposal of printer cartridges are inevitably factors too. In an editorial illustration workflow, the printer was never needed to print artwork, but some illustrators used them as an integral part of their production process, or perhaps printed samples for clients. A desktop printer will never match an industrial printer in terms of quality which is where most illustrators would turn if needing promotional material, but as discussed previously, the preference from most contributors is to produce and send this material digitally now.

Visual Research

Engaging in visual research is one of the most enjoyable and rewarding parts of the job of being an editorial illustrator. Successful visual research can be liberating, intoxicating and engulfing, by designing a journey of discovery that is often as unique and personalized as the resulting artwork itself. It is the athlete's equivalent of working out in the gymnasium, or the chef's experiments with ingredients in the kitchen. Both of those analogies point to the participant exercising discipline, patience and perseverance. These qualities also define successful editorial illustrators, but how is it possible to design such a journey against the short deadlines of editorial artwork production?

The key message about the collection of visual research is that it should be seen more as a professional undertaking that cements your credibility as a creative practitioner, forged over a career that espouses your values of originality and authenticity. Taking in gallery shows, collecting ephemera and immersing yourself in quality cultural outputs can all provide a nutritious diet of inspiration. But they are undertaken alongside the day-to-day graft of taking commissions, working through assignments and delivering artwork to deadlines. Visual research collections need rationalizing, sorting and cataloguing into useable frameworks. Creating such frameworks allow models of developmental practice that utilize what you have found in answering assignments with regularity and consistency. At the same time the experience will be stored in your memory of experiences, to be drawn upon in the future when another tricky assignment comes in. Being able to dig deep when times are tough, or finding inspiration from unexpected and seemingly incongruous ingredients are where the visual research process can piece clues together to give unexpected results. Other illustrators prefer to visually research and develop digitally, working on screen over visual notes that they have scanned or photographed. Using digital tools to drop in colour to versions of ideas, or trying multiple crops to amplify an idea through compositional changes is seen as an organic and time-saving process and again has the advantage of being portable if undertaken on a laptop or tablet.

The visual research collection and recording process is unique and highly personalized for each illustrator. It forms the very DNA of their professional work output. Being observant, responding and recording what you see, think, hear, say and feel are all legitimate and necessary responses to subject matter. In some instances, recording could take the form of writing or doodling lists of words, phrases and terms that encompass a subject. Illustrators brainstorm ideas using spider diagrams to link these segments of visual research to form ideas that are often translated into no more than a small box with doodles, scribbles or an economy of lines to represent the seed of an idea. This process is repeated again and again, building up content both conceptually by adding or taking away corresponding ideas, continually testing out whether the essence of the idea communicates the essence of the assignment. The independence and autonomy of visual research is further enhanced by the illustrator's choice about where these experiments are recorded. Some illustrators work in physical journals that allow portability, drawing, doodling, annotation and sticking down text, image and found objects. This process fuels further thoughts and ideas and the journals take on an important role as an experimental laboratory but also as a chronological historical record of a developing and maturing practice. Other illustrators choose to work at a larger scale on worksheets that allow them to see the ebb and flow of their ideas emerge across an expansive surface, finding a journal too restrictive and repetitive in scale.

Depending on the type of work produced, the visual research process will also begin to consider what specific information is needed to construct the illustration. If the illustrator creates work realistically then reference for subject matter must form part of that research collection. For example, it will

Figure 11.1
Editorial illustration can be used to visualize subjects that are goals or aspirations, allowing the reader to decode visual information through cerebral connections to their own goals or aspirations. Illustration by Lucy Truman titled 'Book of Dreams' for the Stylemaker section of the US *Better Homes and Gardens* magazine.

Getting underway

There are many routes that illustrators take to begin an assignment. Broadly, research for this book reveals that the majority follow the principle of reading the article, researching the content contextually and continually revising their ideas in correspondence with the commissioner. With new clients, understanding the ethos and philosophy of the publication is important. What are they driving at and what are their stated ideals? What is the publisher's ethos and philosophy? With existing clients, much of that inner knowledge and experience will have been garnered from previous jobs.

Understanding the audience profile is important as many publications have a loyal and ardent readership. Indeed, subscribers become an intrinsic part of a publisher's financial considerations. This context should help form a valuable part of initial discussions with the commissioner and prove that you have an awareness of who you are illustrating for. This flow of information helps discuss initial ideas that arise out of reading the article and mapping it against a wider contextual

be necessary to solve how key actions happening in a static or sequence are articulated for the reader. How faces, hands and body positioning of figures in relation to their environment or other figures and objects must become part of the narrative strategy. If the illustrator uses collage as their production method, collecting source materials that are relevant and empathetic to the subject is a central part of visual research collection and analysis at this point. These examples reinforce the notion that visual research collection is a continuum that occupies much time in an editorial illustrator's existence. You never know when an observation, an idea or a visual solution in the form of a colour sketch, dynamic composition or media experiment will come in useful for future projects.

Figure 11.2
The evolution of ideas for the Fox News article illustrated by Frazer Hudson for *The Guardian*.

Figure 11.3
This illustration for *The Guardian* newspaper by Frazer Hudson is based on an article about Fox News being thwarted from expansion of its UK market base. Hudson takes his inspiration from Sky dishes littered across the urban landscape and reimagines them as the base for the foxes face, a take on urban foxes being a blight on the landscape in some people's eyes, but more fundamentally a social comment on our media landscape being swamped by unscrupulous subscription broadcasting.

understanding of the subject at large. Spend time finding this information out as it will reap dividends later in the process.

Gathering research

With the brief agreed and the collaborative working principles established between commissioner and illustrator, the process of gathering research material can begin in earnest. Many illustrators like to surround and immerse themselves with research material, and certainly visual prompts can aid further discussion with the commissioner. In some instances, publishers may send examples of screenshots or attachments of visual research material that they think will be useful for consideration in the development of the illustration. It is also not unheard of for licensed visual assets to be sent for the illustrator to incorporate into some assignments, particularly if they work using a collage or assemblage-based process.

Researching subject matter is a very enjoyable part of the job for many editorial illustrators;

Figure 11.4a–c
Mr Slowboy's development sketches for the cover of Monocle magazine are created quickly, mapping out the essence of the illustration as briefed, rather than dwelling on precise details which will come later into the development process.

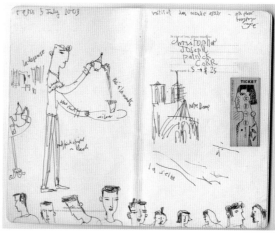

Figure 11.5

These range of visual notes, rough sketches, preparatory drawings and colour notes by Christopher Corr show the intensity and energy created by working under pressure to observe and record situations, play with ideas and develop content. Often recorded under time pressure, and often in locations away from studio comforts, his visual language is immediate, incisive and direct. This is achieved through continual application to sharpening his ideas and developing his editing skills about what to include as vital information in an image, and what to extract as being superfluous visual clutter.

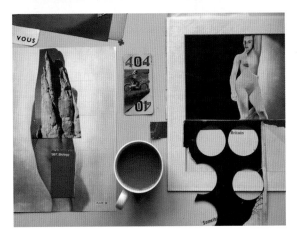

Figure 11.6a–e
Michelle Thompson's working process involves sourcing, cutting, scanning and assembling pictorial elements through collage and assemblage in Photoshop. Having a vast source of material is a necessity – finds from bookshops, car boot sales and flea markets are all valuable hunting grounds in the process of collecting ephemera that will form the basis of successful illustrations.

Figure 11.7

An avid watcher of people, Lucy Truman takes a tablet on vacation to make location drawings of observations on her travels. These visuals often inform her developmental work, allowing her to work out figurative postures, compositional placement and how to integrate subjects into environments. This hybridized way of working has been developed from analogue sketchbooks onto digital screen which allows portability on location, and transferable resources back in the studio.

the intellectual challenge is what many thrive on to produce high-quality work. Sorting and synthesizing research into useable commodities to help generate concepts and ideas is a selective process that places the illustrator at the heart of triangulating the needs of publisher, creative and reader. Having a working method that manages this process in a tidy and accessible format will pay huge dividends in being efficient and professional. Editorial illustrators are usually working on multiple jobs with overlapping stages and deadlines, so having job bags or folders to collect research material is a necessity. A research management system, whether labelled alphabetically, numerically or colour-coded, is time well spent when you have an exacting deadline to meet.

Be wary of how you collect research source material – Google image search may provide visual suggestions to a search term, but it doesn't provide answers! Varying your research process to collect visual ephemera or firsthand research material can prove rewarding as a way of keeping creative work fresh and inspired. Allocating time to peruse bookshops, flea markets and charity shops can also turn up surprising finds, but this is not always possible in the spur of the moment during a busy editorial commission. Planning

research trips to supplement your personal visual library is one of the best things about being a visual creative and a very therapeutic way of investing back into your creative career at relatively little cost. Set aside a specific time for research where you will be focused, uninterrupted and alert and, if necessary, set yourself a timer so that you can keep workflow efficient.

For editorial illustrators beginning their careers, it is very important to be aware of visual plagiarism. Knowingly stealing or borrowing another illustrator's work, or incorporating elements where you do not have permission from the original creator, is likely to cause problems regarding infringement of the copyright laws of the country you are working in. Serious infringements can result in criminal proceedings, fines and severe damage to a creator's career. Whilst illustrative ideas themselves are not copyrighted, their interpretation and manifestation into original artworks are. Having work stolen is a horrible experience for those who have suffered such occurrences and the effort required to chase down, accuse and seek justice for infringements is arduous and frustrating. Illustrators, as can be seen by the multitude of examples in this book, produce visual outputs that are immediately recognizable and attributable by other practitioners and in many cases by the wider media-consuming public. With many illustrators enjoying greater global exposure through digital platforms such as social media outlets and web portals showcasing talent, some may argue that the temptation to copy is greater. But that exposure also makes work easy to identify, trace and cite as evidence of wrongdoing. However great the temptation, the moral and ethical view is clear – it is wrong.

Many authors have written extensively about what exactly constitutes copyright from various perspectives and are worth seeking out, as laws are specific to different countries and regions. As a point of principle, admiration and inspiration for fellow illustrators work is acceptable; lifting and reappropriating their work and claiming it as your own is most definitely not.

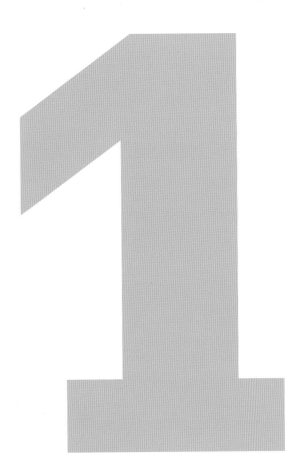

Ideation

The process of ideation enables the illustrator to develop visual ideas and make decisions about directions in answering a client's assignment. As ideas flow they create a chronological and conceptual map of the illustrator's thoughts, influences and adoption of visual and textual research, synergized into a visual statement. These may take the form of thumbnail-sized initial drawings to capture essential components of content that act as carriers or signifiers for an idea. Time spent crafting more elaborate images may lose the flow of inspiration or the sense of clarity in translating the editorial angle suggested by the writer, or details in the text. Creation of thumbnail drawings allows the quality of ideas to be assessed, measuring their tone of voice in keeping with the thrust of the article the illustration will sit alongside. Creating ideas at speed helps remove superfluous detail and also offers opportunities for one good idea to feed another. At this stage, all ideas should be considered in the round, but it is worth emphasizing that adding further ideas to an original can dilute and obstruct clear messaging. Again, this will depend on how the final illustration is going to be used – impactful cover illustrations require acute and focused messaging, whereas more contemplative internal spreads may have a lead idea with other supportive narrative concepts also working as sub-plots in the composition.

The advantage to an ideation work-flow offers opportunities to achieve some objectivity with the subject matter and the process. Some illustrators like to share initial thoughts and ideas with the editorial client to gauge reaction and to talk through potential directions. Other illustrators prefer to work their favoured ideas up into more complete proposals, working on the principle that an idea will have greater clarity and connection to a client if it is presented with more refined and resolved visual informa-tion. Both approaches are possible, but should be agreed between client and illustrator ahead of the assignment being undertaken. The evolution of ideation is useful where differing points of view

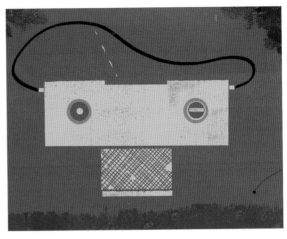

Figure 12.2
Illustration produced for *The Guardian*, based on the article 'Fake Photos' highlighting the history of manipulating and editing documentary photographic imagery and passing it off as real. This illustration by Frazer Hudson manages to balance the anonymity of source material with the intense clamour of recognition we see in contemporary society.

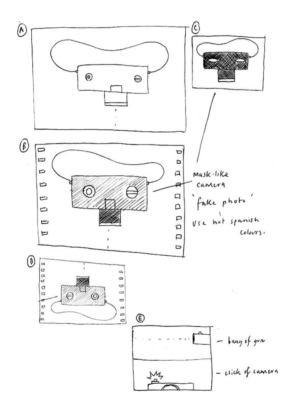

Figure 12.1
Early roughs show the germ of Frazer Hudson's ideas for answering an article about fake photos illustration for *The Guardian*. Playing with the shape and profile of the camera starts to open up the possibility of a visual link between a mask and the concept of disguise through masking off a face, with the film winder and shutter button signifying eyes and the strap being read as hair.

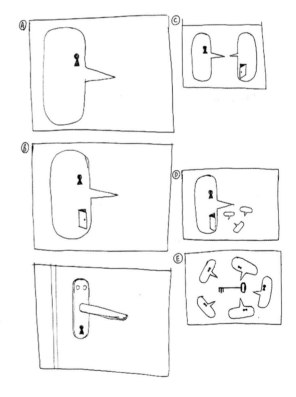

Figure 12.3
Frazer Hudson's sketchbook drawings for *The Guardian* 'Open-Closed Inquiry' article are drawn at speed in response to the ideas being generated. Newspaper illustration deadlines are notoriously short and capturing the essence of an idea is important in not getting too bogged down with superfluous details.

Figure 12.4
This illustration was produced by Frazer Hudson for *The Guardian*, responding to an article titled 'Open-Closed Inquiry'. The ideas here develop out of possible interpretations of the relationship between open and closed associations that allow the reader to associate linking. The illustration aims to encourage finding common solutions through discourse.

are encountered, allowing the illustrator to revisit the process at the point of disagreement, rather than necessarily starting the translation and interpretation of subject matter from scratch. As previously mentioned, discarded ideas may yet have another life in future work with some further development and visual decision making.

Creating visuals and decision making

Sorting and evaluating ideas into workable solutions for the brief is the next step in the production process. Considering how visual ideas can be amplified through changes to viewpoint, composition and placement of individual pictorial elements and their corresponding relationship to one another is a crucial part of creating recognition and readability for the audience. Critically, exercising choices and options of these structural components also controls how the audience receive and respond to this visual information. For example, if the subject matter is placed in a way that occupies the majority of the panel, the reader is arrested by the image and the subject

is permitted a degree of control and authority over other aspects of the image. By contrast, if the landscape or environment gulfs other objects through reducing their scale, then their presence becomes diminished or inconsequential. A subject that seemingly towers over a reader induces a feeling of power and strength, whilst placing the readership in a position where they look down or over a subject reduces its presence and impact.

Such compositional choices structurally affect the content and create a tone of voice that needs to correspond and be sympathetic to the essence and spirit of the written content the illustration will accompany. The creation of visuals therefore become important assets to help communicate with the commissioner about how the proposed artwork will answer the brief. They also act as a safeguard to track back previous communications if later problems arise. Historically, illustrators created a sketch of the proposed final artwork to send to a client. Whilst many ideas may have been developed and shortlisted, most illustrators prefer to send a visual solution that answers the brief and creates an unambiguous step to create final artwork from. Sending several ideas can confuse the issue and possibly create an unwelcome scenario where a further set of sketches are requested that blend or amalgamate ideas beyond the illustrator's original intention. It is better to keep ideas and developed sketches in reserve if the commissioner feels the presented sketch doesn't fully answer the brief.

In a contemporary setting, digital production methods have proved advantageous for the visual process, but they have also created some problems. Certainly having the ability to scan, clean up and send visuals through email attachments, or through file transfer services for larger files, has improved workflow and created direct communication channels. Taking the time to explain the visual as an attachment in a well-crafted email helps formulate a context for the work, explains the approach you have taken and clarifies visual elements that are perhaps difficult to decipher.

Reception of a visual is more likely to be positive using this process and can lead to a swift agreement to proceed to final artwork. This is especially useful if decision making over content resides with an editorial team, rather than one point of contact. In this regard, the communication of why an approach was adopted becomes extremely useful in filling in the gaps of knowledge and contextualizing the proposed work. Additionally, online communication services such as FaceTime, WhatsApp and Skype are also useful if further explanation is required to confirm content or approach, or if receiving feedback about submitted visuals from the commissioner that require alteration.

At all times, maintaining a professional communication stance is key. If changes are required, as is often the case, make changes and send the revised visual with appended notes if necessary. Creating these as a digital file allows the opportunity to index numerical versions so that iterations of changes can be stored and avoids confusion when discussing any changes. This also creates a useful record of the project and will often mean not having to start any changes from scratch. Reaching an agreed solution that works for both parties is the ultimate goal here and allows the final production of artwork to commence.

Figure 12.5
American illustrator Greg Clarke's visual development process maintains a strong degree of drawing at its heart. Clarke constructs his illustrations through drawing and designing particular elements on tracing paper, and then placing the layers over each other to achieve a compositional fit. Many iterations of this process happen in the construction phase, allowing the slight shifts in compositional structure to occur that create slight differences to the inference of the illustration.

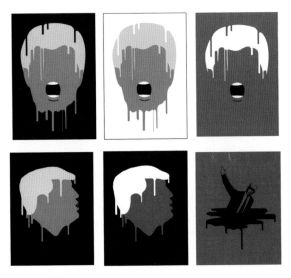

Figure 12.6
Edel Rodriguez's sketches for *Time* magazine's 'Meltdown' cover show the evolution of the initial idea and the pairing down of visual elements in order to achieve maximum impact for the readership. These images show how direct and dynamic Rodriguez's working process is, using iterative decisions around colour, shape and composition to grow and synthesize his concepts as loaded visual statements.

Figure 12.7
With a cover sketch agreed by the art director, Greg Clarke's production process uses a mixture of analogue drawing techniques and digital layout to achieve the final artwork. Using grainy pencil on a coquilled paper surface, as seen above, allows him to build up layers of texture that are random and handmade. These drawings are scanned and saved as TIF file layers, allowing Clarke to play with the position of pictorial elements and their relationship to each other to maintain readability and foreground characters that are performing important functions in the composition. The ability to adjust colour, tone, saturation and hues in Adobe Illustrator enables the illustrator to alter the tone of voice of an illustration, heightening or lowering its impact on the reader.

Figure 12.8
The final typeset Chicago Dining Secrets cover sees the successful pairing of Greg Clarke's playful illustration with well chosen typefaces and a successfully orchestrated editorial design grid to create a witty, appealing take on the city's dining experiences.

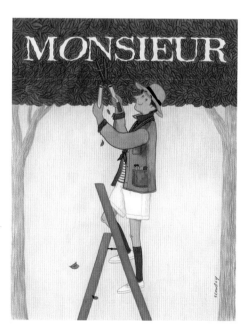

Figure 12.9a–b
A worked up pencil drawing to show compositional placement was presented, approved and used as reference to create the final artwork. Illustration by Mr Slowboy for Monocle magazine.

Commercial Practice Considerations

Illustrators seeking to enter the profession come from different starting points. Some are students of the subject in higher or further education, whilst others have shifted across from related humanities subjects or, indeed, disciplines that have no formal art or design training. Other participants are looking to the editorial illustration world to relaunch careers, to do the one thing they have always wanted to do, but previous circumstances prevented them originally. Some are re-entering the profession after a career break to have children, care for relatives and friends or having successfully recovered from illness. Motivations for succeeding and forming a professional commercial practice may differ, but what unites hopeful creatives is that editorial illustration has been historically seen as a low-risk way in to getting work seen, published and appreciated. An editorial illustration has a short shelf life in comparison to other illustrative output, and fees are correspondingly smaller than for bigger publishing jobs such as children's books or for advertising commissions. If an illustration meets the standard in terms of communicating the intended idea, is technically well constructed and delivered on time it is worthy of publication. That satisfies the base commercial position of being published and paid, but the aspiration should always be to better your last published piece of work and achieve an award-winning standard.

Research into this book reaffirms the view that commissioners and creators of illustration come from wildly differing backgrounds of gender, ethnicity, religion and cultures, but each has experiences to draw upon and opinions to share that make the subject richer and more diverse than at any time in its history. Personal expectation of a successful commercial practice might be getting published regularly for some, or illustrating for a particular publication for others. Achieving a consistent, long-standing commissioned series is a goal for many. Being recognized by peers for output in one of the many annuals or journals dedicated to showcasing high-quality work is the dream for other practitioners. Over the course of a commercial lifetime, it may be possible to achieve a number of these important milestones. The one thing that never fades is the satisfaction of seeing your work published on the cover of a magazine, or turning the page of a newspaper to see your work sitting under a headline in an editorial spread, or seeing positive comments and plaudits under the article posted in the online edition. These accolades keep editorial illustrators returning to the next assignment, eager to test themselves against challenging content and unremitting deadlines.

Figure 13.1
Illustrator Greg Clarke working at his drawing table in his Los Angeles studio.

Experimentation, change and development

Growing a career as an editorial illustrator is about making informed choices based on experience, situation and aspiration. Many contributors express the view that being successful in the field of editorial illustration requires a connected range of personal insights emerging from having an honest connection to personal experiences. Failing that, deep research into a subject is necessary to ensure that you are well informed about the subject you are illustrating. Any failure to convince, either through a comprehensive misunderstanding of the content, or through a lack of attention to detail in crafting the image, will have negative, unwanted repercussions.

Seeing a reaction to your work, on the faces of those who commission, professional illustrators you are in competition with and the readership at large, can be an enlivening or chastening experience, but also a very educational one. Achieving recognition, whether through the success of communicating a concept, uncovering a story or provoking a reaction to generate attention or notoriety for creating work that is challenging and unconventional, is at the forefront of illustrators' minds when undertaking each commission. This is a recognition that the publication is also a marketplace for work to be seen by rival publications, contemporaries and associated professionals such as agents who can potentially help further your career. Responding to that motivation and being excited by the possibility of the next opportunity is the fire that editorial illustrators thrive on.

For new illustrators, having the confidence to fully embrace experimenting with a newly found visual language or stylistic approach is hard. Having worked to develop a visual direction that is coherent and enveloping is a hard journey, involving many hours of painstaking practice, mistakes and learning experiences. The process may have involved learning new analogue processes or digital software packages, and possibly a combination of both, as the search for a way of professional working that is both commercial and rewarding continues. Recent history also suggests that commissioners of illustration have certainly been persuaded by

Figure 13.2a–d
An illustrator's working environment should be a welcoming and comfortable environment that will inspire, facilitate great work and provide safe and secure storage of equipment. Greg Clarke's studio is an extension of the person, shown here through an inspiration wall with collections of promotional cards, ephemera collected on travels and treasured finds that all have a tangible bearing on Clarke's work.

a consistency of approach in the way images were manufactured and presented. Illustration agents encouraged their roster of represented illustrators to make work that fitted a mould of production, partly out of a need to segment their talent and partly in response to produce content for websites that employed keyword search algorithms for content, styles and modes of production. Art directors were encouraged to look at licensed stock images through the lens of the host sites catalogued and framed by similar search methods.

Yet, some of the most internationally recognized, award-winning and critically acclaimed work comes from exponents who embrace different visual stylistic production methods, but whose work is nonetheless recognizable. The roots of this success go back to seeing editorial illustration not simply as a stylistic continuum, but what fundamentally are the raw ingredients to successful editorial illustration output itself. The concept, the idea and the viewpoint derived from textual analysis determine the execution, hence why some ideas may 'work' in pre-production development, but do not translate into successful communicative messaging as final artwork. The entirety of the visual message, including how it is contextualized by the content that it supports, is the sum of its parts.

The process of experimentation is crucial in all stages of the editorial illustration process. Personal identity is not only recognizable through visual production methods, but through the way content is channelled and communicated as a considered whole contribution to the final image. For example, illustrators such as David Hughes and Edel Rodriguez use acerbic wit and incisive vantage points to make cutting and telling statements about their subjects. Imbued often with dark humour and raw emotion, they leave little doubt about their standpoint and commentary on the content of an article. By contrast, illustrators such as Matthew Richardson and Matthieu Bourel invite inspection and suggest connotation and are altogether more subtle in drawing a readership into the accompanying written content. Here, the messaging may be deliberately more obtuse and divergent, leaving gaps for wonderment or ambiguity to reside. In that spirit, the visual language employed may be more abstracted or non-linear in visual depiction, and the metaphorical use of symbology or iconography may be inventively juxtaposed in the composition to create a frizzante of unexpectedness.

Many contributors to this book experiment behind the scenes with works that may never see the light of day for the general public, yet do much to motivate, excite and raise new possibilities for future output. Having a process that can allow that practice to flourish and employing a method of archiving findings will be advantageous in the long run. Examples might include ideas books, private sketchbooks, closed-access research and development websites or personal Pinterest boards. The format should reflect the individualized nature of experimentation, but equally might be curated through an online collaborative platform that seeks and values contributions from others.

Execution of artwork

Facing a blank surface or screen can be an intimidating prospect for many artists. However, for an editorial illustrator's workflow, a significant amount of preparation has already been undertaken in the pre-production of the illustration.

Accepting a commission, reading a brief, talking to a client and creating visual proposals for consideration and approval are all accepted parts of the process of planning to deliver artwork. These steps go a long way to answering the brief by ensuring that there is a harmonious marriage between text and image on page or screen, thereby setting up the conditions for the editorial illustration to be successfully produced with flair and professionalism.

Double-check the finished illustration measurements and either prepare your paper for working on, or set your screen measurements correctly. If you are working with wet media such as ink, watercolour or gouache, the surface may require stretching in advance depending on the weight of paper you are using. Digital work can be enlarged in scale for on-screen working, but always ensure you have set the image proportions to take account of the final size of artwork required for reproduction. For screen-based illustrations, this is 72 dpi (dots per inch) and artwork should be saved in RGB (red, green, blue format). For print-based publications, a minimum resolution of 300 dpi is required and artwork should be saved using the CMYK convention, whose abbreviation matches traditional four-colour print processes of cyan, magenta, yellow and black.

The myriad of illustration styles determine the stages of production that vary from illustrator to illustrator. It is important to take breaks where possible, mindful that artwork deadlines are often short. Some national newspapers expect artwork to be turned round in a matter of hours on occasion, and invariably timescales for magazines, periodicals and journals seldom extend further than a few days. Breaks help ensure that you are able to revisit the work afresh and can be objective about the unfolding image to make necessary adjustments that can improve its quality of execution or the clarity of its communication.

Many clients expect to be kept up to date on progress and it is increasingly common to send versions of works in progress via email or services such as WeTransfer or Dropbox to keep communication flowing effectively. Some illustrators feel that this stifles creativity and interrupts their flow. Others like having the reassurance that they are on track philosophically and practically with the brief. Establishing trust between the illustrator and the art director or commissioner of the work again becomes key as deadlines loom

Figure 13.3a–c
Three illustrations created by Serge Bloch for *The Boston Globe* health supplement which perfectly expose his eclectic working method of combining line and object to create highly original graphic statements that are often carrying significant depth of information. Despite being an experienced practitioner, Bloch's love of experimentation with materials ensures his work remains fresh and surprising.

and nerves need to be held. If possible, schedule these 'in progress' updates at the end of a working day so that you maximize your best working conditions. Ensure you have a system for naming and numbering versions of files so you ensure you are receiving feedback on the correct artwork. Feedback invariably keeps the illustrator waiting, so it is best not to feel like your productivity time

is being wasted. The global reach of editorial illustration often means working with clients in other countries where time zones are different, so build those considerations into any communication schedule.

A busy illustrator is often dealing with creating one piece of artwork, developing another for a different client and taking a brief from another.

Figure 13.4
Translating the energy from an approved sketch or rough to final artwork is an issue that many young illustrators experience difficulty with. This is quite common and occurs under pressurized situations. Depending on production methods, it may be necessary and desirable to create versions of the final artwork to maintain that freedom of expression and prevent images tightening up. Joe Ciardiello's illustration of Thelonious Monk for the *New York Times* Book Review places great emphasis on a variety of mark-making to achieve an energy and liveliness, controlling the focus for the viewer without the subject looking wooden or staged.

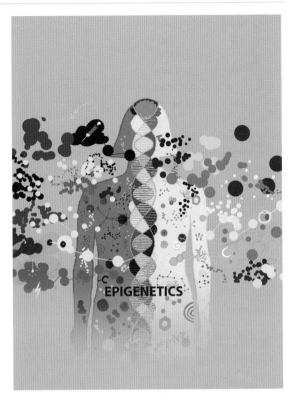

Figure 13.5a–b
Andrew Selby's cover illustration for *The Journal of Allergy and Clinical Immunology* portrays the scientific subject of epigenetics. The artwork formed a central band across the middle of the cover with floating elements designed to work in harmony with the typography.

Email, phone calls and social media posts can quickly turn from punctuating the day into destroying any sense of continuity and consistency unless these interruptions are managed. Decide on your professional approach, inform clients that this is how you choose to operate and stick to it. Corralling email replies into specific segments of the day, turning your phone to silent and keeping social media for coffee breaks are all ways of managing interruptions but still achieving goals. Above all, revel in the art of making artwork that has taken many hours to perfect and that is your professional, unique, creative signature

Dealing with criticism

No book on editorial illustration would be complete without advice about how to deal with criticism. Firstly, editorial work is published in the public domain, in a world where the principle of free speech is championed. Readerships and audiences will always disagree on motives, viewpoints and opinions that are expressed in published communication media. Criticism has always been a part of editorial illustration, even though we perceive we live in a more fractious and contradictory society than previous generations. Whilst it is inevitably hard to compare time periods, it is certainly true to say that the opportunity to criticize through a broader range of visible platforms has increased. Perhaps in contrast, the multitude of platforms has also diluted contemporary focus and scattered opinions.

Developing a thick skin to keep criticism at a managed distance therefore becomes paramount. Most illustrators admit to having creative doubts about their work in private. This is part of the professional drive and determination that keeps the discipline relevant and current – everyone is united in their desire to produce the highest-quality work. The best approach is to develop a publicly professional persona that is robust, polite but firm. Such professional integrity extends from meetings with clients, to receiving critical feedback during an assignment in response to work created, through to dealing with social media commentary after publication. It can be soul-destroying to receive critical feedback when you have genuinely attempted to provide the best solution you can in the time allocated. Developing strategies to absorb and reflect on feedback, and deciding whether and what actions to take in response, is different for every individual.

Developing that professional persona that can receive and respond to criticism takes time and requires effort. It also revolves around the experiences that you have had and understanding your deeper motivations as a professional creative. Considering the following rhetorical questions may be useful in framing a professional persona:

What are your long-term career ambitions?
What are your expectations day to day for how you should be treated and your work used?
How do you portray your professional identity to others and maintain your integrity and right to a voice?

Fundamentally, accepting criticism can be turned into many positives. Your work can improve either in technical acumen, communicative tone or professionalism in turning jobs around efficiently. Often the best advice is to listen to and absorb criticism and then decide which aspects of the critique are worthwhile. If critical opinions of the work don't match or exceed the expectation you have set yourself as a creative, then park them and move on. Asking friends or other acquaintances that you value the opinions of to sense-check criticism is often a good way to see the commentary in context. Never respond to criticism immediately or aggressively. Instead be measured and robust if you must respond. It is wise not to complain about a person or a publication either. The industry is small and well networked. Having the reputation of being a difficult or antagonistic person to work with will create more obstacles than it solves.

In a creative career, there are inevitably times when differences exist and, left unchecked, can escalate. In these circumstances, try and resolve issues before they become problematic. A good deed or a few lines of communication that are well crafted can often be a good tonic in calming a situation. Some illustrators have reported that some difficult relationships caused by jobs going wrong have resulted in commissions from that publisher dwindling and drying up. Equally, others report that post-holders move on in their own creative careers and new people assume commissioning roles, completing the circle of fortune in a creative life.

Agency representation

Historically, most agencies have not engaged with the representation of editorial illustrators. Timescales are often too short and fees not generally lucrative enough to merit their attention. However, more recently newer agencies have sprung up to cater for this market. Established agencies have looked to diversify by wading into the editorial market to keep their illustrators active as commissions from other areas such as publishing or advertising have declined. In instances where illustrators work beyond editorial markets this approach is understandable, but there are clearly a set of specific requirements that editorial illustrations will need to display for commissioners to consider hiring. Inevitably, they will want proof that an illustrators has worked in the editorial arena before, understand the specific demands of working to an exacting brief, tight timelines and with limited wriggle room if changes are sought. Illustrators who have

Figure 13.6
A fun approach to the often complex subject of language and translation in verbal communication in this three-colour illustration by Serge Bloch for *The Boston Globe* Sunday travel supplement. Utilizing Bloch's graphic language across imagery and type ensures that the two work together, but also allows for cultural variation through scale, colour and expressive mark-made representation.

experiences working within advertising are used to the tight timelines, but not necessarily the demands of conceptually linking the brief to a writer's content, whilst those used to the longer timeframes in publishing are often shocked by the quick turnaround times for editorial work.

Agencies have the distinct advantage of massing talent in one central point of contact, even if they represent illustrators from different countries. Some agencies have multiple offices in different countries, with specialist agents who speak local languages which can seriously boost the reach and availability of illustrators to work on a truly global stage. Agencies should act as an umbrella for talent and a magnet for commissioners who then meet a unified approach to dealing with clients as a professional, holistic experience. The external face argument works for some illustrators who do not want to deal with the promotion, negotiation of fees or usage for their work. Agents can negotiate fees that independent illustrators may not have the confidence to charge, and should have an up-to-date knowledge of current pay scales in the market. Most agents expect to see a 20–30 per cent commission for editorial jobs and will push for their representative to command the best fee possible. This continual negotiation forges a working relationship between clients, agents and illustrators which can potentially grow and mature over a career through some positive mentoring – a role some illustrators find useful in what otherwise can be a solitary existence. Other illustrators see the day-to-day dealings as an aspect of their job which allows them some social contact, greater voice with the person commissioning their work and the opportunity of being better financially rewarded as a price worth paying to stay independent. They also relish the autonomy of independence to forge new directions and break free of the constraints of stylization that some agents prefer to label their stable of creators with.

Many editorial commissioners of illustration are wary of working with agents and find concerns about the protracted communication channels off-putting. Central to these factors is the issue of trust. Good agencies will have an excellent rapport with their illustrators and clients, and be able to recommend the right illustrator for the commission being offered, and will be expedient determining fee and usage. There is no reason in a digital age for the commissioner not to communicate direct with the illustrator, and where necessary, copy the agent into communication exchanges. This allows all parties to be kept abreast of developments and head off any potential difficulties before they arise. The communication trail also provides evidence of decisions made and actions undertaken if for any reason a job is cancelled or delayed. There will always be some editorial commissioners who simply want to work with illustrators directly and will bypass agencies and their roster of artists altogether.

An agent's marketing power is amplified by the number of artists they represent and with each paying for a slice of promotion, their ability to reach clients is clearly more powerful than any individual illustrator would achieve. However, big agency marketing can feel like a blanket approach and so targeted marketing of a smaller number of illustrators to a particular client is likely to yield better successful commissions. Chasing commissions down is a time-consuming process of keeping in regular contact with commissioners, understanding what jobs are on the horizon and pitching work to meet those needs. This requires excellent networks of contacts and frequent communication. Often, independent illustrators will argue that they are better at these aspects of chasing work as they are more nimble and fleet of foot. However, the independent illustrator has to do everything and the long, arduous job of requesting feedback or chasing fees through late payments of invoices is time taken away from the creative act of making work. Many students are surprised at the proportion of time established illustrators spend undertaking non-creative work, but as an independent creator, the marketing, promotion, studio maintenance and accountability for your practice are yours. Freelance employment has many advantages in terms of flexibility, but that freedom also needs to be applied creatively to the more mundane and routine parts of the job.

If you are interested in agency representation, then the best advice is to follow them through social media and keep abreast of who they are representing and the types of jobs that they are winning. Finding the correct agency to represent you is worth the investment in time that it takes to find the right fit for both parties. When you are convinced, make an enquiry professionally and show them a representative sample of your work to gauge their interest. The agency may require further work to be undertaken, or they may come back with constructive commentary for developing the work further. They may also want to call you and meet to understand your work in greater depth and to ascertain whether they are comfortable representing you. Building and developing a rapport with an agent is the key to a successful partnership that should last for many years.

In some instances, agents approach illustrators for possible representation, especially where they can see the illustrator is winning jobs. Not surprisingly, agents are first and foremost a business so representing a successful illustrator is much easier than someone who is developing or who has fallen out of favour stylistically. The initial approach may be a welcomed by a busy independent illustrator who needs more time to creatively produce work for the clients they have generated. It is flattering to be approached for representation, but it is worth remembering that other agents may also be interested and so it could be worthwhile discreetly gauging that interest. Time taken to make the next positive career move could be very financially lucrative and creatively rewarding. However, some illustrators may also take the view that they have done the leg work and forged relationships that the agent will simply benefit from without needing to work for their slice of the commission fee. This is precisely where the issue of trust between the illustrator and the agent is tested.

Figure 13.7
The final approved artwork for the cover of Monocle magazine, created by Mr Slowboy and art directed by Thu-Huyen Hoang.

Reflection

Editorial illustration can be a fantastic springboard into other parts of the illustration industry. Having proven an ability to work under tightly pressurized conditions, with short deadlines, changes in art direction and possible updated versions of artwork to satisfy a client, the range of key and transferable skills acquired often surprises illustrators. Demonstrating a versatility of approach, careful negotiation and multidisciplinary presentation skills are often attributes that get overlooked or amalgamated into professional practice as an assumed and expected part of the job, whereas they are becoming increasingly recognized markers that determine how well or otherwise illustrators are at making strategic and defined career decisions that are investments to longer-term survival and prosperity in the wider creative industries.

The general view from contributors to this book is that it is easier to kickstart a career in editorial illustration, but much harder to sustain one. Do not undervalue the skills you will have acquired in developing and enhancing working relationships through the presentation or tendering for commissions process, or developing artwork in collaboration with an editorial team and meeting stringent deadlines. In other disciplines, such versatility and professionalism command respect and recognition. It is worth foregrounding these skills in the pursuit of self-promotion in a commercial context and having personal reminders on days where creativity is in short supply, or where client feedback is not what had been hoped for or expected.

With completed editorial illustrations in your portfolio, you have proven your ability to work under immense pressure. The acerbic wit and satirical elegance of your output may have caught the eye of commissioners of greetings cards and giftware suppliers for a market that is expanding with more celebrations being marked, or more unlikely events celebrated aside from traditional birthdays and religious-inspired calendar festivals such as Easter and Christmas. Equally, the run of sequential narrative panels created for newspapers or supplements may have drawn attention from graphic novel and comic book publishers who are looking to develop storylines or characters that have been created through collaborative projects with other authors, or who see opportunities to publish books without words or encourage the expansion and development of these teasers into larger-scale works with international distribution channels.

For example, Tom Gauld's work for *The Guardian* and *The New Yorker* has led to opportunities to publish collections of works, and new titles, in this vein. Successful editorial covers can spike the attention of the fiction and non-fiction publishing markets, releasing opportunities to create new covers, inside spreads, chapter titles and incidental works involved in the marketing, point of sale and associated presentation support for books to reach their required audience. Successful editorial illustrations can equally catch the eye of advertising clients who value innovative, incisive and persuasive messaging to capture new market segments for products or services, particularly with illustrators whose work can attract a niche following. Works seen in an advertorial context are often good examples of how illustrators are making a successful transition between editorial and advertising.

In essence, using editorial illustration as a springboard to other genres is not new. Many of the best examples of French poster design took their lead from work honed in an editorial setting. Having the dexterity to design with image and text created confidence in skills and a sophistication of handling content for specific audiences. Having a balanced portfolio that contains editorial, publishing, design and advertising output is a happy medium that some illustrators need to find fulfilment in their creative pursuits. The challenge of maintaining such a balance should not be underestimated and, inevitably, choices surrounding what commissions to accept, new work to showcase advertising services and what work to turn down are all highly personalized factors that affect the balance of a creative existence. Work will always be subject to financial, moral, ethical and practical considerations which is what remains taxing about achieving a successful equilibrium between the demands of work and leisure.

Editorial illustration is currently in a very good place to prosper, develop and diversify its appeal and influence. Globally, enough people care about where their news comes from, how it is reported and, crucially, how it is verified as being accurate and balanced. There are more outlets for dissemination of content through the growth of the online market which looks set to stay and develop with the customary developments in technology. Critically, readerships are exercising more control over the choices they make about how to divide their work and leisure time and their aspirations for a happy and healthy future. As illustrated elsewhere in this book, editorial illustrators have continued to learn new skills, experiment with new approaches and educate themselves in software packages that enable their professional output to take advantage of these new platforms, creating rich, immersive experiences for readers. The result is work that has morphed from being two-dimensional and static to limited or full-moving offerings, creating deliberate interplay with text and even moving beyond the confines of the screen by exploring the dimensions of hovering above content through augmented, virtual and/or mixed realities. Issues of authorship, identity and control will surface in the next iterations of editorial illustration development and these will be negotiated by publishers and readerships in tandem rather than isolation.

Editorial illustration isn't just consumed during the home to office commute as it would have been in the age of the broadsheet newspaper. New working from home arrangements, the accelerated gig economy of multi-working solutions and flexible study choices are just some of the examples of how readers' lives have diversified and become more fragmented. Editorial illustration has to function and perform amongst that activity, in a quickly grabbed coffee break, on a phone screen in the airport lounge or as a distraction whilst feeding a baby. Ultimately publishers need readerships and editorial illustration has a huge brokering role to play in presenting, shaping and nurturing those conversations as an expressive, expansive form of visual journalism in its own right. Awareness of the international tussle for control of news media channels and outlets exists. On one level

this could be seen as problematic, with large media organizations snuffing out competition, profiteering from the influence of advertisers or state-supported propaganda, political interference and lobbying from pressure groups with vested interests. But these issues serve to highlight how crucial news media is to people. It matters to contemporary society just as much as it mattered in 1785 with the launch of the first newspaper. Successful societies and cultures are dependent on the rules and regulations they have in place to maintain and uphold the values of freedom of expression, offer spaces to present arguments and debate points of view, and respect differences of opinion.

Figure 14.1
Collaging and montaging are effective ways of communicating to an audience by combining a reader's familiarity with the representation of an object with a drawn element which might be more frivolous or ambiguous. In these illustrations, Serge Bloch combines different codes of symbols, lines and photographed objects into amusing situations involving the presentation and consumption of wine.

Bibliography

Barthes, R. (1964), *Rhetoric of the Image*, Fontana Press.

Barthes, R. (1977a), 'An Introduction to the Structural Analysis of Narrative, 1966', in *Image-Music-Text*, 79–124, Fontana Press.

Barthes, R. (1977b), *Elements of Semiology*, reissue edn, Hill and Wang.

Barthes, R. (1977c), 'Rhetoric of the Image, 1964', in *Image-Music-Text*, Fontana Press.

Barthes, R. (1977d), 'The Photographic Message, 1961', in *Image-Music-Text*, 16–31, Fontana Press.

Barthes, R. (1993), *Camera Lucida: Reflections on Photography*, Vintage.

Barthes, R. (1998), 'The Death of the Author', in *Art and Interpretation: An Anthropology of Readings in Aesthetics and the Philosophy of Art*, ed. Eric Dayton, 383–6, Broadview.

Barthes, R. (2009), *Mythologies*, Vintage.

Bennett, A. and Royle, N. (2016), *An Introduction to Literature, Criticism and Theory*, 5th edn, Routledge.

Berger, J. (1972), *Ways of Seeing*, Penguin.

Berger, J. (2009), *About Looking*, Bloomsbury.

Berger, J. (2016), *Confabulations*, Penguin.

Berger, J. (2020), *Steps towards a Small Theory of the Visible*, Penguin.

Branagan, A. (2019), *The Essential Guide to Business for Artists and Designers*, 2nd edn, Bloomsbury.

Brazell, D. and Davies, J. (2014), *Understanding Illustration*, Bloomsbury.

Breton, A. (1924), *First Manifesto of Surrealism*, trans. A. S. Kline (2010), Editions du Sagittaire.

Brock, G. (2015), *Out of Print: Newspapers, Journalism and the Business of News in the Digital Age*, Kogan Page.

Bucher, J. (2017), *Storytelling for Virtual Reality: Methods and Principles for Crafting Immersive Narratives*, Routledge.

Butler, J. (2006), *Gender Trouble: Feminism and the Subversion of Identity*, Routledge.

Caldwell, C. and Zappaterra, Y. (2014), *Editorial Design: Digital and Print*, Laurence King Publishing.

Chandler, D. (2017), *Semiotics*, 3rd edn, Routledge.

Clarke, B. (2010), *From Grub Street to Fleet Street: An Illustrated History of English Newspapers to 1899*, Revel Barker.

Cohn, N. (2013), *The Visual Language of Comics: Introduction to the Structure and Cognition of Sequential Images*, Bloomsbury.

Cohn, N. (2016), *The Visual Narrative Reader*, Bloomsbury.

Cohn, N. (2020), *Who Understands Comics?: Questioning the Universality of Visual Language Comprehension*, Bloomsbury.

Colebrook, C. (2001), *Gilles Deleuze*, Routledge.

Corner, J. (1983), 'Textuality, Communication and Power', in *Language, Image, Media*. ed. H. Davis and P. Walton, 266–81, Palgrave Macmillan.

De Beauvoir, S. (2010), *The Second Sex*, Vintage.

Debord, G. (1994), *Society of the Spectacle*, Rebel Press.

Deutscher, P. (2005), *How to Read Derrida*, Granta Books.

Doyle, S., Grove, J. and Sherman, W. (2019), *History of Illustration*, Bloomsbury.

Eco, U. (1978), *A Theory of Semiotics*, Indiana University Press.

Eco, U. (1984), *Semiotics and the Philosophy of Language*, Indiana University Press.

Errea, J. (2017), *Visual Journalism: Infographics from the World's Best Newsrooms and Designers*, Die Gestalten Verlag.

Errea, J. (2018), *Newspaper Design: Editorial Design from the World's Best Newsrooms*, Die Gestalten Verlag.

Embury, G. and Minichiello, M. (2017), *Reportage Illustration: Visual Journalism*, Bloomsbury.

Foucault, M. (1994), *The Order of Things*, Random House USA Inc.

Gannon, R. and Fauchon, M. (2021), *Illustration Research Methods*, Bloomsbury.

Gilroy, P. (2002), *There Ain't No Black in the Union Jack*, Routledge.

Gilroy, P. and Gilmore, R. W. (2021), *Selected Writings on Race and Difference* (Stuart Hall: Selected Writings), Duke University Press.

Gombrich, E. H. (2000), *Art and Illusion: A Study of Pictorial Representation in Pictorial Representation*, Princeton and Oxford University Press.

Hall, S. (1973), *Encoding and Decoding in the Television Discourse*, University of Birmingham.

Hall, S. (2021), *Writings on Media: History of the Present*, Duke University Press.

Hébert, L. (2019), *An Introduction to Applied Semiotics: Tools for Text and Image Analysis*, Routledge.

Heck, J. G. (1988), *The Complete Encyclopaedia of Illustration*, Merehurst Press.

Heller, S. and Arisman, M. (2000), *The Education of an Illustrator*, Allworth Press/School of Visual Arts.

Heller, S. and Arisman, M. (2004), *Inside the Business of Illustration*, Allworth Press.

Heller, S. (2014), *Merz to Emigré and Beyond: Avant Magazine Design of the Twentieth Century*, Phaidon Press.

Heller, S. and Anderson, G. (2018), *The Illustration Idea Book*, Laurence King Publishing.

Herman, E. S. and Chomsky, N. (1995), *Manufacturing Consent: The Political Economy of the Mass Media*, Vintage.

Hoogslag, N. (2014), 'On the Persistence of a Modest Medium', PhD thesis, Royal College of Art, London.

Kovach, B. and Rosenstiel, T. (2007), *The Elements of Journalism*, Three Rivers Press.

Kress, G. and van Leeuwen, T. (2001), *Multimodal Discourse: The Modes and Media of Contemporary Communication*, Arnold Publishers.

Kress, G. and van Leeuwen, T. (2006), *Reading Images: The Grammar of Visual Design*, 2nd edn, Routledge.

Leski, K. (2015), *The Storm of Creativity*, MIT Press.

LeWitt, S. (1967), 'Paragraphs on Conceptual Art', *Artforum* 5 (10): 79–83.

Male, A. (2014), *Illustration: Meeting the Brief*, Bloomsbury.

Male, A. (2017), *Illustration: A Theoretical and Contextual* Perspective, 2nd edn, Bloomsbury.

Male, A. (2019), *The Power and Influence of Illustration*, Bloomsbury.

Manea, N. (1992), *On Clowns: The Dictator and the Artist*, Faber & Faber.

Manovich, L. (2020), *Cultural Analytics*, MIT Press.

Manovich, L., Malina, R. F. and Cubitt, S. (2002), *The Language of New Media*, 2nd edn, MIT Press.

McCloud, S. (2001), *Understanding Comics: The Invisible Art*, W M Morrow.

McLuhan, M. (2001), *Understanding Media*, Routledge.

McLuhan, M. and Fiore, Q. (2008), *The Medium is the Massage*, Penguin.

Nail, T. (2018), *Being and Motion*, Oxford University Press.

Nail, T. (2019), *Theory of the Image*, Oxford University Press.

Noble, I. and Bestley, R. (2011), *Visual Research*, 2nd edn, AVA Publishing.

Peirce, C. S. (1958), *Collected Papers of Charles Sanders Peirce*, Harvard University Press.

Rauch, J. (2021), *The Constitution of Knowledge: A Defense of Truth*, Brookings Institution Press.

Rubin, P. (2020), *Future Presence: How Virtual Reality is Changing Human Connection, Intimacy, and the Limits of Ordinary Life*, HarperOne.

Sabbagh, D. (2011), 'Guardian and Observer to Adopt "Digital-First" Strategy', *The Guardian* [online] 16 June. http://.theguardian.com/media/2011/jun/16/guardian-observer-digital-first-strategy.

Sabbagh, D. (2012), 'Leveson Inquiry: The Essential Guide', *The Guardian*, 28 November.

Selby, A. (2009), *Animation in Process*, Laurence King Publishing.

Selby, A. (2013), *Animation*, Laurence King Publishing.

Stuart, A. (2006), *Online News: Journalism and the Internet*, McGraw Hill International.

Weil, S. (2020), *The Power of Words*, Penguin.

Wells, P. (1998), *Understanding Animation*, Routledge.

Wells, P. (2006), *The Fundamentals of Animation*, AVA Publishing.

Weinstein, S. B. (2005), *The Multimedia Internet*, Springer New York.

Willows, D. M. (1987) *The Psychology of Illustration*, Springer-Verlag New York.

Zada, J. (2021), *Veils of Distortion: How the News Media Warps Our Minds*, ISBN Canada.

Zeegan, L. (2020), *The Fundamentals of Illustration*, 3rd edn, Bloomsbury.

Žižek, S. (1997), *The Plague of Fantasies*, Verso Books.

Žižek, S. (2006), *How to Read Lacan*, Granta Books.

Acknowledgements

This book was written over the course of the Covid-19 pandemic which has affected so many people in so many ways. My grateful thanks are therefore due to my editors at Bloomsbury, Louise Baird-Smith and Leafy Cummins who commissioned and shaped the content and were generous with their advice, encouragement and deadlines to accommodate my writing. Thanks to all of the research participants, interviewees and organizations for your valuable insight, help and support in providing details, leads and permissions to content that exemplifies the context, content and creation of editorial illustration.

I am immensely honoured to include so many editorial illustrators in this book who I admire and am in awe of. Thank you for letting me reproduce your work here to illustrate the text and hopefully provide insight and inspiration to a new generation of editorial illustrators. In alphabetical order: AhoyThere, Peter Allen, Simoul Alva, Anna and Elena Balbusso, Gary Baseman, Eva Bee, Jon Berkeley, Serge Bloch, Matthieu Bourel, Steve Brodner, Marc Buckhardt, Ben Challenor, Doug Chayka, Stanley Chow, Joe Ciardiello, Christopher Corr, Andy Robert Davies, Eleanor Davis, Camilla Falsini, Malika Favre, Felicia Fortes, Tom Gauld, Julian Glander, Olaf Hajek, Matthew Hancock, Rebecca Hendin, Frazer Hudson, David Hughes, Rod Hunt, Janne Iivonen, Javier Jaén, Jean Jullien, Olivier Kugler, Anita Kunz, Jianen Liu, Adam McCauley, Francesco Muzzi, Victo Ngai, Stina Persson, Hanoch Piven, David Plunkett, Eglė Plytnikaitė, Andy Potts, Matthew Richardson, Edel Rodriguez, Sergio Sánchez, Guy Shield, Yuko Shimizu, Lasse Skarbøvik, Paul Slater, Mr Slowboy, Brian Stauffer, Studio Feixen, Patrik Svensson, Gary Taxali, Michelle Thompson, Caroline Tomlinson, Lucy Truman, Armando Veve, Paul Wearing.

Image Credits

Figure 0.1: © Edel Rodriguez
Figure 0.2: © Lasse Skarbøvik / *Time*
Figure 0.3: © Adam McCauley / *The New York Times*
Figure 0.4: © Brian Stauffer / Len Small / *Nautilus Magazine*
Figure 1.1: © Lasse Skarbøvik / *The Economist*
Figure 1.2: © Simoul Alva / *The New York Times*
Figure 1.3: © Simoul Alva / *Medium*
Figure 1.4: All rights reserved ©Victo Ngai www.victo-ngai.com / Subterranean Press
Figure 1.5: © Yuko Shimizu / Todd Spangler / Robert Festino / *Variety*
Figure 1.6: © David Plunkert / *Sojourners Magazine*
Figure 1.7a-b: © AhoyThere / *The Big Issue*
Figure 1.8: © Serge Bloch / *The Boston Globe*
Figure 1.9: © Janne Iivonen / *Die Zeit*
Figure 1.10: © Paul Wearing / Dennis McLeod / David Armario Design / *Stanford Medicine*
Figure 1.11: © Paul Slater
Figure 1.12: © Matthew Richardson / *The World of Interiors*
Figure 1.13: © Michelle Thompson / Perou / *The Sunday Times Magazine*
Figure 1.14: © Malika Favre
Figure 1.15: © Milton Glaser Inc. All Rights Reserved / Columbia Records 1967
Figure 1.16: © Javier Jaén / *The New York Times*
Figure 1.17: © Gary Baseman
Figure 1.18: © Jonny Hannah / *The Sunday Telegraph*
Figure 1.19a: © Matthew Richardson / *Morningstar Magazine*
Figure 1.19b: © Mesmerise Studios / *Morningstar Magazine*
Figure 1.20: © Malika Favre / *The New Yorker*
Figure 1.21: © Armando Veve / Alexandra Zsigmond / *The New Yorker*
Figure 2.1: © Stanley Chow
Figure 2.2a-b: © Edel Rodriguez / D. W. Pine / *Time*
Figure 2.3: © Marc Burckhardt / Burckhardt Studio, Inc.
Figure 2.4a-d: Illustrations by © 2020 Balbusso Twins @ balbusso_twins
Fig 2.5: © Francesco Muzzi / Deb Bishop / *The New York Times*
Figure 2.6: © Edel Rodriguez / D. W. Pine / *Time*
Figure 2.7: © Brian Stauffer / NAACP / The Crisis
Figure 2.8: © Javier Jaén
Figure 2.9: © Felicia Fortes / *Göteborgs-Posten*
Figure 2.10: © Simoul Alva / *The New York Times*
Figure 2.11: © Eleanor Davis / *The New York Times Book Review*
Figure 2.12: © Malika Favre / *Resist! Magazine*
Figure 2.13: © Patrik Svensson / Susannah Haesche / *Harvard Business Review*
Figure 2.14: Eva Bee / Angel List
Figure 2.15: © Brian Stauffer / *Playboy*
Figure 2.16: © Yuko Shimizu / Megan Rabbitt / Jessica Downey / *Real Woman Magazine*

Figure 3.1: © Serge Bloch / *Time*
Figure 3.2: © Matthew Richardson / *World of Interiors*
Figure 3.3: © Brian Stauffer / *The New York Times*
Figure 3.4: © Javier Jaén / *The Guardian Saturday Review*
Figure 3.5: © Janne Iivonen
Figure 3.6a-b: © Doug Chayka / *The Washington Post*
Figure 3.7: © Brian Stauffer / *Scientific American*
Figure 4.1: © Brian Stauffer / *The Wall Street Journal*
Figure 4.2: © Joe Ciardiello / *Columbia Magazine*
Figure 4.3: © Paul Wearing / Dennis McLeod / David Armario Design / *Stanford Medicine*
Figure 4.4: © Guy Shield / *AirBnB*
Figure 4.5: © Marc Burckhardt / Buckhardt Studio, Inc. / *Scientific American*
Figure 4.6a-b: © Michelle Thompson / *Prospect Magazine*
Figure 4.7: © Edel Rodriguez / Svenja Kruse / *Der Spiegel*
Figure 4.8: © Eglė Plytnikaitė / *Scientific American*
Figure 4.9: © Serge Bloch / *The Boston Globe*
Figure 4.10: © Jean Jullien
Figure 4.11: © Hanoch Piven
Figure 4.12: © Anita Kunz, All Rights Reserved / *The Dallas Times Herald*
Figure 4.13: © Tom Gauld
Figure 4.14: © Gerald Scarfe / *The New Yorker*
Figure 4.15: © Steve Brodner
Figure 4.16: © David Hughes / *The Times Saturday Review*
Figure 4.17: © Lucy Truman / Royal Horticultural Society
Figure 4.18a-d: © Olaf Hajek
Figure 4.19: © Ian Bott / *Financial Times*
Figure 4.20: © Rod Hunt / *Bloomberg Business Week*
Figure 4.21: © Rod Hunt / *Bloomberg Business Week*
Figure 4.22: © Stina Persson
Figure 4.23: © Malika Favre
Figure 4.24: © Olivier Kugler / *Dem Krieg Entronnen* / Edition Moderne 2017
Figure 4.25: © Lucy Truman / *Better Homes and Gardens*
Figure 4.26: © Lucy Truman
Figure 4.27: © Lucy Truman / *Better Homes and Gardens*
Figure 4.28: © Camilla Falsini / *Uppa Magazine*
Figure 4.29: © Tom Gauld / *New Scientist*
Figure 4.30: © Andy Potts / *BBC Science Focus*
Figure 4.31: © Studio Feixen / MIT The Engine
Figure 4.32a-b: © Julian Glander / *The New York Times*
Figure 4.33: © Studio Feixen / *Wired Magazine*
Figure 5.1: ©Malika Favre / Berenberg
Figure 5.2: David Hughes / *Entertainment Weekly*
Figure 5.3: © Javier Jaén / *The Atlantic*
Figure 5.4: © Paul Slater / *The Times Saturday Review*
Figure 5.5: © Anita Kunz, All Rights Reserved
Figure 5.6: © Ben Challenor / *The Sunday Times*
Figure 5.7: © Jon Berkeley / *The Economist*
Figure 5.8: © Doug Chayka / *LA Times*
Figure 5.9: © Frazer Hudson / *The Guardian*

Figure 5.10: © Edel Rodriguez / D. W. Pine / *Time*
Figure 6.1: © Matthieu Bourel / *The New Yorker*
Figure 6.2: © Sergio García Sánchez / *The New Yorker*
Figure 6.3: © Brian Stauffer / *Dallas Observer*
Figure 6.4: © Joe Ciardiello
Figure 6.5: © Malika Favre / *The New Yorker*
Figure 6.6: © Gary Taxali
Figure 6.7: © Edel Rodriguez / Svenja Kruse / *Der Spiegel*
Figure 6.8: © Michelle Thompson
Figure 6.9: © Andrew Selby / *The Journal of Allergy and Clinical Immunology*
Figure 7.1: © David Plunkert / *National Geographic*
Figure 7.2: © Jean Jullien
Figure 7.3: © Frazer Hudson
Figure 7.4: © Sergio García Sánchez
Figure 7.5: © Serge Bloch / Manfred Jarisch / *Süddeutsche Zeitung Magazine*
Figure 7.6: © Matthew Hancock / *Fare Magazine*
Figure 7.7: © Tom Gauld
Figure 8.1: © Lasse Skarbøvik / *The New York Times*
Figure 8.2: © Malika Favre / Brummell
Figure 8.3: © Anita Kunz, All Rights Reserved
Figure 8.4: © David Plunkert
Figure 8.5: © Gary Baseman
Figure 8.6: © Simoul Alva / *MIT Technology Review*
Figure 8.7: © Javier Jaén / *The New Yorker*
Figure 8.8: © Doug Chayka / *The New York Times*
Figure 8.9: © Janne Iivonen / *The New York Times*
Figure 8.10: © Christopher Corr
Figure 8.11: © Doug Chayka / *The New York Times*
Figure 8.12: © Andy Robert Davies / *FT Weekend Magazine*
Figure 8.13: © Malika Favre / *The New Yorker*
Figure 8.14: All rights reserved © Victo Ngai www.victo-ngai.com / Black Dragon Press
Figure 8.15: © peterandallen / *The Radio Times*
Figure 9.1: © Edel Rodriguez / D. W. Pine / *Time*
Figure 9.2: © David Hughes / *The Times*
Figure 9.3: © Jianan Liu / *IPPR Progressive Review*
Figure 9.4: © Simoul Alva / *HuffPost*
Figure 9.5: © Paul Slater / *The Times*
Figure 9.6: © Brian Stauffer / *Phoenix New Times*
Figure 9.7: © Christopher Corr
Figure 9.8: © Ben Challenor / *The Sunday Times*

Figure 9.9: © Joe Ciardiello
Figure 9.10: © Mr Slowboy / Thu-Huyen Hoang / *Monocle Magazine*
Figure 9.11: © Janne Iivonen / *FT Weekend Magazine*
Figure 9.12: © Matthew Richardson / Association of Illustrators / *Varoom Magazine*
Figure 9.13: © Simoul Alva / *The New York Times*
Figure 9.14a-b: © Serge Bloch / *The Boston Globe*
Figure 9.15: © Eva Bee / *The Observer Life & Style Magazine*
Figure 10.1: © Michelle Thompson / People of Print
Figure 10.2a-d: © Michelle Thompson / People of Print
Figure 10.3: © David Hughes / The Maverick Festival
Figure 10.4: © Caroline Thompson / *Geo Magazine*
Figure 10.5: © Christopher Corr
Figure 10.6: © Lucy Truman / *CN Traveler*
Figure 10.7: © Simoul Alva / *The New York Times*
Figure 11.1: © Lucy Truman / Laura Engel / *US Better Homes and Gardens*
Figure 11.2: © Frazer Hudson
Figure 11.3: © Frazer Hudson / *The Guardian*
Figure 11.4a-d: © Mr Slowboy / Thu-Huyen Hoang / *Monocle*
Figure 11.5: © Christopher Corr
Figure 11.6a-e: © Michelle Thompson / People of Print
Figure 11.7: © Lucy Truman
Figure 12.1: © Frazer Hudson
Figure 12.2: © Frazer Hudson / *The Guardian*
Figure 12.3: Frazer Hudson
Figure 12.4: Frazer Hudson / *The Guardian*
Figure 12.5: © Greg Clarke / *Chicago*
Figure 12.6: © Edel Rodriguez
Figure 12.7: © Greg Clarke
Figure 12.8: © Greg Clarke / *Chicago*
Figure 12.9a-b: ©Mr Slowboy
Figure 13.1: © Greg Clarke
Figure 13.2a-d: © Greg Clarke
Figure 13.3a-c: © Serge Bloch / *The Boston Globe*
Figure 13.4: © Joe Ciardiello / *The New York Times*
Figure 13.5a: © Andrew Selby
Figure 13.5b: © Andrew Selby / *The Journal of Allergy and Clinical Immunology*
Figure 13.6: © Serge Bloch / *The Boston Globe*
Figure 13.6: © Mr Slowboy/ Thu-Huyen Hoang / *Monocle*
Figure 14.1: © Serge Bloch

Index

Italic page numbers indicate figures.

A

Abstract Expressionism 20
academic journals and conferences 30
accountability of editorial illustration ix
advertising 79
agency representation 193–5
AhoyThere, cover for *The Big Issue 15*
Allen, P. *150*
alternative publications 21–2
Alva, S. *4*, 5, 6, *48, 144, 156, 160, 170*
analogue tools 165–8
animation 103, 105, *105*
annuals, illustration *149*, 149–50
Apple MacIntosh computer,
        introduction of 26
appropriation 52
A-priori/A-posteriori truths 65
archiving work 170
Art Brut 25
Art Deco *17*, 17–18
art movements
        Abstract Expressionism 20
        Art Brut 25
        Art Deco 17–18
        Bauhaus 17
        Conceptual Art 22–3, *23*
        Constructivism 15, *15*
        Dada 14, *14*
        Expressionism 13
        Folk Art 24–5
        Futurism 13–14
        growth and evolution of 13
        humour 110
        Lowbrow 23–4, *24*
        Moderne 18
        Outsider Art 25
        Pop Art 20–1, *21*
        Pop Surrealism 23–4
        Post Modernism 18–20
        Primitivism 16, *16*
        Psychedelia 22, *22*
        Supramatism 14–15
        Surrealism 16–17
associative relations 123, *123*
attitudes towards illustration 27–9, *29*
        damage done by 29–30
audiences 71
authorship 71
authors' prejudicial attitudes towards
        illustration 28

B

backing-up work 170
Balbusso Twins *40*
Baldessari, J. 23
Bar, N. 111
Barthes, R. 61, 71
Baseman, G. 24, *24, 144*
Bauhaus 17
beauty, definitions of 64–5
Bee, E. *51, 161*
Behance 146, *146*
Benjamin, W. 66
Berger, J. 61, 68–9
Berkeley, J. 113, *113*
Big Idea 82–3
The Big Issue, AhoyThere's cover for
        15
Bloch, S. *16, 57, 85, 130, 160, 191, 194,*
        197
Borges, J. L. 121
'borrowing' of ideas 52, 113
Bott, I. *93*
Bourel, M. *118,* 190
Brodner, S. *89*
Burckhardt, M. *37, 81*
Butler, J. 70–1

C

calligraphic line work 85, *85*
cameras 169–70
capitalism
        Benjamin and 66
        Marx and 65–6
career as an editorial illustrator 137
        growing 188
        recognition for work 188
        see also commercial practice;
                promotion
caricatures 86–9, *89*
cartoons 86–9, *88, 89*
Cassandre, A. M. 18
chairs 165
Challenor, P. *113, 157*
Charlie Hebdo terrorist attacks 36
charts, bar, pie and line 92
Chayka, D. *63, 114, 146, 147*
Chow, S. *34*
Ciardiello, J. *76, 120, 158, 192*
Clarke, G. *184, 185, 188, 189*
clear line work 85

clever thinking
        art movements 110
        balance in 110
        humour 109–15, *110, 111, 112, 113,*
                114, 115
        innuendo *114,* 114–15
        irony 113–14, *114*
        parody 112–13, *113*
        pastiche 113, *113*
        readers and 110
        sarcasm 115, *115*
        satire 112, *112*
        visual puns 111
        wit 111, *112*
clients
        communication with 183–4, *184,*
                185, 190–2
        meeting 156, 158, *158*
        visiting with portfolios 141
co-creation of knowledge 36–7
code and decoders 76–8
cognitive reception of images 61
Cohn, N. 126, 132
collage 52
comedy
        as approach to clever thinking 109
        art movements 110
        balance in 110
        innuendo *114,* 114–15
        irony 113–14, *114*
        parody 112–13, *113*
        pastiche 113, *113*
        readers and 110
        sarcasm 115, *115*
        satire 112, *112*
        visual puns 111
        wit 111, *112*
commercial practice
        agency representation 193–5
        ambitions for 188
        communication with clients 190–2
        criticism, dealing with 192–3
        execution of artwork 190–2
        expansion into new areas 196
        experimentation and development
                188–90
        growing a career 188
        motivation for 187
        recognition for work 188
        skills developed in 196